T0361457

PRAISE FOR
THE STIGMATISTS

"When I returned to the Catholic Church, I shied away from purported private revelations, apparitions, relics, stigmatists, and other supernatural and/or preternatural phenomena. I couldn't shake the sense that there was a whole lot of gullibility passing as faith. But to raise questions was to risk being regarded as an unbeliever and a skeptic.

Now we have a professional historian and committed Catholic, Dr. Paul Kengor, speaking candidly about what can be verified and what should be discarded as inauthentic. He focuses on seven Church-approved stigmatists—especially those declared as blessed and saint. These include St. Francis of Assisi, St. Catherine of Siena, Bl. Anne Catherine Emmerich, St. Gemma Galgani, St. Padre Pio, Bl. Elena Aiello, and St. Faustina. He combs through their visions, revelations, messages, prophecies, and their warnings about the end times and the return of Christ. He listens carefully to their own sense of mission. They are living crucifixions, vividly portraying before the world Christ's atoning death. They make visible what all Christians are called to do in less dramatic form. For example, St. Paul says to the Christians of Rome, "I urge you, brothers and sisters, in view of God's mercy, to offer your bodies as a living sacrifice, holy and pleasing to God—this is your true and proper worship" (Rom 12:1). Kengor's study of these stigmatists moves the discussion away from spectacle and reintroduces them to us as brothers and sisters in Christ who are specially gifted to exhort us to take up our cross. The stigmatists are not part of a religious freak show. They are usually psychologically stable and mentally and emotionally balanced people whose company is enjoyed by family and friends. Kengor's *The Stigmatists* forces us to ask how comfortable we would be with a little Christ as a member of our parish family."

—Al Kresta, President and CEO of Ave Maria Communications, host of *Kresta in the Afternoon*

"*The Stigmatists* is the kind of book that forever changes the way one looks at the supernatural gift of the mark of the stigmata. Impeccably researched yet infused with the faith of a devout follower of Christ, Paul Kengor provides readers with the riveting stories of the visions, the revelations, and the warnings of the Church-approved stigmatists. Some of the prophecies that these holy men and women provide are terrifying, but Kengor reminds us that even as the world may seem to be falling apart, passionate mystics like St. Catherine of Siena provide us with hope by offering up their suffering for the expiation of the sins of the world—just as Christ had done. This has resonance for us and the ways in which we take up our own cross and follow Him."

—Dr. Anne Hendershott, Director of Veritas Center for Ethics in Public Life, Professor of Sociology

"One of the most mysterious and scientifically defying phenomena within the Catholic Church is the sacred stigmata. In his riveting exploration, *The Stigmatists*, Dr. Kengor takes you on a journey into the mystical and often misunderstood world of those who bore the wounds of Christ. To date, this is one of the most comprehensive works exploring the complex terrain of private revelations with a balanced and discerning approach. This book is an indispensable resource for scholars, theologians, and anyone interested in the mystical. Trust me when I tell you, *The Stigmatists* is a crucial addition to your spiritual library and a testament to the power of God's love and mercy in salvation history."

—Drew Mariani, nationally syndicated radio talk show host, author, and award-winning writer, producer, and director

"A fascinating work of spiritual storytelling, *The Stigmatists* is a collection of biographies, messages, and insights inspired by an exclusive group: recipients of the rarest supernatural gift bestowed by Christ Himself. Should the visions, revelations, prophesies, and warnings of stigmatists shape the way we understand and interact with the modern world? Paul Kengor's enjoyable, expertly researched book—which urges readers to live a holy life and help get family and friends to heaven—makes a compelling case that the stigmatists are a crucial part of God's plan for our salvation."

—Kimberly Begg, author of *Unbreakable: Saints Who Inspired Saints to Moral Courage*

"*The Stigmatists* is yet another testament to Paul Kengor's unwavering commitment to his Catholic Faith and his research pursuits. Working closely with him (we co-authored *The Divine Plan*), I've witnessed firsthand his dedication to delving into the mysteries of Faith with scholarly rigor."

—Robert Orlando, filmmaker and author of *The Shroud: Face to Face*

"Paul Kengor's work is first-rate, and *The Stigmatists* is no exception. The material is intriguing, and the research is both careful and reliable. Excellent and highly recommended."

—Julia Meloni, author of *The St. Gallen Mafia*

THE STIGMATISTS

Their Gifts,
Their Revelations,
Their Warnings

PAUL KENGOR, PHD

TAN Books
Gastonia, North Carolina

Unless otherwise noted, Scripture quotations are from the Revised Standard Version of the Bible—Second Catholic Edition (Ignatius Edition), copyright © 2006 National Council of the Churches of Christ in the United States of America. Used by permission. All rights reserved.

Cover design by Andrew Schmalen

Cover image: *The Stigmata of Saint Catherine of Siena*, Alessandro Franchi (1838–1914). Painting, Sant'Elisabetta della Visitazione. Public Domain / Wikimedia Commons.

Library of Congress Control Number: 2024935097
ISBN: 978-1-5051-3294-6
Kindle ISBN: 978-1-5051-3296-0
ePUB ISBN: 978-1-5051-3295-3

Published in the United States by
TAN Books
PO Box 269
Gastonia, NC 28053
www.TANBooks.com

Printed in the United States of America

CONTENTS

PREFACE

There have been very few books that offer a serious, reliable, careful look at stigmatists and, specifically, what one might call *visionary stigmatists*. Then again, is there any other kind of stigmatist? This question makes a crucial point and sets the theme for this investigation.

It is quite interesting, intriguing, and revealing—and I would venture to say no coincidence—and above all, something not to be ignored, that almost all Church-approved stigmatists have also been just that: visionaries. Call that providence. As Pope St. John Paul II once said, "In the designs of providence, there are no mere coincidences."[1]

A genuine stigmatist is certainly no coincidence but indeed the design of providence. Truly, such a person was providentially chosen and marked with a providential purpose, which was often a prophetic one stretching well beyond the individual's time and place—in some cases, extending to the very days we are living in right now.

This book gives special attention to Church-approved stigmatists—especially those declared blessed and saints—and their visions, their revelations, their messages, their prophecies, and their warnings. In some cases, the prophetic warnings dramatically relate to the end times and the second coming of Christ. One might rightly interpret the mark of the stigmata as a heavenly affirmation of their authenticity, which, in turn, adds authenticity to their expressed visions.

So many of these stigmatists had visions that the gift of prophecy seems almost an accompaniment to the gift of stigmata. Of course, not all such visions were pleasant ones—quite the contrary. Yes, many of them saw Jesus, the Blessed Mother, their guardian angels, saints, and images of heaven, but they often saw opposing forces. St. Frances of Rome (1384–1440) endured terrifying visions of hell. St. Veronica Giuliani (1660–1727) saw hell and purgatory. St. Catherine de Ricci (1522–1590), a woman of extraordinary experiences, was said to have spiritually descended into purgatory every Sunday night, and her earthly suffering was often offered up for the release of souls in purgatory.[2] In fact, such penitential-sacrificial suffering was commonplace for numerous stigmatists. And above all, many stigmatists issued dire prophetic warnings, which they claimed were given to them by Christ Himself or by His Blessed Mother, about a final day's fire from the sky that will chastise man for his sins, purify the earth once again, and initiate the end times and Christ's second coming.

The prophetic visions of stigmatists speak to us in both an earthly and eternal way. It is interesting that many non-Catholics—and even many non-Christians—are intrigued by stigmata. As a former Protestant, I experienced many occasions when the mention of stigmata was an attention grabber—one which was not reflexively or cynically dismissed out of hand. I have seen evangelicals and even secularists who think that Catholics can be a little strange concerning mystical things, thinking that we see the Virgin Mary swirling daily in our cups of coffee, yet they stop to give full attention when stigmatists are talked about. Maybe they are more willing to take someone like Padre Pio seriously when they glimpse the modern-day photos, read news reports, or hear testimonies from the countless witnesses who attested to his undeniable bleeding marks. Here was a modern figure who died in 1968, nearly two thousand years after the time of Christ, astonishingly bearing the wounds of Christ for fifty years of his life.

Many people find claims of stigmata fascinating; there do not seem to be the scoffers one might expect in our derisive, cynical age. Even when the notion of stigmata is raised by Hollywood (albeit sensationally and sometimes blasphemously), eyes are wide open. And really, such is what it takes: eyes to see. People want to see with their own eyes. When they see the nail marks, they find it hard to deny their own eyes. As the doubting apostle Thomas said of the risen Christ, "Unless I see in his hands the print of the nails . . . I will not believe" (Jn 20:25). Thomas saw them, but more than that, he touched them. And with that, he was a believer.

Interested parties today, unlike in the time of history's most famous stigmatist, St. Francis, who lived eight hundred years ago, can see the holes in the hands of modern stigmatists. At a minimum, they can see photos and sometimes even videos. While this is not as good as being there—seeing the marks in person and putting your finger in the wounds—pictures are enough to give anyone pause. As we shall see with the stigmatists profiled in this book, clergy and physicians alike, believers and nonbelievers, stood beside many of these stigmatists and saw and touched them. And when they did, their beliefs and lives were dramatically changed. How could they not be?

This book opens with a comprehensive overview of the phenomenon of stigmata, beginning with the words of St. Paul in the New Testament, which some believe suggest that he was the first recorded case of someone receiving the stigmata. Aside from St. Paul, St. Francis (1181/1182–1226) is generally believed to be the first stigmatist. The opening chapter looks at data and cases to which we have access. Thereafter, the book provides individual chapters focused on St. Francis, St. Catherine of Siena, Bl. Anne Catherine Emmerich, St. Gemma Galgani, St. Padre Pio, Bl. Sr. Elena Aiello, and finishing, appropriately, with St. Faustina Kowalska, the first canonized saint of the new millennium, who had profoundly consequential messages for our times. These are the seven stigmatists featured in this book.

Notably, not all of these stigmatic saints and blesseds had dramatic visions of the final days. Some of these special visions were along the lines of St. Francis's transformational conversations with Jesus at the San Damiano cross, which had a significant historical purpose: "*Francesco*," pleaded Jesus, "*ripara la Mia chiesa*" (Francis, repair My church).[3]

Francis proceeded to do just that. What followed was a wonderful historic moment for the Church and the Faith—one that, through the death of Catherine of Siena in 1380, produced some tremendous figures for the Faith. Unlike Martin Luther in the 1500s, Francis in the 1200s embarked upon a genuine reformation. Francis, who was an instrument of the Lord's peace, was a true reformer in the best sense. Whereas Luther rebelled, Francis reformed.

These stigmatists and their revelations have spoken to us in profound ways from the time of Christ to the Middle Ages to our times and will to the end times. And now, in the twenty-first century, there is no more imperative time to take a sober, prayerful look at what they have told us. And though this book accords specific chapters only to Church-approved saints and blesseds, it does not ignore the extraordinary visions claimed by other reported stigmatists of recent times, such as Therese Neumann, Sr. Agnes Katsuko Sasagawa (the visionary of Our Lady of Akita), and many others from the twentieth century who are still living today.

To that end, I shall wrap up this brief preface with a personal note. A driving impulse for writing this book was not merely my fascination with stigmatists, including with some of those allegedly living among us in our modern day, albeit without the stamp of the Church's approval (not yet, anyway). A key personal motivation was to sort through the information and disinformation about certain stigmatists, extract the facts from the great amount of misinformation found on the internet, and strive to uncover reality rather than being misled by fictitious nonsense. Sadly, there is an incredible amount of fake material out there, including much that can be found on Catholic websites, as well as dubious books filled with undocumented sources.

I wanted to learn the truth. Like many of you reading now, I just want to know the truth. If this or that reported stigmatist/seer is said to have had this or that astonishing vision for humanity—genuinely given by divine messengers, whether Jesus Himself or the Blessed Mother or other heavenly sources—I want to know if it is genuine. For my own sake and the sake of my family and friends and my times, I want to find out what is real, or at least have a reasonable sense of what we can place our faith in. I want to know what we are supposed to know, and I want to be prepared—for my own soul and the souls of my loved ones—for what is to come.

We all need to be ready at any time and any day to meet our Maker and hopefully get to heaven, regardless of whether our times are the end times. And if we are given extraordinary messages from stigmatists, past and present, about the state of our souls and of our times, and the end times in which we may be living, I want to heed them. And I would like to help others to heed them.

But alas, which of the purported statements are authentic, as opposed to which are the product of some slipshod online "reporting"? My own intense curiosity and desire to know the truth about what could be the most important things to know about ourselves and our times compelled me to launch my own in-depth investigation of what the stigmatists have told us.

This book is the product of that search. I have done my best to exercise caution regarding what we (namely, the Church) can and cannot confirm. I try to speak candidly about what seems verifiable and what does not. My prayer is that I have gotten it right or at least have come close enough to perhaps assist others in what they need to know. And as we proceed, above all, rest assured in knowing this: no matter what the claims, disputed or verified, legitimate or not, simply seek to live a holy life. Have your soul prepared to receive the place that the Lord has prepared for you.

CHAPTER 1

STIGMATISTS
THROUGH HISTORY

Stigmata are physical marks reflective of and representing a participation in the sacrificial passion of Jesus Christ at His crucifixion.
The marks are wounds that are granted to the so-called victim soul as a
special spiritual gift. Stigmata are the rarest supernatural gift bestowed
by Christ Himself only upon particularly blessed individuals who are
willing to sacrifice themselves for the sins of others as their Lord and
Savior did at Calvary.

"The stigmata is not given to the stigmatic for his or her benefit
but for the benefit of others," writes Deacon Albert E. Graham in his
Compendium of the Miraculous. "The stigmatic represents the Crucified
Christ to a world continually in need of a loving sacrifice that atones
for our sin." The stigmatic becomes a loving sacrifice himself or herself,
"transformed into a living crucifix who shares in the Lord's Passion for
the redemption of the world."[4]

In no way does this suggest that the stigmatists in any way replace
Christ or that His atonement is insufficient for us. The stigmatic
receives these marks from Christ as a gift of Christ to share in His
expiation for the sins of mankind. The chosen stigmatists are intensely
holy souls, willing to give of themselves entirely to help atone for the
sins of the world. They are blessed by a living Christ who chooses them
as a living crucifix to participate in His atonement.

For non-Catholics who find this hard to theologically assimilate, consider a few analogies: God the Almighty could end poverty if He so desired, but here on earth, He calls Christians to establish charities to feed and clothe and minister to the homeless. Though Jesus Christ can heal or rescue anyone, He nonetheless has servants in this world who help humanity as doctors, nurses, firemen, and first responders in hospitals, surgical rooms, fire stations, and ambulances. It is interesting that the stigmatist Padre Pio often told those seeking his counsel regarding a medical condition that they would be healed, but God wanted them to get the surgery nonetheless. "God wants us to help ourselves in seeking healing," Padre Pio explained, "and we have the duty to submit . . . to medicines and other treatment."[5] We are called to be living servants who serve as the Almighty's hands and feet on this earthly terrain, and surgeons and nurses can glorify God by using their talents to serve Him and help His people.

Christ, too, gave us the Gospel, but He asks His followers to go forth to spread His word. As Christians, we should eagerly and rightly evangelize, even though God alone can save, because by evangelizing, we can help Jesus save souls. Why did Billy Graham hold countless crusades if Christ alone can save? Christ wants us to play a role in His Great Commission. In fact, St. Paul described Christians as God's coworkers or colaborers in Christ's vineyard (see 1 Cor 3:9).

It pleases God immensely to have earthly souls willing to serve Him faithfully to assist in heaven's divine ambitions. That is servanthood or discipleship. Thus, imagine Christ's joy in learning that some unique souls are so willing to assist Him that they are willing to bleed and suffer as He did during His passion. Few have ever served Him like stigmatists. Their service, like His, is a service of suffering. And all stigmatists do this with humility, bowing to Him alone.

As for Protestants looking to the Bible for evidence of such sacrificial offerings by Christians, consider that Christ urged His followers to pick up their crosses and follow Him. Matthew 16:24–25 states, "Then Jesus told his disciples, 'If any man would come after me, let him deny himself and take up his cross and follow me. For whoever would save his life will lose it, and whoever loses his life for my sake will find it.'" Even more to the point of stigmatists' sacrifices, St. Paul said in Romans 12:1, "I appeal to you therefore, brethren, by the mercies of God, to present your bodies as a living sacrifice." Paul added in Colossians 1:24, "I rejoice in my sufferings for your sake, and in my flesh I complete what is lacking in Christ's afflictions for the sake of his body, that is, the church." Was Paul here saying that Christ's suffering and atonement on the Cross was insufficient, and he personally had to make up for it? No, of course not. But Paul was willingly suffering in his flesh, as Christ had, and he was rejoicing in it.

So devoted are these sacrificial servants that their wounds, in many cases, come not just once in a lifetime on a single Friday afternoon during one Easter season but repeatedly. In certain cases, the wounds come every Thursday or Friday, sometimes for years or decades, bleeding again and again. They then heal again on Saturday, only to start anew the next week. In other cases, the wounds are always there. Some of the suffering souls bear wounds in their feet or hands only, others in their heads or sides or elsewhere. Some bear multiple wounds. Some even display actual nail protrusions.

Do the wounds hurt? Absolutely. Of course, they do. But as the saying goes, no cross, no crown. The sacrifice is intended to spare souls, snatching them from the flames of perdition and hell itself. The process is literally miraculous.

It is widely said that St. Francis of Assisi, early in the thirteenth century, was the first stigmatist. But some have argued, not unjustifiably, that St. Paul might have been the first many centuries earlier, in the first century AD. Note Paul's words in Galatians 6:17: "I bear on my body the marks of Jesus."

We do not know for certain if Paul was referring to what we today would call stigmata. It is possible that Paul was speaking more figuratively, asserting that he suffered as Christ did. As Paul made clear elsewhere in the Scriptures, he suffered in almost every conceivable way: he was flogged, imprisoned, stoned, left adrift at sea, three times beaten with rods, three times shipwrecked, five times received forty lashes minus one, went without food and water and sleep, and still more (see 2 Cor 11:23–27). As noted, Paul, in his Epistle to the Romans, urged his fellow Christians to offer their bodies as a living sacrifice to God and personally rejoiced in their sufferings. He certainly did that, and perhaps to the point of stigmatic sacrifice.

Two stigmatists noted in this book, the German mystics Servant of God Therese Neumann and Bl. Anne Catherine Emmerich, were granted vivid visions of past figures in the Church, such as St. Francis receiving the stigmata. Both of these mystics claimed that the world's first stigmatic after Jesus's ascension was indeed St. Paul.[6] So, it is highly possible that St. Paul was the first stigmatic. But if not St. Paul, it was St. Francis some twelve centuries later.

Hands versus Wrists, Real versus Faked

A key aspect of the stigmata worth clarifying up front relates to the contention by some modern commentators that Jesus Christ was nailed to the Cross not through His hands but through His wrists, which, they assert, was the more likely procedure by the Roman executioners to ensure the victim was best secured to the cross. This has led some to doubt stigmatists who show the bleeding marks of Christ in the palms of their hands. One will sometimes hear this objection from Protestant skeptics.

And yet, if one goes to the Bible, as Protestants claim to do as their authority for all religious claims, we will find that St. Thomas the Apostle said to the other disciples after the crucifixion of Christ, "Unless I see in his hands the print of the nails, and place my finger in the mark of the nails, and place my hand in his side, I will not believe" (Jn 20:25). Note that Thomas said "hands," not "wrists." Moreover, Jesus said to Thomas when he saw him after the Resurrection, "Put your finger here, see my hands" (Jn 20:27). Again, Sacred Scripture, quoting the words of Jesus, says "hands," not "wrists." Stigmatists show these marks in their hands, too, just as the Bible said that Jesus did.[7]

Some might object that when Jesus and Thomas said "hands," this included Christ's wrists, though that would not be an exact interpretation of the biblical text. This objection is even proposed by some scholars who argue that there is no direct equivalent for the English word *wrists* in Hebrew and Greek. (I cannot resolve that debate here.)[8] From a practical standpoint, though, it is hard to imagine Thomas successfully sticking his fingers through Christ's bony wrists. It seems that palms would be much easier to stick a finger through. Some have speculated that perhaps the long nails went into the palms but were driven downward and exited through the back of the wrists. However, most stigmatists, including Padre Pio, had exit marks through the back of their hands, directly opposite the holes in their palms. As we shall see, observers said that one could see all the way through the holes in Pio's palms.

Some have also attempted to claim that certain cases of stigmata might be the diabolical work of the devil, intended to deceive, or the work of fakers, intended to mislead. The Church is always alert to such possibilities, as are physicians, psychologists, and other authorities. Examiners, medical and ecclesiastical, start from a point of skepticism, seeking to rule out other causes,[9] and serious cases are usually subject to formal investigations.

As to the work of Satan, the devil certainly was not the causal factor for the victim souls accorded specific chapters of this book. In these cases, it was clear that only the Lord could have imposed the types of lasting marks on these extraordinarily holy, pious, and virtuous individuals. The Church always looks for precisely such signs of holiness—as well as signs of the diabolical—before approving certain cases. Moreover, as this book will make clear, Satan detests stigmatists with a ferocious passion. The devil has brutally attacked many stigmatists. That, too, was observable. Sts. Gemma Galgani and Padre Pio were not pulling themselves across the floor by their hair with invisible third hands. Demons were doing that.

In his 1974 book *The Stigmata and Modern Science*, the Rev. Charles M. Carty stated, "It can be confidently stated that there has been no case within the last hundred years in which the external, physical marks of the stigmata . . . have been produced by natural means such as hypnotism, by diabolical agency, or by a combination of both."[10]

The archaic charge of hypnotism has always struck me as utterly absurd and ridiculously unscientific, as has the charge of hysteria (often applied to female stigmatists by male psychiatrists) and psychosomatic suggestion. Many of these charges stem from screwball psychiatry or "medical science" of centuries past (albeit, sadly, into the twentieth century) that no one today takes seriously. It is the height of sophistry to suggest that Padre Pio could have been hypnotized to bleed daily from his hands, feet, and side for fifty years or that he could do so by autosuggestion. Where are the lab results and peer-reviewed studies to support that? Such a belief would be, in fact, a leap a faith!

When confronted with such criticism from a "medical expert" that he was imagining into existence the copious daily bleeding wounds that saturated his gloves and socks and cloak, Padre Pio humorously responded, "Tell him to think intensely about being an ox. Let's see if he grows horns."[11]

A key test of authentic stigmatization—neither faked nor of diabolical origin—is the character of the individual. Confirmed stigmatists are usually psychologically stable; they are mentally and emotionally well-balanced.[12] They do not strike friends and family and clergy and medical and psychological experts as "crazy." They are not demented masochists who would drive nails into their own hands every day for a lengthy, sustained period of time, such as decades or even half a century in Padre Pio's case. (What type of person would or could do such a thing? Think about that.) Moreover, if they did inflict such damage to themselves, even if only a few times, the wounds would not instantaneously heal on, say, Saturday morning, twelve hours later, with no signs of infection or scarring. Yet, this has miraculously occurred with many stigmatists, leaving doctors astounded. For a scientist examining such a case, especially a skeptical one, a faker of such a thing would not be difficult to expose.

As an additional sign of authenticity, true stigmatists tend to exude heroic virtue. They do not want these wounds. Yes, they consented to them when the Lord accorded the marks, but their humility is such that they consider themselves wholly unworthy. Those around them, particularly religious authorities, stand in awe of their palpable holiness. Witnesses easily sense that they are dealing with a suffering servant who seems saintly (even though not all stigmatists have been declared saints). At a minimum, these stigmatists do not seem diabolical. Their words, their actions, and their visions are heavenly ones, relating messages that are inspiringly good and seek to guide the faithful. These individuals exude a saintly quality, not a demonic one. As for those individuals who instead seem infested with the demonic, the difference becomes obvious, especially to trained ecclesiastical authorities.

This consideration of non-authentic versus authentic stigmata raises another crucial distinction going forward. As we shall see in this book, many of these stigmatists endured terrible suffering not only from their wounds provided by the Lord but from notably unsaintly men and women—not only lay people and scientists but priests and nuns and even bishops of the highest rank—who treated them with suspicion and contempt and who often were filled with jealously, envy, a lack of charity, and vice rather than virtue. Padre Pio, now formally declared a saint and widely perceived as a saint in his own time, endured such treatment. He was not alone. This, too, seems to be part of the earthly suffering that heaven ordains these unique servants to forebear during their time on earth.

Living Crucifixes

Given these remarkable figures, some of them living in our own time, the lack of news stories about stigmatists is rather astonishing. Open your local newspaper or typical news website, glimpse at your latest internet alert, or turn on your television for local or national news, and there are stories on just about anything and everything, including the utterly superficial. And yet, somehow, a potentially miraculous story about a pious man or woman alleged to be bleeding from his or her hands or head or feet or side manages to get no attention from the media. If it does get covered, the treatment might be scornful. Even less so do academics devote scholarly studies to these alleged phenomena. How can this be? Whatever the theory, the lack of attention is shocking. It is another sign of the shallowness of modern journalism and academia that these extraordinary mystical figures who have lived among us get so little attention. Do reporters think there would be no audience for such a story? Surely, they do not.

One of the few serious works on the subject was a 1989 book by Michael Freze, titled *They Bore the Wounds of Christ*, published by Our Sunday Visitor. Freze gave the topic careful and thoughtful attention. Among his sources was a Franciscan priest from Brooklyn, New York, Fr. Joseph Martin, OFM Cap., who, having been at Padre Pio's side daily for the final three years of the holy friar's life at San Giovanni Rotondo, was as close to him as anyone. Martin told Freze that the stigmata were given to Padre Pio not for his own benefit but for that of others. "He told me that the mission of the stigmatist was a gift and sign for the world," wrote Freze. "The stigmatist represents the crucified Christ to a world continually in need of a loving sacrifice that atones for our sin. The stigmatist is this loving sacrifice, a living crucifix who helps in the plan of God's redemptive action. . . . Perhaps above all, they show a Christ who is very much alive today."[13]

Freze's work is valuable and inspiring, and like this work, he struggled to find reliable, up-to-date estimates on stigmatists. There is no authority—perhaps including at the Vatican (to my knowledge)—that keeps a running tab of alleged or even Church-approved stigmatists. Freze quoted the renowned Parisian scholar Dr. Antoine Imbert-Gourbeyre, who did groundbreaking work on the subject. In his monumental two-volume work *La Stigmatisation*, Dr. Imbert-Gourbeyre reported that there had been 321 authentic stigmatists in Church history, sixty-two of which had been canonized or beatified. But alas, that work was published more than a century ago, in 1894. It is long outdated. As Freze acknowledges, since that time, numerous others have borne the marks of Christ either partly or completely, whether visible or hidden. (I will address hidden stigmata later.) Freze noted Padre Pio, Therese Neumann, and Marthe Robin among the major cases following Dr. Imbert-Gourbeyre's study, but there have been many others since then.[14]

In fact, there have been so many that Freze noted that the twentieth century might be rightly called the "era of the stigmatist." He went on to relate that more than two dozen reputable cases had been reported and investigated in the twentieth century, though few had yet been authenticated by Church authorities. Still, the rising number of stigmatics in recent centuries and even recent decades is significant; it does make one wonder why there are so many, seemingly more than ever. One might say that we simply know of more cases today because of the mass media—though, as lamented above, they unfortunately often get no significant media attention. And frequently, when they do, they are ridiculed.[15]

Still, as Freze notes, there have been numerous cases in the twentieth century that have undergone extensive investigations by medical experts and theologians. And oftentimes, there are pictures and even videos. What might be dismissed as medieval fables in cases like St. Francis eight hundred years ago cannot be so easily shrugged off today in an age when technology allows us to see for ourselves.

Stigmatists by Gender, Country, Order, and Religion

Quickly noticeable when looking at lists of stigmatists is that most have been women, and among countries and regions, the majority have been from Italy. And nearly all have been Catholic. In his classic study, Dr. Antoine Imbert-Gourbeyre found that of the 321 authentic stigmatists in Church history, 229 came from Italy (including ten from Sicily), which is about 70 percent. Beyond Italy, seventy stigmatists in Dr. Imbert-Gourbeyre's research were from France, forty-seven from Spain, thirty-three from Germany, fifteen from Belgium, thirteen from Portugal, five from Holland, five from Switzerland, three from Hungary, and one from Peru.[16] Nearly all of them were from Europe. Hilaire Belloc once famously proclaimed that "the faith is Europe and Europe is the faith." One might observe that Dr. Imbert-Gourbeyre's country breakdowns are reflective of saints from those areas. More saints have come from Italy, by far, than any other country. And France is second.

Far and away, most stigmatists have been women. It thus seems odd that the first stigmatist was male, whether St. Paul or St. Francis, and the most famous stigmatist, Padre Pio, was male. Nonetheless, the vast majority have been women. Dr. Imbert-Gourbeyre calculated that of his 321 authentic stigmatists, 280 were female. That means nearly 90 percent were female.

Michael Freze asked Fr. Joseph Martin, the Capuchin friar and very close friend and aide to Padre Pio, to offer an opinion on why so many stigmatists have been women and why so many hailed from Italy. "Well, I think it has to do with the character of the people here," observed Martin, a non-Italian. "They're more emotional, and therefore they love easier. Actually, there are more women stigmatists than men, probably because they are more sensitive and emotional."[17]

Freze also got an insight into female stigmatists from Fr. Ulrich Veh, a German Capuchin who was the vice postulator for the cause for beatification for Therese Neumann. Asked why there were so many more female stigmatists, Fr. Veh proffered, "Women have been called to love in a more sensitive way than most men. They seem to be able to suffer more at the same time they love. A woman is a great lover."[18]

Dr. Imbert-Gourbeyre also found that most stigmatists came out of religious orders. Among them were 109 who were Dominicans (the order of St. Catherine of Siena), 102 were Franciscans (the order founded by St. Francis), fourteen were Carmelites, fourteen were Ursulines, twelve were Visitation nuns, eight were Augustinians, and three were Jesuits. Lay stigmatists were much less common.[19]

Even more dominant is the category of the religion of the stigmatists. Dr. Imbert-Gourbeyre identified all 321 stigmatists that he could authenticate as being Catholic. We shall see that more recent studies have found a few Protestant stigmatists, albeit a tiny minority. That should not surprise us, given that the very notion of stigmatists is much less accepted by Protestants.[20]

Of course, only the Lord Himself could explain why He primarily chooses Catholics to share in this suffering, but surely the reasons relate to Catholic theology and its teachings on the value of redemptive suffering. Catholics are more likely to willingly accept suffering and to unite their suffering to that of Christ's, more so than other Christians, and particularly much more so than modern Protestant evangelicals. Long dominant in American evangelical circles are questions like

"Why does God allow bad things to happen to good people?" which they find perplexing. Yet, Scripture is clear on this point when Christ Himself says that following Him requires one to pick up his own cross. For whatever reason, however, the idea of picking up the cross seems to have eluded much of modern American evangelical thinking, especially those sucked into the so-called health and wealth gospel.

Catholics generally understand that bad things happen to good people all the time. This is no mystery. It is part of living in this fallen world. The lives of biblical figures and saints alike have shown that. In the Old Testament, we have the example of Job, and in the New Testament, we have the Blessed Mother. These sufferings are captured with representations like the *Pietà* and so many other depictions commonly found in Catholic art. It is shown in Catholic portrayals of Christ's bleeding, beaten body nailed to their crucifixes throughout their parishes and homes. These images of our crucified Lord remind us of His salvific and eternal sacrifice on the Cross. While Catholics have plenty of crosses without a corpus or of the glorified Christ not bloodied, most of the representations of Christ's crucifixion display His wounds—the stigmata.

In all, Catholics more readily understand the value of suffering, fasting, honoring Lenten sacrifices, and generally undergoing mortification. And when they accept suffering, they willingly "offer it up"— that is, offer up their suffering to be united to Christ's for a heavenly purpose that the Lord might use. Even the phrase "offer it up" is alien to many non-Catholics, including modern evangelical churches, especially in the United States, where, at best, it would elicit a blank stare. In fact, there are entire Catholic penitential orders devoted to mortification. Look at the order started by St. Francis or St. Clare, or Mother Teresa's Sisters of Charity in Calcutta, in comparison to modern American evangelical megachurches with coffee shops, concert-like stages and atmospheres, and cushy seats. In fact, some Catholic penitential orders embraced such severe forms of self-imposed deprivation that the Vatican had to step in to stop members from doing long-term health damage to themselves.

Given this keen Catholic identification with the suffering Christ, it seems hardly any surprise that the vast majority of stigmatists would be Catholic—nor would it be a surprise to learn that many non-Catholics find it puzzling that Christ would ask certain Christians to take on stigmata, while others might find it theologically outrageous and scandalous and, therefore, deem these occurrences dubious.

And yet, in so many cases with Catholic stigmatists, they begged Christ to let them join in His suffering. As we shall see, many, amidst that intense suffering, asked Christ for the honor of doing still more for Him. They would happily accept more thorn wounds, as if to say, *What, Lord, only one thorn wound for me?*

That is not something commonly heard among evangelical Protestants. Incidentally, nor is veneration of the Blessed Mother common to Protestants. Thus, it is also no surprise that visions of the Holy Virgin occur with Catholics rather than with Protestants. We will also see that Marian apparitions happen with special intensity among stigmatists.

More Recent Studies of Stigmatists

Michael Freze's book was published in 1989, and Dr. Imbert-Gourbeyre's research was published a century before that, in 1894. Other research that brings us closer to our modern day is that done by the Ruusbroec Institute of the University of Antwerp in Belgium.

Launched in 1925, the Ruusbroec Institute specializes in academic research on religion and mystical spirituality.[21] The institute has compiled a database that lists stigmatists from the period of 1734 to 1934 (the earliest and latest dates of birth of the stigmatists). The database lists 245 claimed cases and asserts that, among them, forty were fraudulent. Those who are listed as fraudulent were either declared fraudulent by a local Church authority or by the Vatican itself when investigated.

As with the research by Dr. Imbert-Gourbeyre, the institute's breakdown of specific categories is illuminating. All of the stigmatists listed by Ruusbroec were Catholic, except for five, among whom was one each of Anglican, Congregationalist, Methodist, and Presbyterian, plus one Protestant of an unspecified denomination. Once again, there were more from Italy than any other country (over one-third), followed by France, Germany, and Spain, plus a sizable number from Belgium, which may be reflective of and perhaps the reason for the interest by the University of Antwerp.

Another set of data, much closer to our current day, comes from Deacon Albert Graham, author of the 2013 volume *Compendium of the Miraculous*, who continues to compile research on stigmatists. Now in his nineties, in May 2021, Graham shared with us at TAN Books a sample of his research at its current stage of progress. As for twentieth-century stigmatists, which he categorized as having died in the twentieth century (although many of them were born in the nineteenth century), Graham had identified eighty-nine in total. Among them, eighty-two were women, seven were men, and all but two were Catholic (one Lutheran and one Episcopalian). Once again, Italy was the most common country of origin. Perhaps also of interest is that, among the women, most were named after the Blessed Mother (Mary/Marie/Maria), followed by six bearing the name Therese/Theresa (with or without the *h*).

As for stigmatists currently living or who had lived into the twenty-first century, Deacon Graham, in this 2021 list, had already found forty-five. Once again, most were Catholic (there was one Baptist and one Lutheran), but more unusual in this list is that eight (or close to 20 percent) of the stigmatists were male, a higher portion than in earlier centuries. Once again, Italy is the country most represented, being home to eleven of the forty-five (nearly a quarter). Quite different, however, was the diminished representation of stigmatists from France, Germany, and Spain, which seems a fitting reflection of the aggressive secularization of those countries in our modern era. More prominently represented than in previous centuries were stigmatists from South America, Africa, India, the United States, Syria, South Korea, and Asia.

In all, when looking at the data from Dr. Imbert-Gourbeyre, Michael Freze, the Ruusbroec Institute, and Deacon Albert Graham, the list of generally known and accepted stigmatists since the time of

St. Francis of Assisi seems to run in a range of about four hundred to five hundred and is still counting and growing today.[22]

Common Sufferings and Traits

We will see in the lives of stigmatists in this book a few common character and spiritual traits and tendencies. Here are a few.

A period of trial

Among the stigmatists, there seems to be a period of trial and preparation by which the victim soul suffers physically and spiritually before receiving the marks. This might include hidden wounds at first, attacks by demons and the devil, or even persecution by clergy, high-ranking Church officials, and nuns who dismiss the stigmatists, accuse them of hypocrisy, fraud, or even worse. It seems almost like a test of their spiritual mettle, as if Christ is assessing whether they are ready to go still deeper in their shared suffering. God permits this trial period as a way of preparing them for what is to come.

Inedia

Inedia is the scientific term applied to persons able to live by eating little to almost nothing. This is different from anorexia. A number of stigmatists have subsisted on virtually no food at all, with one exception: the Eucharist. This inedia has been accompanied, especially in female stigmatists, by a desire to eat nothing but the Body and Blood of Christ in the Holy Eucharist. It becomes their Daily Bread.

In some cases, the stigmatist vomits up any other form of nourishment. Incredibly, some stigmatists have lived on nothing but the Eucharist for decades. We will see examples in the pages ahead, most notably with St. Catherine of Siena and Servant of God Therese Neumann. Other such reported stigmatists characterized by this phenomenon include St. Angela of Foligno (1248–1309), who was only recently canonized by Pope Francis, the French mystic Marie-Julie

Jahenny (1850–1941), and the Belgian stigmatist Louise Lateau (1850–83), among still others.[23]

Lack of sleep

Also curious among many stigmatists is their ability to subsist without much sleep in spite of their intense physical and spiritual sufferings. Padre Pio lived with very little sleep, often despite long, continuous, arduous hours hearing confessions. Therese Neumann likewise carried on with little sleep, as did Sts. Catherine of Siena and Gemma Galgani. Amazingly, it is said that St. Catherine de Ricci slept for only about one hour each week.[24]

Death at the age of thirty-three

Among the most intriguing characteristics among a number of stigmatists, though in no way a majority, is the striking fact that several—virtually all women—died at the age of thirty-three. Of course, that was also the age of Jesus Christ, whose wounds they bore, when He perished on the Cross. Dying at the age of thirty-three were the likes of Sts. Catherine of Siena and Faustina Kowalska, both profiled with chapters in this book, as well as Louise Lateau (1850–83), the Canadian-American Marie Rose Ferron (May 24, 1902–May 11, 1936), and Sr. Josefa Menéndez (1890–1923).[25]

Hidden stigmata

A number of stigmatists suffered from invisible stigmata. Naturally, in our skeptical age, claims of hidden stigmata will incline many observers to doubt whether they really existed. Like St. Thomas at the side of the risen Christ, we want to be able to see the wounds ourselves.

Nonetheless, for whatever reason, certain suffering souls were given wounds that they alone could see and feel, perhaps to keep them humble and away from the sin of pride.[26] And yet, in certain key cases, the already humble stigmatist pleaded with the Lord for the wounds to be kept invisible. These souls were anything but prideful or exhibitionists. Some of them were granted that wish only later (St. Gemma Galgani, for instance) after the wounds had been visible for a time. Others still had invisible wounds at first, which were later made visible for the purposes of others to see, according to the higher intentions of the Lord's plan (we will see this with Bl. Anne Catherine Emmerich). The two most prominent cases of hidden stigmata were Sts. Catherine of Siena and Faustina Kowalska.

The Incorruptibles—Lucy and Friends

Another common trait exhibited among stigmatists is the rare phenomenon that, after their deaths, their exhumed bodies were found to be incorrupt. That was the case for extraordinary figures such as St. Frances of Rome (1384–1440), St. Catherine de Ricci (1522–1590), St. Veronica Giuliani (1660–1727), Bl. Anna Maria Taigi (1769–1837), and Padre Pio (1887–1968), among others.[27] Their exhumed corpses years, decades, and sometimes centuries after their deaths showed little to no sign of decay, often looking almost identical to their condition before they died, or well before they died. Padre Pio's body looks fresher today, long after his death, than it did in his final weeks of his life in 1968.[28] For the bodies of these stigmatists to ultimately end up incorrupt—with several of them also accompanied by a perfumed, sweet-smelling odor of sanctity—seems only fitting as a capstone to the incredible things that happened to their bodies while they were alive in our realm.

Among these, a striking case of incorruptibility was the stigmatist Bl. Lucy of Narni, then called Narnia (1476–1544). That name ought to immediately perk the attention of fans of C. S. Lewis's classic series *The Chronicles of Narnia*. The similarity is no coincidence. For Lewis, his Lucy of Narnia was a fictional character called Lucy Pevensie, who became queen of Narnia. In Lewis's rendering, Lucy mystically traveled between her original 1940s wartime Britain and the other world of Narnia. It is a fantasy, of course. And yet, the real-world Lucy of Narni seems more fantastic because her story is not made up. That Lucy, who lived among us mortals, kept up constant communication with her other world as a stigmatist, visionary, ecstatic, mystic, and Dominican tertiary in central Italy in the fifteen to sixteenth centuries.[29]

Lucia Brocadelli's fifteen-century Umbrian village caught the notice of C. S. Lewis. It was said that the Englishman "instantly fell in love with" the town of Narnia.[30] As a faithful Christian and medieval scholar, Lewis was drawn to this historic section of Italy, where he was doubly drawn in by learning of the intensely mystical life of a young girl that captured his creative imagination.

The oldest of eleven children, Lucia Brocadelli lived in the small village of Narni. From her early youth, she had many mystical experiences. These were said to include playing with angels and cradling the infant Christ (her "Christarello") during a three-day vigil fast as a mere child engaging in acts of mortification.[31] She claimed visions and visits from the Virgin Mary and St. Catherine of Siena, who had died a century before Lucia's death. At the very young age of just seven, Lucy was granted the gift of divine espousal. It was said that there she beheld "a glorious company of saints and angels [standing] round the Person of Jesus Himself."[32] To the right of Jesus was His Virgin Mother; to His left was St. Catherine and the great Dominican patriarch St. Dominic, among still other figures. It was said that during this mystical experience came the ceremony of divine marriage, with the Lord placing a ring on the young girl's finger. Also coming at this moment was the placement of Lucy under the protection of Dominican Sts. Catherine of Siena and Dominic, as well as Lucy's commitment to one day join the Dominicans.

Under the social pressures of everyday life, the young Lucy was later obliged to enter an arranged marriage with the Count of Milan. But Lucy had made an earlier promise to her Lord. She and the count, Pietro de Alessio, agreed to honor the previous vows she had made to Christ of consecrated virginity. They would live effectively as brother and sister. (The English version of Pietro is "Peter," which was the name of the dominant male character in Lewis's *Chronicles of Narnia*. That Peter becomes Lewis's king.)

Lucy lived a holy life of service in the world, accompanied by saints and experiencing visions and miracles on a constant basis. Eventually, she entered a convent as a Third Order Dominican, whereupon, at the age of twenty, she received the stigmata. This occurred on February 25, 1496, at a convent in Viterbo, where she had been sent after a period in Rome.[33] Her stigmata were visible and appeared every Wednesday and Friday. What happened was no secret. Everyone knew and wanted to see, and it became a near spectacle, a sensation.

Multiple physicians examined Lucy. Word quickly reached Rome, and Pope Alexander VI sent his own physician, Bernardo de Recanati, to examine her. Three successive papal commissions, composed of physicians and theologians, examined Lucy before declaring her wounds unexplainable. The wounds were pronounced genuine. The pope himself said that the wounds were not from this world but from God, and he asked Lucy to pray for him.[34]

Ultimately, it was said that Count Pietro was so struck by the visible wounds of Christ that he ceased his increasingly aggressive demands of Lucy. After three years of celibate marriage, Pietro had reversed his pledge and demanded his marriage rights. He was belligerent in that respect, near-violent, prompting her to flee to a Dominican convent in Rome. But the appearance of the stigmata certainly prompted a change in attitude. Pietro himself became a religious, joining the Friars Minor.[35]

Experiencing the ecstasy of Christ's passion meant significant suffering for Lucy of Narni. She unintentionally gained notoriety for her unusual piety—attention she did not seek. She was admired by many for her holiness. But unfortunately, for many others, the wounds were a source of spectacle, of entertainment. Others still were envious, scornful, or disbelieving. That included her fellow sisters at the convent.

In 1505, Lucy was replaced in her position as prioress at the Convent of St. Catherine of Siena. The new superior confined Lucy to the convent, closing her off for the remaining four decades of her life in what was effectively a form of house arrest. There, she lived in silent obedience, though frequently receiving heavenly visitations during moments of ecstasy, even as some fellow sisters doubted her sanctity. She had been closed off for so long that at the time of her death, the townsfolk in the community of Ferrara were surprised to learn that she had still been alive; they had assumed that she must have passed away long ago.[36]

But when she did die, the miraculous signs only continued. The sisters who had treated her badly were astonished to hear angelic voices singing from Lucy's cell at the time of her death, and they also reported that the whole convent was filled with a beautiful smell of an extraordinary perfume. They fell to their knees, praying for forgiveness for how they had mistreated Lucy.[37] (This notion of a divine fragrance is not a wholly unique phenomenon among certain saints, especially stigmatists; it has long been associated with Padre Pio as well. We will also see it in the account of St. Rita that follows.)

Four years after her death, Lucy's body was exhumed, and the same lovely perfume was smelled by all. More than that, observers were stunned to discover a body that appeared exactly as it had when it was first interred. Most remarkably, long after, in the year 1710, when Lucy was beatified by Pope Clement XI, her body was again disinterred and found in the same excellent condition—almost two centuries after her death. Also observed at that moment were the marks of the stigmata, which were still visible.[38] Two centuries later, in May 1935, the body was translated to the town of Narni, where it today lies in repose in a glass reliquary in the city's cathedral.

All the misunderstanding that Lucy endured throughout her life was merely humbling to the saint, but through postmortem miracles, including total incorruptibility and the odor of sanctity, it can surely be asserted that God revealed Lucy's holiness in life beyond doubt in her death, including the still enduring marks of Christ's passion on her corpse.

Lucy persevered despite the scorn she received. C. S. Lewis was so inspired by her strength that he dubbed his visionary heroine "Queen Lucy the Valiant." Walter Hooper, Lewis's personal aide and secretary, once marveled to Lewis that his Lucy "bears such a very strong resemblance to your saint—the inner light of Faith, the extraordinary perseverance. . . . I think Blessed Lucy of Narnia has furnished the world with one of the most loved, and spiritually mature characters in English fiction."[39]

For Lewis, what better inspiration for his story than that of a truly inspired visionary? He found the vision through the eyes of a medieval mystic, Lucy of Narnia, visionary and stigmatist, who faced earthly torment but, in death, was protected from it by the same Lord who gave her the gift of His espousal and a sharing in His wounds of the Passion.

Partial Stigmata—Saint Rita of Cascia (1381–1457)

It is common among stigmatists to have borne the wounds of Christ in their hands and feet and sometimes in their sides and heads. Some had more wounds, and others had less. And some were gifted with only a partial wound. And in the case of one of the most extraordinary women in the history of the Catholic Church—St. Rita of Cascia—she was given a mere single thorn. For Rita, that was enough. In the Lord's providence, it was done.

Rita was born Margherita Lotti in 1381, just a year after the death of St. Catherine of Siena, almost, in a sense, an unseen passing of a torch from one remarkable Italian stigmatist to another. She hailed from the little town of Roccaporena in central Italy, a small suburb of Cascia in the region of Umbria, which is in the province of Perugia. This was truly an area where saints were made, including Sts. Francis and Clare of nearby Assisi a century earlier. It was a sign of the devoutness of the times that in Rita's village of Cascia, there were no less than four religious options for women. One was Augustinian, another was Franciscan, a third was Benedictine, and the fourth was the St. Mary Magdalene Convent, which Rita one day would join.[40]

Another sign of the times—a much less edifying one—was the conflict among these towns and regions. Rita's home province, Perugia, was warring with Assisi at the time of St. Francis. That atmosphere was one of the things that had so soured Francis on military life. This time also saw conflicts between families, during the terrible era of the *vendetta*, when families took revenge against one another for generations. In fact, it was this toxic environment of familial conflict and revenge that caused the loss of St. Rita's husband and sons, and it was in this environment that she would make her mark.[41]

Rita sought to change this destructive attitude of vengeance and would become known as "the Peacemaker" for her attempts to make peace among warring families. St. Rita's efforts for peace are similar to that of other female stigmatists from Italy, such as St. Catherine of Siena just years earlier and Sr. Elena Aiello many centuries later (with Elena's outreach being to Benito Mussolini). In fact, Rita "the Peacemaker" was so successful that she would also become known as the "Precious Pearl of Umbria" and, most famously, as the patron saint of impossible causes.

Rita had been very devout from the time of her childhood. Her parents, Antonio and Amata Ferri Lotti, certainly noticed her piety. Known to be kind and decent parents, they understood that their little girl craved the religious life. But her parents were also elderly, and they feared their daughter being left alone in the world when they died, so they sought to arrange a marriage for her. However, they did not make a good choice. At a young age (some sources say as young as twelve), Rita was married to a nobleman named Paolo Mancini. He was wealthy, which seemed the only motivation for the choice of Paolo, who was reputed to be an immoral man who led a licentious lifestyle and had a nasty temper. He has long been reported to have been cruel and abusive toward Rita, who, throughout eighteen years of marriage, offered up her suffering.[42]

The trial ended when her husband was killed, possibly by a rival family, possibly by bandits, or simply by men he had wronged. The murder set Rita's two sons on an angry course of revenge. Rita prayed to the heavens that the Lord would take her boys before they could act on the mortal sin of murder on behalf of avenging their father, and the boys soon died of sickness from an outbreak of the plague. Rita was relieved that they had not committed murder, but she was devastated nonetheless.

Now a widow with no husband and no children, Rita at long last entered the Augustinian convent in Cascia. There, she had many mystical experiences, including visions of her patron saints: John the Baptist, Augustine, and the thirteenth-century saint Nicholas of Tolentino—a visionary himself.[43] She died just three days after receiving a vision of the Lord and His Blessed Mother.

Particularly fascinating about St. Rita were two physical phenomena: her stigmata and her incorruptibility after so many years—nearly six centuries, in fact. The stigmata were granted to her on Good Friday 1442, fifteen years before her death.[44] It was inspired by a sermon preached by St. James of the Marches (1392–1476), a renowned Italian Franciscan of the era, which convinced her to embrace suffering and accept mortification of the flesh rather than eschew it.

When Rita returned to the convent that afternoon, after hearing the sermon by James, she went to a corner of the convent that held an image of Jesus in a portrait known as *Jesus of the Holy Saturday* (also known as the *Resurgent Christ*). This image is renowned for its portrayal of Christ crowned with thorns during His passion, along with His pierced hands and feet. Moved more than ever this time by a deep identification with her Lord's suffering, Rita expressed a willingness at that moment to have the honor of sharing a mere small part of Christ's suffering on the Cross.[45] And then it happened. "Her offer was accepted, her prayer was answered," writes one biographer, "and Rita was united with Jesus in a profound experience of spiritual intimacy. In this moment of ecstatic union, a thorn from Jesus's crown penetrated Rita's forehead and the wound it caused remained open and visible for the next fifteen years until the day of her death."[46]

As with St. Francis in front of the San Damiano cross or Padre Pio inside Our Lady of Grace chapel at San Giovanni Rotondo, the image of Christ on the Cross penetrated Rita in a profound way. Rita had implored her Savior to let her partake in His passion, and she was rewarded most acutely with a divinely implanted thorn in her forehead. It was her own part to share in the crown of thorns. To the wonderment and often shock of onlookers, this thorn would remain for fifteen years until her death at age seventy-six.

Notably, the oozing wound produced a foul odor, so much so that people avoided Rita, and she sought seclusion. Her death, however, changed everything. Akin to that of stigmatist Bl. Lucy of Narni, it was said that at the time of Rita's death, her cell was filled with a lovely perfume smell, accompanied by a ray of light that was said to emanate from the thorn wound in her head. The nuns who were present were astounded. The beautiful smell did not go away, accompanying Rita's corpse long after.

Hence, we can add to the phenomenon of Rita's thorn stigmata another related wonder: her sweetly perfumed corpse. Inexplicably, after her death, her corpse gave off a sweetly perfumed scent that eventually filled the church where she was laid. That sweet fragrance has been interpreted as a heavenly reward for Rita's unique form of earthly suffering. The aroma remained constant for centuries and, reportedly, still happens intermittently.[47]

Of course, news of these supernatural occurrences spread throughout the Umbrian countryside. Pilgrims flocked to the church where Rita's corpse lay enshrined beneath the altar. Travelers came to venerate the corpse, the freshness of which went still further beyond the attractive smell. How so? Rita's body was not decomposing. How long would this last?

Before Rita was declared a blessed in July 1627 by Pope Urban VIII, her corpse was examined by Church authorities and found incorruptible—some 150 years after her death. "The body was carefully examined and found to be as perfect as it had been on the day of her death," writes Joan Carroll Cruz in her classic *The Incorruptibles*, "with the flesh still of a natural color. The excellent condition of her body after the lapse of over 150 years seems quite extraordinary since it was never properly entombed."[48]

This was just the start of Rita's post-death earthly journey. In 1946, a church was built in her honor and specifically for her body, which was encased in glass. And even then, her body remained incorrupt. "St. Rita's body, as viewed by countless pilgrims, appears only slightly discolored and is perfect in all its members," recorded Joan Carroll Cruz in 1977, "except for one eyebrow, which moved in its position about the year 1650, and a right cheek bone, which became dislodged. These were repaired with wax and string as the two medical examinations of 1743 and 1892 indicate."[49]

As Cruz's documentation attests, Rita's incorruptibility is not some superstitious flight of imagination by locals. Medical personnel and Church officials have observed it rigorously for over a half millennium. It has amazed all as a work of the truly miraculous, right up until and through the intense investigation leading to her canonization four and a half centuries after her death. Today, visitors to places like Assisi—home of Francis and Clare—are struck by the presence of prayer cards to St. Rita, in addition to Francis and Clare.[50]

Cruz and others have reported claims of Rita's eyes having allegedly opened and closed unaided at various times in her tomb and of her body shifting on its own. There have also been claims of her body rising (floating) to the top of the reliquary.[51] The Church, of course, was not present as a witness and cannot affirm these individual claims.

While Rita died on May 22, 1457, which is now her feast day, she wasn't canonized until May 24, 1900, by Pope Leo XIII. It is hard to believe that it took that long—almost impossible, it would seem, given her saintliness. Then again, Rita would come to be known as the saint of impossible causes. Today, her seemingly impossibly incorrupt body remains in the Basilica of Santa Rita da Cascia.

As noted by biographer Fr. Michael Di Gregorio, though Rita, unlike other stigmatists, bore only one wound, that thorn "was truly and fully a sharing in the physical and spiritual suffering of our Lord."[52] With St. Rita, nothing seems impossible, including sharing in a mere thorn of the suffering of her Savior—a most distinctive form of stigmata.

✝

Whether it's the story of St. Rita, Bl. Lucy, or the other stigmatists to be profiled in the pages that follow, none of this seems possible. In essence, none of the stigmatists seem possible, at least to modern science and the natural world. And yet, they have been among us, bringing the supernatural to us for millennia. They go back to St. Francis some eight hundred years ago, if not to St. Paul some two thousand years ago. They are men and women from all over the world, admired for their exceptional piety as well as for their wounds.

We have had them among us through history by the hundreds, sometimes bleeding from their hands and feet and sides and heads, and sometimes gifted with merely one thorn, as with St. Rita of Cascia, saint of the impossible. In all, they show that nothing is impossible with God. And behold, if you have been struck by these stories of the impossible thus far, quite a few accounts still more miraculous are yet to come in the pages ahead.

CHAPTER 2

SAINT FRANCIS OF ASSISI
(1181/1182–1226)

Born at either the end of the year 1181 or the beginning of the year 1182, St. Francis—known for everything from flowers to birds to crèches to poverty and penance and more—is one of the most revered names in the Catholic Church, if not in Christendom as a whole. He was born in Assisi, a lovely Italian village in the heart of the beautiful region of Umbria, in the Spoleto Valley area of the Apennine Mountains.

His father was Pietro di Bernardone, a wealthy silk merchant, who, upon returning from a trip to France, was so captivated by his visit that he told his wife, Giovanna (known as "Pica"), that he desired to name his newborn son "Francesco." It was not the typical Italian name, but by the time the infant grew to manhood and ultimately sainthood, it would become one of the most popular Italian names ever for boys and even girls ("Francesca"). It would one day, some eight hundred years henceforth, even inspire the name of a pope.

Fittingly, the baby's mother had initially named him Giovanni, or John, after John the Baptist. The name was appropriate given the ascetical, penitential life in the wilderness that Francis, like John, lived. But the father had a different name in mind, and perhaps that was just as well, as Francis of Assisi would, like John the Baptist, have a uniqueness that no other figure ever could quite match. There has never been anyone else like him.

The boy and especially his father harbored dreams of him becoming a soldier, a crusader, and a gallant knight, whether taking up arms against the rival city of Perugia or going abroad to the Holy Land to take back Christian lands from Muslim invaders. And when he was not training to be a warrior, he was up late at night partying with friends and the ladies—living the high life, drinking, carousing, and doing so with his father's hard-earned money. Perhaps the drinking was a way to cope with the stress of warring, which Francesco clearly did not enjoy as much. Privately, it tore at him.

During one particular battle with Perugia, the troops from Assisi were defeated, and Francis was captured and tossed into a dark dungeon. He was very depressed and wondered if he would eventually be ransomed and freed. That incarceration certainly affected him, but it had not yet dampened his spirits so much that he was willing to stand up to his father and give up a life of war.

But God had other plans for Francis. As Francis set out from Assisi for a crusade—namely, the Fourth Crusade (1202–1204)—all fitted in the finest cloak (courtesy of Pietro's cloth-trading business), armor, and sword, making his father proud, he had a revelation, the first of many provided by the divine. He did not get far before God spoke to him, telling him to turn around and give up this path of war and find a path of peace.

It was not easy to turn back to Assisi. Francesco knew that his father's fellow businessmen and his peers would laugh at him or consider him a coward. Nonetheless, Francis went home. This began, for the young man, a steady path of intense conversion, supported by his mother and the Bible that she gave him during this time of personal crisis when his father scolded him.

He emerged from an effective exile in his own home as a changed person. Father and friends and townsfolk alike marveled at this young man suddenly so on fire for the Lord that he was kissing lepers and giving away his father's money to the poor. When Francis stood in the middle of the town square and shed all his clothes, forsaking all worldly goods and Pietro's inheritance, many were convinced that he had lost his mind. His father, no doubt, was losing his mind at what his son had become. He was furious, though Francis's Father in heaven was jubilant.

The Lord now had a warrior—a warrior for Christ. He became, in the words of his first biographer, Thomas of Celano (writing in the year 1228), a "knight for Christ." Or, in the words of a modern biographer, prayer and ascetism were now his "sword and shield."[53] This was a different type of armor; it was the armor of God. Here was a new and altogether different type of knight, a soldier willing to be wounded for Christ. Here was a young man willing to suffer and offer it up for God in a way few had in history.

Francesco di Bernardone had become fully alive, a child of God in a way he never felt before. He would now escape into the countryside, alone, to find himself and his mission in the world.

The San Damiano Vision

Francesco retreated to the countryside just outside of Assisi, where he found a cave and the remains of the delapidated church of San Damiano. There, he escaped the wrath of his earthly father and found the welcoming arms of a heavenly Father and the wide-open arms of Christ on the Cross.

One day, in the year 1205, Francesco sought solace at the church of San Damiano.[54] It was a church that had been abandoned, akin to what was happening in the Catholic Church of the day. There, Francesco had an extraordinary vision. Kneeling in prayer, he looked up at an icon of Jesus Christ crucified and was shocked when the image of Christ literally spoke to him, eyes open and lips moving. His animated Savior said to him, "*Francesco, Francesco, va, ripara la Mia chiesa, che, come potete vedere, sta cadendo in rovina* (Francis, Francis, go and repair My church, which, as you can see, is falling into ruins)."[55] Christ issued this order three times, repeating the phrase verbatim.

Stunned by what he saw and heard, Francis set forth to repair the church of God that lay in ruins all around him, namely, that fallen countryside church of San Damiano. He rebuilt it with his own hands, soon joined by others inspired to help. But in retrospect, Christ had in mind a much larger mission—a larger Church that was falling and needed to be repaired: the Catholic Church. And that would be Francis's mission.

Of course, given that Christ communicated to Francis audibly rather than by way of a written text, we do not know if He used the word *chiesa* (lowercase *c*). But He actually meant *Chiesa* (uppercase *C*). For Francis, in due time, it would apply to both that little church of San Damiano and the bigger one, the Catholic Church, headquartered in Rome. He would visit both and seek to repair both. "It was a moment of ecstasy and great consolation for Francis," writes one author. "He had received from God a mission, a vocation. He left the San Damiano Chapel irrevocably transformed."[56]

His call would deeply affect not just him but those who rallied to him, desiring this strange form of penitential joy. Soon, Francis had been so inspired and was now himself so inspiring of a figure that many men entered the hills and valleys to join him. Women, too, wanted to be a part of what he was founding. One of them, the lovely Clare of Assisi, would follow him and start her own order—the Poor Clare sisters.

After the death of Francis, it was fitting that Clare and her Poor Clare sisters would secure that special San Damiano cross when they left San Damiano in 1257 and place it in safekeeping. Since 1958, it has hung high in their Church of Santa Chiara (St. Clare), where pilgrims to this day can come and venerate it, sitting under the very crucifix that literally spoke to St. Francis eight centuries ago.[57]

Receiving the Stigmata

The experience with Christ on the cross at the chapel at San Damiano was apparently preparation for a still deeper transformation of spirit and of body for Francesco di Bernardone. Francis would feel an even more intimate connection to that Christ on that cross. The icon showed a triumphant Christ, with a black silhouette behind him, representative of the empty tomb. It also showed the living Christ's pierced hands and feet. Therein, too, Francis would find a keen identification.

The penitential friar had taken a liking to a retreat spot on the mountain of La Verna, where he and other Friars Minor would go to fast and pray. Francis had a special devotion to St. Michael the Archangel, whose feast day is September 29, and so he went to La Verna for a forty-day fast in preparation for that feast day. It was during that time of penance, specifically on September 14, 1224, the feast of the Exaltation of the Cross, that something extraordinary happened.

Br. Leo, who was Francis's closest friend, companion, and secretary, was a witness to the event. Later, after the death of Francis, he described what happened very simply and succinctly. He noted that it occurred two years before Francis's death, at La Verna, during a fast that for Francis had been a personal "Lent" done "in honor of the blessed Mary, mother of God, and of the holy angel, Michael, from the feast of the Assumption of the Virgin right up to the feast of Saint Michael in September." Leo attested to the presence of a seraph and the subsequent "impression of the stigmata on his body."[58]

Such first-person witnesses are crucial because Francis himself refused to write about the phenomenon and had forbidden those few individuals who saw and touched his wounds and cared for him during the final two years of his life from talking about it. (This explains Br. Leo's terseness in describing the phenomenon.) It was only after his death and before he was buried that others, including friars in his own order who had not been close to the humble man, had the chance to observe the wounds themselves.[59] Unlike another Franciscan friar centuries later, Padre Pio, whose stigmata were removed by the Lord shortly before his death, Francis's wounds remained on his corpse.

Upon Francis's death, Br. Elias, the leader of the Friars Minor, immediately dispatched a formal letter to the entire order, describing the stigmata and affirming that the spectacular wounds were indeed of supernatural origin. He sent his encyclical letter the very day of Francis's death, October 4, 1226, writing jubilantly:

> I announce to you a great joy, a miracle of a new kind. One has never heard tell of a similar wonder in the whole world except

in the person of the Son of God, Christ our Lord. Indeed, a
little before his death, our brother and father (Francis) appeared
as if crucified, bearing in his body the five wounds which are
truly the stigmata of Christ. In fact, his hands and feet had had
something like perforations made by the nails, front and back,
that retained scars and showed the blackness of the nails. As to
his side, he seemed to be pierced and blood often flowed out.[60]

One can feel in this detailed missive Br. Elias's excitement and long-
ing to inform the world of what those closest to the suffering servant
from Assisi had the incredible privilege to witness. The leader of the
Friars Minor was explicit in describing the perforations, the nails, the
wounds, and the blood and did not hesitate to affirm that this was
"truly the stigmata of Christ." In life, the humble servant could try to
hide these wounds received at La Verna, but now, in death, it was time
for his associates to shout the news from the mountaintop. Note, too,
that Br. Elias used the word *stigmata*, which means "marks" of Christ.
This may have been one of the first uses of the term since the time of
Christ. Such was the mark left by St. Francis.

Three years later, published in 1229, came the first *Life of Francis*
biography by Thomas of Celano, which would become the primary
source for most subsequent biographers chronicling the life of the little
poor man, known as *Il Poverello*.[61] Unlike Br. Elias in his quick letter
upon Francis's death, which almost felt akin to a thirteenth-century press
release, Thomas, in his biography, went into further detail, including
where, when, and how the stigmata were first received.

Interestingly, Thomas related that Francis had been having doubts
about his vocation. Three times during these doubts, he opened his
book on the Gospels and just happened to come upon passages concerning Christ's passion. It was only during the third time that he
looked up and glimpsed the figure appearing as a seraph fixed to a cross
with arms outstretched.[62]

According to Thomas of Celano, this seraph-looking figure had six
wings, two above its head, two at the bottom of the body, and two in
the middle that were extended outward as if in flight. He said it had the
appearance of an Old Testament seraph (noted for their grand powers),

with the notable exception that this seraph was suspended from a cross. Thomas described the scene this way:

> Two years before Francis gave his soul back to heaven, while he was staying in a hermitage called "Alverna" after the place where it was located, he saw in a vision from God a man with six wings like a seraph, standing above him with hands extended and feet together, affixed to a cross. Two wings were raised over his head, two were extended in flight, and two hid his entire body.
>
> When the blessed servant of God saw these things he was filled with wonder, but he did not know what the vision meant. He rejoiced greatly in the benign and gracious expression with which he saw himself regarded by the seraph, whose beauty was indescribable; yet he was alarmed by the fact that the seraph was affixed to the cross and was suffering terribly. Thus Francis rose, one might say, sad and happy, joy and grief alternating in him. He wondered anxiously what this vision could mean, and his soul was uneasy as it searched for understanding. And as his understanding sought in vain for an explanation and his heart was filled with perplexity at the great novelty of this vision, the marks of nails began to appear in his hands and feet, just as he had seen them slightly earlier in the crucified man above him.

The seraph was crucified, and now Francis was about to share in the same sad and yet happy ordeal. Thomas then went into detail, describing not only what Francis himself had felt but what those who saw the wounds had perceived and tried to understand:

> His hands and feet seemed to be pierced by nails, with the heads of the nails appearing in the palms of his hands and on the upper sides of his feet, the points appearing on the other side. The marks were round on the palm of each hand but elongated on the other side, and small pieces of flesh jutting out from the rest took on the appearance of the nail-ends, bent and driven back. In the same way the marks of nails were impressed on his feet and projected beyond the rest of the flesh.

Moreover, his right side had a large wound as if it had been pierced with a spear, and it often bled so that his tunic and trousers were soaked with his sacred blood.

Alas, how few were worthy of viewing the wound in the side of this crucified servant of the crucified Lord! How fortunate was Elias, who was worthy of seeing it while the holy man lived, but no less fortunate was Rufinus, who touched the wound with his own hands. For once, when the aforesaid brother Rufinus put his hand on the holy man's chest in order to rub him, his hand fell to his right side, as often occurs, and he happened to touch that precious wound. The holy man of God suffered great anguish from that touch and, pushing the hand away, he cried out to the Lord to forgive him. He carefully hid the wound from outsiders and cautiously concealed it from those near him, so that even his most devoted followers and those who were constantly at his side knew nothing of it for a long time. And although the servant and friend of the most high saw himself adorned with many costly pearls as if with precious gems, and marvelously decked out beyond the glory and honor of other men, he did not become vain or seek to please anyone through desire for personal glory, but, lest human favor should steal away the grace given to him, he attempted to hide it in every way possible.[63]

Thomas of Celano went on to note how these wounds further exacerbated (not surprisingly) Francis's already intense physical sufferings—which included a worsening condition of near blindness—especially given the severe forms of self-imposed mortification to which he subjected his body: "During this period Francis' body began to be beset by more serious illnesses than previously," added Thomas. "He suffered frequent illnesses because for many years he had castigated his body perfectly, reducing it to servitude. For during the preceding eighteen years his flesh had scarcely or never found rest, but traveled constantly throughout various wide areas so that the prompt, devout and fervent spirit within him could scatter God's word everywhere."

Despite the nails pressing into his flesh, Francis pressed on, preaching the Word and offering up his sufferings as expiation for the sins of the world. His weakened frame grew only weaker. He would be able to withstand the pain for only two more years in his young life. He was in his early forties, but he surely felt much older. He was certainly carrying his cross, and then some.

There is still another source worth quoting on this subject: St. Bonaventure, a Doctor of the Church, who entered the Franciscans in 1243 and, in 1257, was elected minister general. A major scholar and theologian educated at the University of Paris, he wrote what many consider the definitive biography of Francis. He played such a crucial role in the early decades of the Friars Minor that he is often considered the "second founder" of the Franciscans, second only to Francis himself. St. Bonaventure wrote of the stigmata, which provides yet another authoritative statement on this first stigmatist.

> As the vision was disappearing, it left in his heart a marvelous fire and imprinted in his flesh a likeness of signs no less marvelous. For immediately the marks of nails began to appear in his hands and feet just as he had seen a little before in the figure of the man crucified. His hands and feet seemed to be pierced through the center by nails, with the heads of the nails appearing on the inner side of the hands and the upper side of the feet and their points on the opposite sides. The heads of the nails in his hands and his feet were round and black; their points were oblong and bent as if driven back with a hammer, and they emerged from the flesh and stuck out beyond it. Also his right side, as if pierced with a lance, was marked with a red wound from which his sacred blood often flowed, moistening his tunic and underwear.[64]

This miraculous occurrence made Francesco di Bernardone perhaps the first stigmatist in history, even earning him among some the title of *alter Christus*, meaning "another Christ," though certainly not comparable to Christ Himself—as Francis himself would have affirmed emphatically. As noted at the start of this book, it is possible that

St. Paul might have also been a stigmatist, given his words in Galatians 6:17: "I bear on my body the marks of Jesus." But we do not know if that referred to what we understand today as stigmata or something symbolic in which Paul simply meant to say that he suffered as Christ did. As to what we now understand a stigmatist—that being a person with bleeding wounds akin to those of Christ on the Cross—St. Francis is generally understood as the first.

Francis's Mission and Ours: Reforming Rather than Rebelling from the Church

The extraordinary and yet humble Francis and his extraordinary and yet humble Order of Franciscan friars became not merely the talk of the Umbrian region but of Italy, Rome, the Vatican, and the Church. The order experienced explosive growth, so much so that Francis himself— and his order—almost became overwhelmed by it. After his death, it would be left to successors, better educated and better schooled in the art of administration—which most certainly was not Francis's calling—to manage the growth of the order and keep the Franciscans' commitment to their rule.

That order, thanks to the example of Francis, in the year 1209, received approval from the pope, namely, Innocent III. Many Christians were inspired to join the order, but many more were simply inspired by it to the point that they wanted to recommit themselves to the Church, which, prior to Francis's encounter with the cross in the church of San Damiano, seemed to have fallen into ruins. It no doubt needed to be repaired.

Sadly, another friar, not known for his humility, came to the conclusion three centuries later that the Church needed to be repaired much more drastically. That was the doing of Martin Luther, based on his own personal assessment of what was wrong and what needed to be fixed. Christ did not convey that need to Luther by way of spoken words from a crucifix. He did not tell Luther to go and repair His Church. Luther had his own vision and his own plan. Rather than repair Christ's Church, as Francis did, Luther rebelled from Christ's Church.

Martin Luther insisted on doing things his way, outside of the approval of the pope, whom he mocked, insulted, cursed, and denounced as the antichrist. Francis obediently yearned for the pope's approval and walked all the way to Rome to plead for it. It was not easy, with Innocent III's curia very suspicious of the strange hermit and his grimy, unshaven friends in dirty, tattered brown robes, who seemed to eat even less than they washed and yet somehow seemed filled with joy. But with the guidance of the Holy Spirit, sought by both sides, the Holy Father granted Francis approval to preach penance everywhere. Francis's whole mission, thereafter, was one of penance, submitting wholly to Christ's way. Martin Luther's mission was one of arrogance, convinced that the pope and Church needed to wholly submit to his way.

The two divergent attitudes had profound effects in so many ways, including in their personal lives. When Luther met a nun who loved him, they both rejected their vows of celibacy and married. They did not seek the lives of purity, holiness, abstinence, and celibacy that Francis and Clare did. It is believed that there was an attraction, even perhaps a burning passion, between Francis and Clare, but they forced it aside to serve their orders and their Church. Luther and his ex-nun, by contrast, did things their way. Francis and Clare did things the Church's way.

What Martin Luther led is what we today call the Reformation. But in truth, Luther did not reform the Catholic Church. That might have been his initial intention, but what he ultimately did was rebel against the Church. What Luther led is what we today ought to call the Rebellion. It was not a Protestant Reformation—the very word "Protestant" means "Protest," that is, a protest forever against the Catholic Church—but a Protestant Rebellion.

By contrast, the humble and obedient Francesco di Bernardone and his friars led a very real reformation. They genuinely helped to reform—to repair—a Church that appeared to have fallen into ruins. One might argue that the Friars Minor's reformation/repair was so inspiring and so successful that it helped to keep the Church intact for all of the thirteenth century and even sustained it for centuries to come. However, the Church is always in need of reform. As this book will show, the next century after Francis's death, the fourteenth century, would require the inspiring assistance of another Italian stigmatist, this one a female, St. Catherine of Siena, whose efforts brought the pope back to Rome from Avignon, France.

Reform and repair seem to be a constant process and ever-going battle within Christ's Church, which often seems to be falling into ruin not because of Him but because of His people. Still, the gates of hell shall not prevail against it.

What the Church continually needs is a faithful flock and shepherds who seek to keep it standing. It does not benefit the Church nor Christendom as a whole when priests and laity pull away to create their own churches. We see today a world of endlessly expanding denominations and even nondenominational churches—each fashioning their own doctrines based on their own interpretations of the Scriptures, as Martin Luther had demanded. It is a world of religious relativism and chaos that has led many to ruin.

It has led many a *chiesa*—many a church—to ruin.[65]

The task of reparation is always one of self-sacrifice. It often requires submitting to suffering—severe suffering—and sometimes painful forms of mortification. Few felt that like Francesco di Bernardone. As part of his call, his mission, his vocation, his Lord and Savior went so far as to ask him to share in the suffering of His very wounds on the cross.

✝

In the spring of 1226, Francis visited Siena, where he was extremely weakened from a life of extraordinary mortification. He began dictating a final will and testament. He slowly and steadily made his way back to his Portiuncula in Assisi. It was there that he died during the night of October 3–4, at the age of forty-four. His body was taken first to the monastery at San Damiano, where Clare and her sisters could say goodbye and where the Pierced One on the Cross had first commissioned him.

It took little time thereafter for the pope to canonize Francis. In less than two years, on July 16, 1228, Pope Gregory IX canonized the poor little man—*Il Poverello*—who exchanged wealth for poverty and war for peace.

St. Francis's feast day is October 4. The marks of Christ that he carried made him the first known stigmatist. They and he would leave their mark on history and the Church in a profound way.

CHAPTER 3

SAINT CATHERINE OF SIENA (1347–1380)

One of the most remarkable women in the history of the Church is St. Catherine of Siena. Along with St. Teresa of Avila, she was eventually chosen by Pope St. Paul VI in 1970 as one of the first female doctors of the Church. (Two other women would follow: St. Hildegard of Bingen and St. Thérèse of Lisieux.) At present, there are only thirty-seven doctors of the Church. The designation of the title "doctor" means "teacher," which was appropriate given Catherine's nearly four hundred letters, twenty-six prayers, and famous *Dialogue*. Pope Ven. Pius XII made her co-patron of Italy, along with St. Francis, and Pope St. John Paul II made her a co-patron of Europe.

Caterina Benincasa was born in the lovely medieval Italian city of Siena on March 25, 1347, the feast of the Annunciation. At the Annunciation, the heavenly messenger Gabriel transmitted to the Virgin Mary a divine message from the Creator of the universe. The Church's commemoration of that event is a fitting birthdate for this extraordinary Sienese woman who would receive and carry so many heavenly messages from the Creator Himself and His Blessed Mother.

Catherine's father, Giacomo Benincasa, was a cloth dyer who ran the business out of the family home along with his sons. Her mother, Lapa Piagenti, was nearly forty years old when she gave birth to Catherine and a twin sister, Giovanna. Giovanna and Catherine were, respectively, Lapa's twenty-third and twenty-fourth children, most of whom did not survive infancy. After birth, Giovanna was fed by a wet nurse, while Catherine was nursed by Lapa. Unfortunately, Giovanna did not live long. When Lapa gave birth to her twenty-fifth and final child, she and Giacomo named the little girl Giovanna in honor of her late sister.

Catherine's parents immediately saw in her very special spiritual gifts. At age five, she learned the Hail Mary and repeated it constantly. One routine had the little girl reciting the prayer on each step up and down the staircase. At each step, she stopped to kneel in homage. Her mother would later tell Catherine's spiritual director that, at times, she heard her daughter get from the bottom of the steps to the top so quickly that it scared Lapa. How could this happen? Her spiritual director, Bl. Raimondo di Capua, asked Catherine about it, pressing her to answer him in confidence. She confirmed that (in Raimondo's words) "frequently, indeed more often than not, when she was going up and down stairs she felt herself being lifted up into the air and her feet no longer touched the stairs." Raimondo believed that this repeated phenomenon may have been a reward for her prayerful habit of repeating the Hail Mary on every step from a young age.[66]

Despite these obvious spiritual gifts, Catherine's parents nonetheless insisted upon and prepared her for marriage, as was the custom for young women of the day. When her beloved sister Bonaventura died during childbirth when Catherine was sixteen, Lapa and Giacomo proposed that Catherine marry Bonaventura's husband, but Catherine fought against it, going so far as cutting her attractive long hair to try to degrade her appearance. Lapa was militantly opposed to Catherine's resistance to the proposed marriage and reacted hysterically, befitting her emotional personality. Giacomo, a kind and gentle man, pressed for Catherine's wishes to be honored, knowing keenly that this girl was quite different. Eventually, the family, seeing the striking depth of her obvious spiritual gifts, consented to give her a single small room in the house—a "cell"—in which she devoted herself wholly to Christ. She would eventually, at the age of twenty-one, enter into a mystical marriage with Jesus Christ.

For Catherine, that moment seemed a kind of sealed commission for this Third Order Dominican. Around the age of sixteen, she joined a group of penitent laywomen who called themselves the *Mantellate* (plural for *Mantellata*). The word translates into "cloak" or "cape," the distinctive form of dress worn by these women. They wore a black mantle or cape over a white habit. They lived not in community and in convents but in their homes, and they met at the Dominican church in Siena.

From there, Catherine devoted herself to the service of God and to those in need. She provided care to the poor, the sick, and the lame in incredible ways. Moreover, she served as nothing less than an emissary to popes, urging the pontiffs of the day to leave their current displaced home in Avignon, France and return to Rome, the home of St. Peter, the true seat of the papacy and the Catholic Church. These leaders of the Church eventually conceded to Catherine's urging, albeit reluctantly, as she steeled their waning courage. The respect and even fear that this humble, demure, but strong medieval woman struck in popes was astonishing and yet another unmistakable sign of her widely recognized holiness. For those who want to argue that the Catholic Church has long repressed and ignored women, they should study the life of St. Catherine of Siena.

This frail but mighty figure was blessed with numerous visions, the gift of prophecy, and the ability to see into souls and predict future events. She also received the stigmata—in her case, hidden stigmata.

A key element of what Pope St. John Paul II called her "lived theology" is that Catherine emphasized the imperative to have correct knowledge of the truth.[67] She said that defective knowledge of the truth leads to sin. Like the great Italian poet Dante, who lived about a hundred years before Catherine and hailed from Florence, about seventy-eight kilometers from Siena, she shared the view that sin is often based in loving the wrong things. You can love, but you need to love the right things. Your love needs to be a properly ordered love, not a disordered love. As we see in the time of St. Catherine, the world has always been replete with disordered love, with people loving the wrong things—including things that are sinful.

Catherine's influence in her lifetime was profound. She quickly grew in esteem and was widely heralded. Unlike other stigmatists in this book, such as St. Faustina, Catherine's gifts were known in her lifetime. Everyone heard about this remarkable woman and wanted to meet her, and she was widely sought out until the day of her death in Rome on April 29, 1380. Like her Savior, she was thirty-three years old when she experienced death after a period of intense suffering, offering up that suffering for the sins of the world.

Catherine's Visions and Stigmata

The admiration for Catherine is so longstanding that she has been a popular source for biographers, including a much-acclaimed 1951 work by Sigrid Undset, finished just months before the Norwegian, Nobel Prize–winning author's death.[68] Most of these works, however, rely almost exclusively (even when curiously not citing it) on the foundational work on Catherine's life, the book *The Life of St. Catherine of Siena*, written by her spiritual director, Fr. Raimondo di Capua (Raymond of Capua).[69]

Raimondo, today recognized by the Catholic Church as blessed, was born in 1330 and was thus seventeen years older than Catherine. In 1364, he replaced her previous spiritual director and fellow Dominican, Tommaso della Fonte. Raimondo was highly regarded when he was granted that special assignment. He was a leading Dominican who, in 1380, the year of Catherine's death, became the order's master general, a position he held until his own death in 1399. He had already served as the first biographer of another remarkable Dominican woman, St. Agnes of Montepulciano, who died thirty years before Catherine was born—and whom Catherine came to know through mystical communications.[70]

A respected spiritual director, theologian, and biographer, Raimondo was with Catherine constantly. He was very close to her as a spiritual director, a confidante, and, at times, like both a father and son until her death. He was an eyewitness to what later biographers of Catherine's life could only try to capture from his recorded notes.

With skilled writing and detail, these notes produced a fascinating biography that still surprises readers over six hundred years later.[71] To revisit all those details here would be, of course, impossible and unnecessary. Given the focus of this particular book, we will look at what Bl. Raimondo recorded about Catherine's astonishing visions and her stigmata.

The first vision of consequence came when Catherine was just six years old. One day in Siena, which Raimondo estimates to be around 1353, the girl was with her brother Stefano on an errand to visit their older sister Bonaventura and her husband, Niccolo. On their way back home, they were walking down the Valle Piatta when the little girl was halted in her tracks by a stunning vision. She looked up at the sky and saw a striking scene above the roof of the church of the Dominicans. Raimondo provided the details:

> Hanging in the air in front of her over the roof of the church of the Friars Preachers, she saw a most beautiful bridal chamber decked out in regal splendor, in which on an imperial throne, dressed in pontifical attire and with the tiara on His head (that is to say, the monarchical papal mitre), sat the Lord Jesus Christ, the Savior of the world. With him were the Princes of the Apostles Peter and Paul and the holy Evangelist John. At the sight of all this the little girl remained rooted to the ground, gazing lovingly with unblinking eyes upon her Lord and Savior, who was revealing Himself to her in this way in order to captivate her love. Then, gazing straight at her with eyes full of majesty, and smiling most lovingly, He raised His right hand over her, made the sign of the cross of salvation like a priest, and graciously gave her His eternal benediction.[72]

This was the first and defining image of Catherine's life and mission to come. Most of her mystical visions would be of Christ the King as well as with His apostles and other heavenly sources.[73] Among her most momentous, divinely ordained missions was to guide the popes of her lifetime. Thus, it was fitting that her first image of Jesus would be one in which He was dressed in pontifical attire with the tiara on His head.

"The grace of this gift was so immediately effective upon the little girl that she was taken right out of herself and entirely into Him she lovingly looked upon," added Raimondo. She was fixated, frozen to that spot, and people and animals alike passed the odd child, going around her, as she stared upward, motionless, totally absorbed. Her brother Stefano had moved well ahead of his little sister before realizing she was no longer at his side. He went back to retrieve her, shouting at her. As he continued to call her, she remained unresponsive. Finally, he grabbed her arm, shook her, and pulled her away. "What are you doing?" he asked in frustration. "Why don't you come along?" This deeply saddened the little girl, who protested to her older brother, "If you could see what I can you would not be so cruel and disturb me out of this lovely vision."[74]

With that, the vision ended, and Catherine burst into tears. That reaction, too, was a harbinger of later incidents. The adult Catherine often would fall deep into a mystical state, as others stood by thinking that she was in a near coma or even dead, though with eyes wide open, unblinking, and totally fixated on the vision at hand and its message. She was always distraught when the vision was over, never wanting it to end, never wanting to stop her truly heavenly moment of divine union. For the remaining twenty-seven years of her life, she would tell witnesses that she never wanted separation from Christ. By comparison, this world was almost torturous, given what the next world looked like and offered. She simply wanted to stay with Jesus all the time, forever, eternally. The moment that she was plummeted back to earth indeed always felt cruel.

This first visionary experience was almost mild compared to the intensity of Catherine's countless mystical moments in the years to come. At first, these were private experiences, but they often became public as well.

One of the most legendary of these experiences came when Catherine, praying to the Lord in a state described by Raimondo as "utmost fervor," requested, "Create a clean heart within me, O God." She claimed that, at that moment, her Heavenly Bridegroom appeared, opened her left side, and literally removed her heart from her body and then left. She claimed to have continued to live without a heart.

In fact, she told friends and her confessor that she was living without a heart. This went on until one day, at the same Dominican church where she had her first vision as a six-year-old, the Lord Jesus appeared to her and said, "Dearest daughter, as I took your heart away from you the other day, now, you see, I am giving you mine, so that you can go on living forever." To this astonishing process of exchange, Raimondo recorded, "With these words He closed the opening He had made in her side, and as a sign of the miracle a scar remained on that part of her flesh, as I and others were told by her companions who saw it. When I determined to get to the truth, she herself was obliged to confess to me that this was so, and she added that never afterwards had she been able to say, 'Lord, I give you my heart.'"[75]

She could no longer say, "I give you my heart," because she had already given it to Him. The Lord had taken it and shared His with her. It was after this reception of this Divine Heart of Jesus, said Raimondo, that Catherine's greatest works, most marvelous of revelations, and most abundant of graces proceeded to pour forth. She was a different person, telling her confessor, "Can't you see, Father, that I am not the same person I was, but am changed into someone else?"[76]

Indeed, all could see that such was the case. Whether feeling no need for food, living strictly off the Eucharist (all other forms of food sent her into violent retching pains), or other phenomena, such as witnesses seeing her body at times rise in the air with nothing (earthly) lifting and supporting it, Catherine of Siena had been transformed.[77]

Catherine Receives the Stigmata

On the fourth Sunday of Lent in the year 1375, the twenty-eight-year-old Caterina Benincasa was in Pisa on one of her many diplomatic missions attempting to bring peace between warring districts in the region. And as always, she was also on a spiritual mission.

On that Sunday, Catherine was absorbed in prayer at the Santa Cristina chapel in Pisa. Friends and companions were there, along with her confessor and spiritual director, Fr. Raimondo, who had celebrated Mass. After receiving communion, Catherine, as was typical, went into a state of ecstasy. But this time, something altogether different transpired. Fr. Raimondo recorded:

> We were waiting for her to come back to herself, so as to receive some kind of spiritual encouragement from her, as we often did on these occasions, when to our surprise we saw her little body, which had been lying prostrate, gradually rise up until it was upright on its knees, her arms and hands stretched themselves out, and light beamed from her face; she remained in this position for a long time, perfectly stiff, with eyes closed, and then we saw her suddenly fall, as though mortally wounded.[78]

This remarkable moment, captured with striking beauty in the artistic image on the cover of this book, was the instance in which St. Catherine of Siena received the stigmata from her Lord and Savior. The wounds were hidden, though she did not hide what had happened from her confessor. Raimondo continued his narrative:

> A little later, her soul recovered its senses. Then the virgin sent for me and said quietly, "You must know, Father, that by the mercy of the Lord Jesus I now bear in my body His stigmata." I replied that while I had been watching the movements of her body when she was in ecstasy I had suspected something of the sort; I asked her how the Lord had done all of this. She said, "I saw the Lord fixed to the cross coming towards me in a great light, and such was the impulse of my soul to go and meet its Creator that it forced the body to rise up. Then from the scars of His most sacred wounds I saw five rays of blood coming down towards me, to my hands, my feet and my heart. Realizing what was to happen, I exclaimed, 'O Lord God, I beg you—do not let these scars show on the outside of my body!' As I said this, before the rays reached me their color changed from blood red to the color of light, and in the form of pure light they arrived at the five points of my body, hands, feet, and heart."[79]

It is interesting to hear from Fr. Raimondo that he had suspected something like the stigmata transpiring in that instant. Like other stigmatists in this book, those around Catherine had repeatedly witnessed the extraordinary preparation that had brought her to that point. By then, such a unique gift as the stigmata was deemed by her priest to be not as surprising, given her spiritual state; she had reached a level that few others achieved. She truly was in the rarefied company of the likes of St. Francis or a later Padre Pio. Note, too, that like other stigmatists, the moment came while in prayer before the cross, from which the rays of light shot out and into her.

Raimondo probed deeper, asking his special subject, "So then, no ray reached your right side?" She replied with detailed clarity, "No, it came straight to my left side, over my heart; because that line of light from Jesus's right side struck me directly, not aslant." When her confessor asked if she felt any residual pain at that moment, Catherine heaved a great sigh and answered dramatically, "I feel such pain at those five points, especially in my heart, that if the Lord does not perform another miracle I do not see how I can possibly go on, and within a few days I shall be dead."[80]

After Catherine finished telling Raimondo "what she wanted [him] to know," they ventured back to the house in Pisa where their group was staying. Upon arriving back at her room, Catherine collapsed right away. As Raimondo put it, "Her heart gave out and she fell senseless." She had not merely passed out. This was different. "We were all called, and gathered round her," related Fr. Raimondo, "and as the occurrence seemed more serious than usual, we all started weeping, afraid that we were going to lose her." He conceded that they had "often seen her rapt out of her senses" or "considerably weakened by the abundance of her spirit; but until this moment we had never seen her stunned in quite the same way."[81]

Fortunately for her companions, after a short time, Catherine did seem to return to herself, though not fully recovered. She reiterated to Fr. Raimondo that if the Lord did not cure her, she would soon be dead. Her spiritual director took Catherine's claim eminently seriously, summoning all her spiritual sons and daughters. The Dominican priest tearfully implored them to plead to the heavens that the Lord would spare their beloved Catherine for their earthly sake.[82]

The prayers were working. Evidently, Catherine was thus informed by the heavens. The following Saturday, Catherine said to Raimondo, "It seems to me that the Lord wills to satisfy you." The next day, Sunday, upon receiving Holy Communion from Fr. Raimondo's hands, she suddenly seemed energized with more life than ever. When the priest asked his subject if she still felt the pain of the invisible wounds, Catherine answered, "The Lord, to my great displeasure, has granted your prayers, and those wounds no longer give my body any pain; instead they have made it stronger and healthier and I can feel quite clearly that the strength comes from the places where the agonies came from before."[83]

Once again, Catherine of Siena had been elevated to yet another spiritual level. The more intimately she entered into bodily communion with Jesus Christ, the more spiritually strong she became. What more would the Lord do with her? What else would He tell her? What messages did the God of the universe share with her to speak to us still today?

Messages and Warnings on Homosexuality and Sexually Corrupt Clergy

The Dialogue is considered St. Catherine's master work. It was instrumental in her being chosen six centuries later as a Doctor of the Church. The book is a dictated transcript related verbatim from the saint, the heavenly words given to her in a mystical state during the final three years of her life, after she had been imbued with the hidden wounds of stigmata that ultimately made her stronger.

The Dialogue is divided into four sections, each called a treatise. These include the "Treatise of Divine Providence," "Treatise of Discretion," "Treatise of Prayer," and "Treatise of Obedience." These sections include God the Father's response—yes, God Himself—to various questions from Catherine.

God states that He is divulging these messages to this woman whom He has blessed with the gift of prophecy, of knowing the things of the future: "Oh, how sweet is the taste of this union to the soul, for, in tasting it, she sees My secrets!" states the Almighty. "Wherefore she often receives the spirit of prophecy, knowing the things of the future.

This is the effect of My Goodness, but the humble soul should despise such things, not indeed in so far as they are given her by My love, but in so far as she desires them by reason of her appetite for consolation, considering herself unworthy of peace and quiet of mind, in order to nourish virtue within her soul."[84]

Catherine was indeed humbled by this. And just in case she had any temptation to pride, the Lord let her know explicitly: "Do you know what you are to Me, and what I am to you, my daughter? I am He who is. You are she who is not." Catherine knew her place. She often referred to herself as "I Caterina, humble servant." And that servant was given the spirit of prophecy so that she might warn others. That especially included priests, and so *The Dialogue* is packed with admonitions to the clergy.

In fact, a series of particular messages that Catherine of Siena received concerned the sins of homosexual acts, including these acts and other sins of sexual impurity and corruption among Catholic clergy.[85] The section of *The Dialogue* that deals with priests and with God's purported own statements on clergy is mostly in chapters 110–34, a crucial section of the book. Thomas McDermott, the Dominican scholar and top authority on Catherine, notes, "It is here that Catherine manifests great respect and love for priests who, the eternal Father tells her, are His 'christs,' sent 'like fragrant flowers into the mystic body of the Holy Church.'"

Note the lowercase *c* in "christs." The Church teaches that Catholic priests operate *in persona Christi*. This would seem to affirm what the eternal Father told Catherine about His "christs." They are beloved sons, especially blessed, and so they need to act like it.

Because of God's—and Catherine's—great love for priests, Catherine was candid in exposing and criticizing the failures of priests and bishops. "In fact," notes McDermott, "she is so indelicate in her criticism that portions of the *Dialogue*—such as chapter 121, on homosexuality among the clergy—have been excised from various editions of the work."[86]

One section that particularly stands out from chapter 124 carries the subtitle "How among the said ministers reigns unnatural sin; and of a beautiful vision which this soul had on the subject." There, God starts by telling Catherine that "I wish thee to know, dearest daughter, that I require in this Sacrament from you and from them [priests] as great a purity as it is possible for man to have in this life." Below, this section is reproduced from an 1896 edition of her *Dialogue*:

> [T]hese wretches . . . do worse, committing that accursed sin against nature, and as blind and fools with the light of their intellect darkened, they do not know the stench and misery in which they are. It is not only that this sin stinks before Me, Who am the Supreme and Eternal Truth, it does indeed displease Me so much and I hold it in such abomination that for it alone I buried five cities by a Divine judgment, My Divine justice being no longer able to endure it. This sin not only displeases Me as I have said, but also the devils whom these wretches have made their masters. Not that the evil displeases them because they like anything good, but because their nature was originally angelic, and their angelic nature causes them to loathe the sight of the actual commission of this enormous sin. They truly enough hurl the arrow poisoned with the venom of concupiscence, but when their victim proceeds to the actual commission of the sin, they depart for the reason and in the manner that I have said. Thou rememberest that I manifested to thee before the plague how displeasing this sin was to Me, and how deeply the world was corrupted by it; so I lifted thee with holy desire and elevation of mind above thyself, and showed thee the whole world and, as it were, the nations thereof, and thou sawest this terrible sin and the devils fleeing as I have told thee, and thou rememberest that so great was the pain that thou didst receive, and the stench of this sin, that thou didst seem to thyself to see no refuge on this side of death, in which thou and My other servants could hide so as not to be attacked by this leprosy.[87]

Note that this "enormous sin," this foul "stench," this "leprosy" of homosexuality, repulsed the devils not because they like things that are good but because their nature was originally angelic, and that angelic nature prompted them to recoil in disgust at this act against nature.

The demons might well "hurl the arrow poisoned with the venom of concupiscence," perhaps leading the sexual sinner to sin, but when the victim goes forth with the actual commission of the sin, the demons flee from the scene; they cannot bear to watch. They are too disgusted. And so, God, through Catherine, wanted her to warn the world of this sin against nature so that transgressors could accept God's gift of mercy and come to repentance:

> I retain My just wrath and do not command the rocks to roll down on them, nor the earth to swallow them up, nor the animals to devour them, nor the devils to carry them off body and soul; on the contrary, I seek for ways and methods for doing them mercy, in order that they may correct their life. Wherefore I place in their midst My servants who are healthy and not leprous, so that they may pray to Me for them.[88]

God continued in this specific admonition against homosexual conduct. He told Catherine that He found it especially appalling among members of the clergy. The offense was even greater when committed by a priest:

> See, therefore, dearest daughter, how abominable this sin is to Me in every creature. Think, then, how much more so it is among those whom I have drawn out of the world and who live in a state of continence, among whom some have left the world to enter religion, and others are planted like flowers in the mystical body of the holy Church among whom are My ministers. Thou couldest never understand how much more this sin displeases Me in them than in men of the world and private persons practicing continence, of whom I have spoken to you.[89]

God's words to St. Catherine of Siena ought to speak today to the likes of Fr. James Martin, apologist for the homosexual lifestyle in the Church today, who wants to change the *Catechism*'s condemnation of homosexuality to "differently ordered" rather than "disordered." In the next sentence, God stated, "For these as lights placed on the candlestick are the administrators of Me, the True Sun in the light of virtue and of their holy and honorable life, and yet they minister in darkness and are so darkened that they do not understand My Holy Scripture." They are filled with "inflated pride and lasciviousness," and "their soul is not rightly ordered, but rather corrupted with self-love and pride, and their reins are full of impurity; for they desire to fulfil their disordinate delights, committing their sins publicly and without shame."[90]

The lesson here for modern-day Catholics trying to change the Church's teachings ought to be clear: homosexuality should not be accepted, period. It must not be acted upon. The act must be considered shameful and not something to celebrated with "pride." Homosexuals, of course, should not be mistreated or discriminated against, no question. Like all of us sinners, they need to seek forgiveness and mercy. Their conduct is not to be embraced.

And the shame is magnified for priests who engage in such behavior. In turn, God the Father told Catherine that this sexual corruption damages the abilities of priests to minister to their flock. They are morally compromised. God continued to Catherine (chapter 125):

> How can these men full of such terrible sins do justice to, or reprove the sins of their subjects? They cannot, because their sins take from them the ardent zeal of holy justice. And if on some occasion they should do so, their subjects, who are their companions in sin, can reply, "Physician, first heal thyself, and then heal me, then I will take the medicine which thou givest me. This man is in a worse state than I am, and yet he blames me.". . . All these evils, dearest daughter, arrive because my pastors do not correct their flocks with a good and holy example. Why do they not? Because they are blinded by self-love, in which are founded all their iniquities. . . . Alas! Sweet daughter, where is the obedience of religious who have been placed in holy religion like angels, and are become worse than devils? I have placed them there to announce My word in doctrine and in truth, and they cry out with the sound of words alone, and so produce no fruit in the hearts of their hearers.[91]

They are worse than devils. And their superiors at the monasteries fail if they neglect to monitor these sexually corrupt predators. God told Catherine that these superiors are "worthless:"

> All these and many other evils are caused by worthless superiors, who have not kept their eye on their subjects, but have rather let them go loose, and themselves pushed them into sin, and have made as if they did not see their miseries, or that their subject was wearied with his cell; and so through their double fault the subject dies. Thy tongue could not narrate with what terrible sins and in what miserable ways they offend Me. They have become the arms of the Devil, and with their stench they poison everything within, that is, in their monastery, and without among seculars.[92]

And such behavior is the means by which these ministers are "sent to hell." But again, God insisted that He was giving this message to Catherine as a warning, a call to correction by these priests—to repentance. For these and other sins and abuses, the pope himself, the Vicar of Christ, should punish them if they do not amend their ways:

> But if the vicar of My Son should perceive their sins, he ought to punish them, and from the one take away his dignity if he do not amend his evil life; and as for the other who buys, it would be well that he should be sent to prison, as his part of the bargain, so that he may be corrected for his sin, and that others may take warning and be afraid, so that no one else may imitate him.[93] If the Christ on earth do this, he does his duty, and if he does not, his sin will not be unpunished when he has to give an account before Me of his flock. Believe Me, My daughter, today this is not done, and it is on this account that My Church has fallen into such sins and abominations.[94]

That is a bracing thought from the fourteenth century. If such sexually immoral behavior back then could befall God's Church, bringing such sins and abominations, one can scarcely imagine what the Almighty would say about His Church today.

This is just a sample from *The Dialogue* of God's anger at those priests that He repeatedly referred to as "wretches" and "devils." The degree to which Catherine's message here speaks to today cannot be understated and really needs no explication at all. The abuse crisis among Catholic clergy is the modern scourge of the Church. It has severely damaged the Catholic Church. In countries like Ireland, which once produced huge numbers of priests—arguably Ireland's leading export to America—vocations have virtually vanished. And of course, as those who have common sense and are honest enough to concede to the data know, the clergy abuse crisis in the Catholic Church is one of homosexuality.

An Irish American who writes powerfully about this is S. A. McCarthy. In his June 2023 piece for *Crisis Magazine*, titled "The Homosexual Infestation of the Church," McCarthy was prompted by the then latest clerical sex abuse report, this one by the Catholic bishops in Spain, which revealed a staggering 728 Church predators, over 99 percent of whom were male. And not surprisingly, 82 percent of the victims were male as well. These were homosexual males targeting other males, and most of the victims were young males. "This statistic shouldn't be shocking," noted McCarthy, "as it is consistent with clerical sex abuse reports across the globe, demonstrating that the chief and even the root issue behind clerical sex abuse is homosexuality."[95]

McCarthy rattled off other statistics: In 2004, the American bishops had commissioned the now-infamous report from the John Jay College of Criminal Justice, which had found that 81 percent of clerical sex abuse victims were male. In France, a landmark report released in 2021 disclosed that of the 330,000-plus children sexually abused by priests and other diocesan employees, 80 percent of the victims were male. McCarthy gave more examples, from his native Ireland to Portugal. The Portugal study found—again not surprising—that the worst hotbed for homosexual abuses was seminaries. And to quote the words from Catherine's *Dialogue*, "worthless superiors" in these seminaries did not stop the infestation.

It is worth noting here that Pope Francis spoke of the issue of homosexual seminarians: "If there's a doubt about homosexuality, it's better not to have them enter the seminary," Francis told Italian bishops in May 2018. "If you think that the guy is homosexual, don't put him in the seminary."[96]

Later, in an interview published in December 2018, Francis spoke of a conversation he had with a bishop who deemed it no problem that several priests in his diocese were "openly gay" because it was just an "expression of affection." The pontiff emphatically disagreed, correcting the bishop, "This is a mistake. It is not just an expression of affection." Francis insisted, "In the consecrated life and in the priestly life, there is no place for that kind of affection." He urged, "I say to the priests, gay religious men and women, we must urge you to live fully celibate and, above all, to be exquisitely responsible, trying not to scandalize your communities or the holy faithful people of God by living a double life. It is better that you leave the ministry or consecrated life rather than live a double life."[97]

The scandalizing of those communities was precisely one of the concerns voiced in Catherine's *Dialogue*.

"For this reason," continued Francis, "the Church urges that persons with this rooted tendency not be accepted into ministry or consecrated life." He lamented, "In our societies, it even seems homosexuality is fashionable. And this mentality, in some way, also influences the life of the Church."

Here again, on this occasion as well, Francis reiterated his call to keep homosexuals out of seminaries: "Homosexuality is a very serious issue that must be adequately discerned from the beginning with the candidates. The Church recommends that people with this ingrained tendency not be accepted into the ministry or the consecrated life. The ministry or the consecrated life is not his place." He said it "worries me" that these candidates "at the moment they are accepted. . . don't exhibit that tendency, but later they come out."

Thus, insists Francis, they should be kept out.

S. A. McCarthy, in his June 2023 piece for *Crisis Magazine*, gave many more examples of clergy sexual abuse, noting terrible individual cases by the upper echelons of the Church's hierarchy: former cardinal and Washington Archbishop Theodore McCarrick; Marcial Maciel, the Mexican priest who founded the Legionaries of Christ and its lay branch, Regnum Christi; Argentine bishop Gustavo Zanchetta, who in 2022 was sentenced to four and a half years in prison for sexually abusing seminarians; the late archbishop Rembert Weakland of Milwaukee, Wisconsin, who allegedly paid nearly half a million dollars in hush money to a seminarian with whom he had a longtime homosexual relationship; and on and on.[98] These men were Church superiors.

McCarthy cited a *Los Angeles Times* poll from 2002 that estimated that 15 percent of Catholic priests were openly homosexual. Among still more studies, McCarthy also cited Fr. Donald Cozzens's book *The Changing Face of the Priesthood*, which claimed that anywhere from 20 to 60 percent of Catholic priests are homosexuals.[99]

No one knows the exact number. Well, God knows. He knew when speaking to Catherine in the late 1300s, and He knows now.

Homosexual corruption among clergy is not new. Well before St. Catherine of Siena, St. Peter Damian, in the eleventh century, fulminated in his letter *The Book of Gomorrah*, "For God's sake, why do you damnable sodomites pursue the heights of ecclesiastical dignity with such fiery ambition?" In 1049, Damian directly appealed to Pope Leo IX, attempting to alert the pontiff to this rot. Damian, a Doctor of the Church, argued that homosexuality is a "festering disease" and "destructive plague" that "pollutes the flesh, extinguishes the light of the mind, expels the Holy Spirit from the temple of the human heart, and gives entrance to the devil. . . . It defiles all things, sullies all things, pollutes all things." Such perversions harm the pastor's flock: "Who can expect the flock to prosper when its shepherd has sunk so deep into the bowels of the devil who will make a mistress of a cleric, or a woman of a man?" asked St. Peter Damian.[100]

Three centuries after Damian's expression of righteous indignation, this scourge was still active among the clergy. And God told St. Catherine of Siena that it displeased Him very much.

Hence, a Catholic who would not have been surprised by S. A. McCarthy's data on clergy sexual abuse in our time is St. Catherine of Siena. She warned us about it six and a half centuries ago. Her message then ought to be heeded today.

How Catherine of Siena Speaks to Our Times

Clearly, in those unfortunately disturbing ways, Catherine of Siena speaks to our times—and not only on the matter of sinful clergy. "In the wake of so many clerical sex abuse scandals, to many people the Catholic Church appears hypocritical and bankrupt morally and spiritually," writes Dominican Fr. Thomas McDermott, the foremost expert on St. Catherine. "In the midst of such trying times, how can Catholics justify remaining in the Church? The words and deeds of St. Catherine of Siena (1347–1380), Dominican *Mantelatta*—or penitential woman—who lived during an earlier crisis, can offer us some guidance and hope."[101]

McDermott noted that during Catherine's day, not only did the Church seem to be collapsing, but so did larger society and even the world itself. Her beloved home region of Italy was a mess of warring republics, monarchies, and feuding families. Outside of Italy, France and England were mired in a bloody Hundred Years' War, one of the most intractable conflicts of the Middle Ages. Islam, as always, was hellbent on war and conquest—seizing lands and peoples, raping, pillaging, and taking prisoners and slaves alike. (Catherine had some suitably harsh things to say about Islam.)

Catherine was born into a Church where the papacy was in exile in Avignon from 1309 to 1376. No less than seven successive popes reigned from France in those decades, a period that some described as the "Babylonian captivity of the papacy." She admonished the popes in Avignon and in Rome to reject sin in themselves and among their clergy. "Most Holy Father," she had urged Pope Urban VI, "it is time to detest sin in yourself, in your subjects, and in the ministers of holy Church."[102] Ultimately, one of these popes, Gregory XI, listened to the impassioned lady from Siena and moved his court back to Rome, arriving in the Eternal City in January 1377. And though the pope returned to Rome, the Church would soon face a full-blown schism after the death of Gregory XI in 1378, which became known as the Western Schism.

At many levels and in many ways, Catherine faced a Church in crisis and a world of nations in turmoil. And that certainly was not all. Among other issues that Catherine faced akin to what we today face, there was major disease. We had COVID-19, which killed millions worldwide. But even then, the disease she faced was much worse, with a far higher mortality rate. She came into a world wracked by bubonic plague, the Black Death, one of history's deadliest scourges, a pandemic that made COVID-19 look like a mere sneeze. As Fr. McDermott notes, some four-fifths of the population of Siena died from the plague the year that Catherine was born. The infant girl was blessed (no doubt specially chosen) to have survived it. Even then, in her short life that followed, more waves of disease arose. McDermott quotes one chronicler of life in Siena at the time: "And no bells tolled, and nobody wept no matter what his loss because almost everyone expected death. . . . And people said and believed, 'This is the end of the world.'"[103]

Some might well believe just that today. It seems like the end times. In many ways similar but others more dissimilar—given the perverse attacks by an unhinged culture on everything from faith to gender, sexuality, marriage, the unborn, the family, and the whole LGBTQIA+ madness that Catherine could scarcely imagine in its unbridled insanity against God and nature—things are worse. It feels like the end of the world to many today.

But Catherine of Siena still fought for the Church and kept her faith in God. She knew that faithful Catholics really had nowhere else to turn. As Peter said to Jesus, "Lord, to whom shall we go?" To Catherine, the only answer was to Christ and His Church.

"Humanly speaking, Catherine had more reasons for abandoning the Church than we do today," notes Fr. Thomas McDermott, "and yet there is not the slightest indication in her writings that she ever considered doing so. What was the basis of her hope? Undoubtedly, her belief in the human and divine dimensions of the Church undergirded her hope that one day it would be what God intended it to be."

The world might be falling apart, with societies coming apart at the seams, but St. Catherine of Siena placed her hope in God, in Jesus Christ, and in His Church. All along, she suffered, offering up her anguish for the expiation of the sins of the world, just as her Heavenly Bridegroom had done.

This passionate mystic, this stigmatist, would leave her mark. Just as she pondered what Christ's marks meant for her and her mission, we should ponder what her marks mean for us today.

CHAPTER 4

BLESSED ANNE CATHERINE EMMERICH (1774–1824)

Bl. Anne Catherine Emmerich was born September 8, 1774, in the village of Flamsche, near Westphalia, in the western part of Germany. She was given the name Anna Katharina, her middle name invoking the memory of the great Italian saint and stigmatist Catherine (Caterina) of Siena. The sister of nine siblings raised in a humble farming family was said to be able to fully understand the liturgical Latin of the Mass from the first time that she attended as a little girl. She always retained what was described as a "perfect consciousness" of her earliest days.[104]

From an early age, Anne Catherine was in touch with the supernatural. She had visions, visitations, conversations, and interactions with heavenly figures, particularly her guardian angel, so much so that she assumed that everyone had such interactions (Padre Pio likewise had that assumption). Not until later did she realize that this (and she) was exceptional. During family Bible readings, her father would sit her on his knee near the fireplace and gently implore his daughter, "Anna Kathrinchen, now here we are! Now tell me something!" She would then describe to him images that had been shown to her from the New Testament. "But child," the father would implore, "where did you get all that?" She would answer merely, "Father, it is all true! That is the way I saw it!"[105]

As she worked with her family in the fields, Anne Catherine was always in contemplation and continually absorbed in God, often taken somewhere else at the same time. "Working with my parents in the field, or engaged in any other labor, I was, as it were, lifted above the earth," she later said. "Exterior things were like a confused and painful dream." The child Jesus, whom she called the "Little Boy," visited her in the fields and helped her. She also claimed to play with the child John the Baptist. When she played in the sand with other children, she found herself trying to shape models of holy places in Jerusalem that she had mystically seen and knew. "If I had had someone to help me," she said, "I could have made models of most of the roads and places of the Holy Land. They were always before my eyes; no locality was better known to me." She said that every Advent since childhood, she accompanied St. Joseph and the Blessed Mother from Nazareth to Bethlehem.[106]

These were clearly the most unique, special spiritual gifts. Spiritually precocious from her earliest childhood days, all friends and family knew that Anne Catherine was destined for religious life. Still, she was turned down by many convents because she could not bring a significant enough dowry, though she eventually found a place. On November 13, 1803, she entered the Augustinian convent in Agnetenberg at Dülmen, likewise located in Westphalia.[107]

Times at the convent were never easy. Anne Catherine suffered significant physical trials as well as mistreatment by fellow nuns and authorities. The convent was suppressed in 1811 due to the aggressive secularization of the surrounding society. Anne Catherine had to leave the convent, taking refuge at the home of Abbé Lambert, a priest who had fled France and lived in Dülmen. She would remain there at that house, effectively bedridden, for the remainder of her earthly life. But quite a life it was, and her time was hardly uneventful. That bed was a journey, almost like a mystical magical carpet transporting her to worlds unknown.

Anne Catherine Emmerich died at the age of forty-nine on February 9, 1824. During the last decade-plus of her life, she subsisted on merely water and the Holy Eucharist, violently vomiting up any other type of food or nourishment. None of that, however, deterred her incredible voyages to other worlds. It was also during these extraordinary mystical years that this remarkable German nun bore the stigmata.

Sharing the Wounds of Christ

Anne Catherine Emmerich received several markings of Christ, including the wounds of the crown of thorns, a cross over her heart, marks on her hands and feet, and the wound from the lance that pierced Christ on the Cross in her side. The Very Rev. Carl E. Schmöger, her principal biographer, records the circumstances surrounding the start of her visible stigmata in the year 1812:

> On the Feast of Easter she went, though not without great effort, to the parish church to receive Holy Communion, and she continued to do so until November 2, 1812, after which she never rose from her bed of pain. In September she made a pilgrimage to a place called the "Hermitage," just outside Dülmen, where an Augustinian had formerly dwelt and near which was a small chapel. She went in the hope of receiving some alleviation to her fearful sufferings. She had hardly reached the spot when she fell into an ecstasy, becoming rigid and immovable as a statue.[108]

That development, not surprisingly, frightened the young girl who had accompanied Anne Catherine Emmerich and who quickly called out to a woman for help. They thought Anne had fainted and treated her accordingly, but they soon discovered that much more was affecting the patient. They noticed upon her breast a bloody cross, which Emmerich had actually received on the preceding feast of St. Augustine on August 28. They also learned that this was no fainting spell but one of many moments of ecstasy (accompanied by stigmata) that this German nun would experience in her lifetime. They helped her home, but more such moments would follow. Fr. Schmöger continued his narrative:

> On December 29, 1812, the daughter of the widow Roters found Anne Catherine again in ecstasy, her arms extended, and

blood gushing from the palms of her hands. The girl thought it the effect of an accident and drew her attention to it when she had returned to consciousness, but Sister Emmerich earnestly requested her not to speak of it. On December 31st, when Father Limberg took her Holy Communion, he saw for the first time the bloody marks on the back of her hands.[109]

Fr. Limberg was a Dominican priest at the convent and Sr. Emmerich's ordinary confessor. He was clearly taken aback by what he witnessed and immediately informed Fr. Lambert, the priest who resided in her building. Seeing the blood still flowing, and no doubt at a loss for proper words, Fr. Lambert exclaimed to Anne Catherine, "Sister, you must not think yourself a Catherine of Siena!" But unlike Catherine of Siena, whose stigmata had been invisible, these wounds were very visible, and they were pouring out blood. As the wounds continued to bleed until the evening, Lambert said to Limberg, "Father, no one must know this! Let it rest between ourselves, otherwise it will give rise to talk and annoyance!"[110]

Very much like Catherine of Siena, Sr. Emmerich appreciated the priest's desire to keep things silent. According to Schmöger, she rejoiced that the two priests wanted to keep the phenomenon quiet. But that would prove impossible as the bleeding intensified, including from other spots. Fr. Limberg would write down a week later, "January 6th, Feast of the Kings, I saw for the first time the stigmata on the palms of her hands." Three weeks after that, Limberg further recorded, "January 28th—Since the 15th, she has been in ecstasy more or less prolonged. Today, I saw the marks of the wounds on the soles of her feet. Her hands and feet bleed every Friday and the double cross upon her breast on Wednesdays." Moreover, "Since the existence of these wounds has come to my knowledge, she has eaten nothing."[111]

As this condition persisted, Sr. Emmerich doubled down on her personal policy to never mention her stigmata; to the contrary, she anxiously hid them. But the plan was bound to fail. The news of her stigmata rapidly traveled. In short order, an official inquiry was underway.[112]

Thus began for this poor suffering nun much the same ordeal experienced by so many other stigmatists, including a Padre Pio–like period of doubters and accusers, whether medical or ecclesiastical, with charges of everything from faking the wounds to some sort of "hysteria"-induced condition that inexplicably caused bleeding wounds (a greater leap of medical faith than the stigmata).[113] The cynics would never stop, but neither would the stigmata, which she bore for the remainder of her earthly life.

And yet, amid the ever-present skeptics, the authoritative witnesses to Anne Catherine's stigmata stand out more. Their testimony was overwhelming. And those who saw the extraordinary phenomenon, including friends who had known her for years, could not keep quiet about it. How could they?

A key example of this was Anne Catherine's longtime close friend, Clara Soentgen, who had entered the convent with Anne Catherine. She knew her close friend all too well not to miss something so dramatic as bleeding wounds akin to those of their Savior on the Cross. Once Clara saw the wounds, the attempts by Frs. Limberg and Lambert to keep things secret flew out the window. "Her state remained secret till February 28, 1813," recorded Fr. Limberg, "when Clara Soentgen perceived it and spoke to me of it. Once Clara Soentgen had penetrated Sister Emmerich's secret, the news spread far and wide. Toward the middle of March, 1813, it was the talk of the town." Soon enough, her extraordinary case was freely discussed from public alehouses to the offices of physicians to, predictably, the ecclesiastical superiors in Münster.[114]

One of the many physicians who was intrigued was Dr. William Wesener of Dülmen, who first dismissed the talk of stigmata as ridiculous superstition. Wesener had been raised Christian but had lost his faith in college. Still, he was a man of character, honesty, and decency. He was in touch with the aforementioned clergy in Münster and agreed to pay a visit to Anne Catherine with them, look for himself, and offer an unbiased examination. What he saw amazed him. As Fr. Carl Schmöger put it, "The mere sight of the patient produced a deep impression upon him [Wesener]. He knew not how to account for the singular facts he witnessed but, trusting to her rare artlessness, he hoped soon to discover their true cause. After a few visits, he offered his professional services, which were willing[ly] accepted. Upon close observation he arrived at the conclusion that all suspicion of fraud ought to be discarded." There were facts simply beyond Dr. Wesener's comprehension that could be neither denied nor concealed. Thus, Wesener consulted with Dean Rensing, the parish priest, with Fr. Limberg, and with another physician named Krauthausen. They agreed to conduct a joint investigation with both priests and physicians on the scene.[115]

That examination of Anne Catherine Emmerich was done on March 22, 1813. These men let little time pass between the markings that first appeared just weeks earlier and the time of their study. Their report stated:

> On the back of both hands are crusts of dried blood under each of which is a sore, and in the palms are similar smaller crusts. The same thing may be seen on the upper part of her feet and in the middle of the soles. The wounds are sensitive to the touch, those of the right foot had just bled. On the right side, over the fourth rib from below, is a wound about three inches long which, it is said, bleeds occasionally, and on the breast-bone are round marks forming a forked cross. A little lower is an ordinary cross formed of lines, half an inch in length which look like scratches. On the upper part of the forehead are numerous marks like the pricks of a needle which run along the temple back to the hair. On her linen binder we saw blood stains.[116]

Still more reports came, as did more medical and ecclesiastical authorities to take a look. On March 25, 1813, Dean Rensing wrote a letter to the vicar-general of Münster, Baron Clement Auguste von Droste-Vischering, who would later become archbishop of Cologne. The vicar-general arrived in Dülmen on March 28 along with Dean Overberg and a medical adviser, a Dr. von Druffel, to inspect the wounds of Anne Catherine. Dean Rensing wanted the vicar-general to be prepped for what he was about to see. Rensing wrote this to the vicar-general:

Most Noble Baron, Very Reverend Vicar-General:

> With a heart deeply touched and full of religious senti-
> ments, I announce to you, as to my Ecclesiastical Superior, a

fact well calculated to prove that God, at all times admirable in His saints, still operates in them even in our own days of infidelity, wonders which clearly exhibit the power of our holy religion, which lead the most frivolous to reflect, the most incredulous to turn from their errors. The Lord still chooses the weak to confound the strong, still reveals to His little ones secrets hidden from the great. I have up to the present kept the case secret, being so requested, and also through the deference I believed due to the favored soul. I feared, too, the annoyances attendant on its being divulged. But now that God has permitted the affair to be, so to say, proclaimed from the housetops, I deem it my duty to make an official report of it to you. I shall not longer conceal the secret of the King.

Anne Catherine Emmerich, Choir-Sister of the Augustinian convent called Agnetenberg, now suppressed, is the chosen of God of whom there is question, and Clara Soentgen is the school mistress of this place. She took the religious habit on the same day as Sister Emmerich and with her parents the latter resided just before entering the convent. Sister Soentgen testifies that from her early youth Anne Catherine was extremely pious, practicing conformity to the will of God in imitation of our Crucified Saviour.[117]

Dean Rensing here shared Clara's assessment as a long-term character witness to Anne Catherine Emmerich. He also talked about how Clara had observed the mistreatment of Anne Catherine by other nuns in the convent. When her fellow nuns heard of the visions and beheld Sr. Emmerich's piety, including her frequent reception of the Eucharist, they responded very uncharitably and with downright "contempt." "Their treatment was not, indeed, very charitable," noted Dean Rensing. "They disliked her because she received Holy Communion several times a week, spoke enthusiastically of the happiness there is in suffering, performed many good works of supererogation, and thus distinguished herself too much from them." Nonetheless, this suffering nun, who for years had been sick, accepted this mistreatment amid her joyful sufferings. Dean Rensing noted that and more, including

Sr. Emmerich barely eating or drinking beyond her nourishment of the Eucharist:

> If she takes a third or even a fourth part of wine in water, in order to conceal the fact that she lives exclusively upon the latter, she instantly rejects it. Her night-sweats are so heavy that her bed linen is perfectly saturated. She is a living witness to the truth of Holy Scriptures: "Not by bread alone doth man live, but by every word that cometh forth from the mouth of the Lord." Every evening she falls into a swoon, or rather a holy ecstasy, which lasts ten hours and more, at which times she lies stiff and immovable in whatever position she may chance to have been, her face fresh and rosy like a little child's. If the coverlet or even a pillow be held up before her and by stealth, if I may use the expression, and a priest gives her his blessing, she instantly raises her hand which until then had lain immovable as that of a statue, and makes the Sign of the Cross. She has revealed to her confessor, Father Limberg, and also to me after these ecstasies, secrets which she could have known only supernaturally.[118]

Of course, all of that appeared supernatural enough to the likes of Dean Rensing. But especially supernatural, he related to the vicar-general, were the Christ-like wounds on the body of this suffering soul:

> But what distinguishes her still more as the special favorite of Heaven is the bloody crown around her brow, the stigmata of her hands, feet, and side, and the crosses on her breast. These wounds often bleed, some on Wednesdays, others on Fridays, and so copiously that heavy drops of blood fall to the ground. This phenomenon creates much talk and criticism; therefore, I engaged the physicians of this place to make a preliminary examination that I might be able to draw up a report. These gentlemen were greatly affected by what they saw. The result of their investigation is contained in a statement signed by them, by Father Limberg, by the Abbé Lambert, a French priest, who resides in the same house with the invalid, and by myself.[119]

Dean Rensing's letter to the vicar-general said still more. Clearly, the man was in awe at what he had witnessed in the wounds of this German Augustinian nun. And likewise were the vicar-general and his team upon their investigation. His accompanying physician, Dr. Krauthausen, wrote this in his April 1, 1813, report:

> In fulfillment of the charge intrusted to me, on Thursday before Passion Sunday, at eight a.m., I bathed in warm water the spots covered with dried blood in the hands, feet, and head of Anne Catherine Emmerich, formerly an Augustinian religious. I then applied bandages in such a way that neither the fingers nor toes could be moved freely, nor could the said bandages be disarranged, much less removed without my knowledge. The bathing, though performed gently with a fine sponge, and the process of bandaging caused keen suffering for about twenty-four hours. When I had finished the bathing, I perceived on the back of the hands and the insteps an oval wound about half an inch long, which was smaller in the palms of the hands and soles of the feet. They were healthy looking and had no pus.[120]

These examinations by Dr. Krauthausen and others continued. Regrettably, they often wore down the patient physically and made her feel worse as they applied bandages and ointments to try to stop something that only the Lord Himself could cause or halt. They wrote careful, lengthy notes and even drew illustrations of what they saw with their own eyes and instruments.[121]

Not surprisingly, word of this extraordinary patient continued to spread quickly among physicians. In mere hours, let alone days, other doctors demanded to see for themselves. Dean Rensing shared another striking example from yet another suspicious physician who insisted on seeing the patient, only to walk away astounded. Rensing wrote on April 3, 1813:

> A visitor presented himself today who would take no refusal, a Dr. Ruhfus, of Gildhaus, Bentheim. He was so determined on being admitted that only on my promising to ask the invalid's consent would he withdraw for a time. She, at first, objected,

but ended by leaving it to my decision and I allowed the doctor to enter. He behaved with remarkable discretion, examined the wounds carefully, and asked for such information as he deemed necessary. On taking leave, he thanked the invalid for her condescension and expressed himself on the wonders he had just witnessed in a manner that did honor to his candor. As we left the room, he said to me: "What I have seen is truly wonderful. There can be no question of imposture in this case. The religious sentiments of the patient testify to her truth, as does, likewise, her countenance, which expresses naught but piety, innocence, and submission to the Divine Will. The wounds speak for themselves, at least to a man of science. To ascribe them to natural causes such as imagination, induction, analogy, or similar causes, is simply impossible. The whole affair is, in my opinion, supernatural."[122]

Prior to that visit, Dr. Ruhfus, according to Dean Rensing, had been joking about the nun at a local alehouse. Challenged to go see for himself, he did so, and he left a believer. In fact, the physicians who examined Sr. Emmerich often were less hesitant than some of the clergy to dub what they saw miraculous, given that these men of science knew that the laws of nature could not explain what they were seeing.[123]

Despite this wearing her down physically, Anne Catherine emotionally displayed remarkable patience, composure, and acceptance of her sacrificial suffering.[124] She endured these inspections of her body just as she had accepted the petty jealousies of her fellow nuns and other torments.

Notably, the other torments included frightening visits by demons. "I looked and saw a hideous figure covered with filthy rags slowly approaching," related Emmerich of one such occasion. "It stood at the foot of my bed. It drew aside the curtain, and I saw it was a frightful-looking woman with an enormously large head. The longer she looked at me, the more horrible she grew." The ugly creature threatened to harm the nun, who called on the forces of heaven for divine assistance: "Then she leaned over me, opening her huge mouth as if to swallow me. At first I was calm, but soon I became greatly alarmed and began to invoke the holy names of Jesus and Mary, when the horrible apparition disappeared." On another occasion, Satan himself visited in the form of a "hideous beast, an enormous dog."[125] For so many stigmatists, this was par for the course. The devil and his demons detested them. In this, Anne Catherine Emmerich had some saintly company.

Anne Catherine on Her Stigmata— and on Saint Francis's Stigmata

That was what the expert witnesses, medical and ecclesiastical, witnessed themselves in the case of this German nun. They carefully filed these reports right away in 1813. But according to the nun herself, some of these sufferings started earlier.

As for Anne Catherine's personal testimony to the stigmata, she later related that she began feeling the pain in her head much earlier, namely, "for four years before entering the convent," which she had entered in 1803; "it is, as it were, encircled by thorns, or rather, as if all my hair were thorns; I can never rest on the pillow without pain." She "had the pains of the Crown around my head even before my entrance into the convent. I felt them first in the Jesuit church at Coesfeld."[126]

Asked when she first felt the pains in her hands and feet, she explained, "Four years before the suppression of the convent, I went to Coesfeld to visit my parents. While there, I prayed for two hours at the foot of the cross behind the altar in St. Lambert's Church. I was very much distressed at the state of our convent, so I prayed that we might see our faults and live in peace. I also asked Jesus to make me experience all that He suffered. From that time I have always had these pains and this burning."[127] Her convent was suppressed in 1811, meaning that pain from wounds on her hands and feet would have started in 1807.

As for the pains from the other wounds, they "are not like ordinary pains, they go to my heart. A touch or light pressure upon the cross on my breast is not so painful outwardly, but inwardly it is as if the whole breast were on fire. As to the sign above my stomach, it feels like a flame of fire."[128]

Asked when these signs began to first visibly appear, she answered with exacting specificity, connecting each wound to a key religious event: "The sign on my stomach appeared on the Feast of St. Augustine; the lower cross on my breast about six weeks after; the upper one on the Feast of St. Catherine; the wounds of my hands and feet on the last Feast of Christmas; and that of my side between Christmas and New Year." She said that she had prayed much to suffer the pains of Jesus, "but never for the marks of His Wounds." Regarding the cross on her breast, she added, "I begged God from my childhood to imprint the cross upon my heart, but I never thought of an external sign."[129]

She realized how the sight of these signs could sometimes shake up witnesses. During the first Vespers service that occurred for the feast day of St. Catherine of Siena, Dean Rensing reported, "I visited her at three o'clock. As I entered the room the blood was streaming from her head and hands. I was quite unnerved at the sight, and an expression of admiration at the extraordinary favors bestowed upon her escaped me." In response to Rensing being unnerved, Anne Catherine said to him, "Yes, God grants me more than I deserve. I thank Him for them, but I would rather He would hide these graces from the eyes of men, for I fear they will think me better than I am."[130]

Dean Rensing asked her about the shoulder wound: "I asked her once if she had not also a wound upon her shoulder, for I think the Savior surely had His sacred shoulder wounded by the heavy Cross." She replied, "Yes, indeed! The Divine Savior had a painful wound on His shoulder from the Cross; but I have not the wound, although I have long felt its pain." She said that she had "venerated this wound from my childhood, because it is especially pleasing to Our Savior. He revealed to me in the convent that this Wound of which so little is thought caused Him the greatest pain, and that when one honors it, He is as much pleased thereby as if that person had borne the Cross for Him up to Calvary."[131] Indeed, as Christ Himself said in the Scriptures, if we are to follow Him, we must carry the Cross, too. That is, the same Cross that repeatedly felled Him as He struggled to carry it to Calvary.

One Christian who happily carried the Cross was St. Francis, the first stigmatist (again, other than perhaps St. Paul). And quite fascinatingly, among Anne Catherine Emmerich's many visions was one of Francis receiving the stigmata. She had that vision on the feast day of St. Francis, October 4, 1820. She made the following observation:

> I saw the saint among some bushes on a wild mountain in which were scattered grottos like little cells. Francis had opened the Gospel several times. Each time it chanced to be at the history of the Passion, and so he begged to feel his Lord's sufferings. He used to fast on this mountain, eating only a little bread and roots. He knelt, his bare knees on two sharp stones, and supported two others on his shoulders. It was after midnight and he was praying with arms extended, half kneeling, half sitting, his back resting against the side of the mountain. I saw his angel near him holding his hands, his countenance all on fire with love.

Here, Anne Catherine Emmerich described *Il Povarello*, his physical appearance, his clothing, and what happened next:

> He was a slight man. He wore a brown mantle open in front with a hood like those worn at the time by shepherds, a cord bound his waist. At the moment in which I saw him he was as if paralyzed. A bright light shot from Heaven and descended upon him. In it was an angel with six wings, two above his head, two over his feet, and two with which he seemed to fly. In his right hand he held a cross, about half the usual size, on which was a living body glowing with light, the feet crossed, the five wounds resplendent as so many suns. From each wound proceeded three rays of rosy light converging to a point. They shot first from the hands toward the palms of the saint's hands; then from the wound in the right side toward the saint's right side (these rays were larger than the others); and lastly, from the feet toward the soles of the saint's feet. In his left hand the angel held a blood-red tulip in whose center was a golden heart, which I think he gave to the saint. When Francis returned from ecstasy, he could with difficulty stand, and I saw him going back to his monastery suffering cruelly, and

supported by his angel-guardian. He hid his wounds as well
as he could. There were large crusts of brownish blood on the
back of his hands, for they did not bleed regularly every Friday;
but his side often bled so profusely that the blood flowed down
on the ground. I saw him praying, the blood streaming down
his arms. I saw many other incidents of his life.[132]

Anne Catherine Emmerich would likewise relate visions of some of
those other incidents in the life of St. Francis.[133] But is it not fascinating
that this stigmatist of the early 1800s actually could see the stigmatist
of the early 1200s receiving his marks? She was a close, keen witness
to what history records as only Br. Leo glimpsing partially at Mount
La Verna. And, as we shall see later in this book, she was not the only
female German stigmatist blessed with this special stigmatic vision of
the poor man from Assisi.

Stirring Visions of the Life of Christ and His Mother

Anne Catherine Emmerich had a two-fold mission. One was to suffer
for the sins of others. She stated that she "was quite overwhelmed by
the reflection that, in spite of [God's] mercy, so many souls are lost
forever." The other, as she said with exclamation, was "to reveal many
things before I die!"[134] And that task was accomplished with the help
of the pen of Clemens Brentano, whose purpose was less to witness her
wounds and sufferings than to transcribe to the world the stigmatist's
astonishing visions, which he did with great diligence throughout the
final six years of her earthly life.

Of all the figures described in this book, and really of all the figures in the history of Christianity, none can match Anne Catherine
Emmerich for the sheer volume and gripping minute details of her
amazing visions of the life of Christ, the Blessed Mother, and the early
Church. It seems fitting that, in one of these visions, she was told that
her ability to see past, current, and future events was greater than any
other individual in history.[135]

Many books have been written on these visions, which typically went
from her lips to the pen of Clemens Brentano, a prominent literary

figure and celebrated poet of the day. He was a highly acclaimed writer and intellectual, embraced by the secular elite. In September 1818, he traveled to see the nun on a challenge by his peers. He would never leave. Like the skeptical physicians, in no time, he was convinced. Brentano became almost her stenographer, a close companion of the German Augustinian nun and devoted transcriber of her messages.[136] (For the record, Brentano today has detractors and doubters, as does and did Emmerich in her time. He and she also have, of course, plenty of defenders to rebut the detractors.)

Transcripts of Emmerich's visions are published in *The Dolorous Passion of Our Lord Jesus Christ*; in *The Life of the Blessed Virgin Mary*; in the seminal two-volume, 1,297-page *The Life and Revelations of Anne Cathrine Emmerich* (by the Very Rev. Carl E. Schmöger); and in the four-volume, 2,088-page *The Life of Christ and Biblical Revelations of Anne Catherine Emmerich* (also by Rev. Schmöger). These visions are as inspiring as astonishing. The level of detail she provided from 1,800 years prior to her earthly pilgrimage is utterly fascinating and seems too uncannily detailed to be made up. Her descriptions have captivated so many readers, including Mel Gibson for his blockbuster film *The Passion of the Christ*.

The Church, of course, cannot vouch for Anne Catherine Emmerich's private revelations, regardless of how seemingly blessed they were, and all readers should thus deal with them with caution. We cannot accord them the same weight as Holy Scripture, though they are faithful to the Bible. Nonetheless, and proceeding with such caveats, one cannot help but be stirred by her vivid descriptions of everything from Jesus in the Garden to the betrayal of Judas, the arrest of Jesus, the painful interrogation of Christ by Annas and Caiaphas, the denial of Peter, Jesus before Pilate, the dreams of Claudia, the Savior being flogged and crowned and carrying His Cross and crucified between the two thieves, and more. Here is but one example:

"'*Shall I crucify your king?*' said Pilate. '*We have no king but Caesar!*' responded the High Priests." Emmerich's account of this epic exchange conforms to the New Testament account, but she added details like these, which are surely conceivable: "I looked up again and saw the cruel Jews almost devouring their victim with their eyes, the [Roman] soldiers standing coldly by, and multitudes of horrible demons passing to and fro and mixing in the crowd." The demons egged on the bystanders, helping to whip the mob into its hateful frenzy—the same people who just a week earlier had welcomed God's only beloved Son to Jerusalem with cheers of hosanna. As Emmerich watched this spectacle, she was "overcome" by the "ferocious joy of the executioners," the "cowardice and duplicity of this despicable being [Pontius Pilate]," the "triumphant countenances of the High Priests," the "agonizing grief" of the Blessed Mother, and, of course, the cruel injustice inflicted upon the sinless One innocently bearing all the sins of the world.[137]

Her images are filled with such details. She described Jesus before Annas: The latter's heart was filled with "cunning and duplicity" and a "most repulsive . . . infernal joy" as he, in his "pride and arrogance," persecuted the Son of God. She described Judas Iscariot in great torment after betraying his Savior, running and wandering about the countryside "followed by many devils," tormenting him as he succumbed to "black despair" and hung himself (Mel Gibson captures this dramatically in *The Passion*).[138]

Readers of Emmerich's rendering of the Passion narrative are captivated by details of things that the Scriptures do not reveal but which we can easily imagine, such as Emmerich's extended description of the piercing of the side of Jesus by the Roman soldier, the terrified reaction to the consuming darkness and the earthquake at the time of Christ's death on the Cross, the shocking apparitions of the dead rising from their tombs in Jerusalem, and much more. One cannot help but nod and say, "Surely, yes, it happened this way."

Reading Anne Catherine Emmerich's account cannot but put one closer to the suffering Christ. Her visions only seem to make us appreciate more what our Savior went through and what he sacrificed for us.

Likewise, Emmerich's visions of the life of the Blessed Virgin Mary leave one in awe. She somehow seemed to know countless details of Mary's ancestry, conception, presentation in the temple, betrothal, annunciation, visitation, birthing of the Christ Child, flight into Egypt, death, burial, and assumption. So much of it seems too painstakingly detailed to not be true. And what is there merely gives glory. It can only uplift.

There were so many unique visions that this German mystic experienced, of many varied types, well beyond the lives of Jesus, the Blessed Mother, and the saints. She could see into the darkened hearts of many clergy and, interestingly, even the likes of many secular professors spreading toxic teachings to youth. In one case, she entered a spacious academic hall of pupils and professors. She observed, "I saw into the hearts of the professors and, to my amazement, I discovered in each a little black casket."[139] These professors were spreading a message of death. To this day, of course, some of the most damaging apostles of the culture of death have been professors in their classrooms. The worst of modern America's cultural revolution has crawled out of academia.

Thus, Anne Catherine Emmerich is known for her visions of the past, and rightly so—because they seem to beautifully accord to what we might picture those scenes two thousand years ago to have looked like. And yet, much less known are Emmerich's visions of future events to occur almost two millennia after the birth of Jesus Christ.

Unchained

Though most of Anne Catherine Emmerich's images looked into the past, some of them also looked forward, and maybe the most remarkable one is a vision that looked into our own times today. Most chillingly, it began with a look down deep into the pits of hell.

Emmerich's imagery of the underworld is chilling. She described it as a place where "nothing is to be seen but dismal dungeons, dark caverns, frightful deserts, fetid swamps filled with every imaginable species of poisonous and disgusting reptile." It is a place of "perpetual scenes of wretched discord," filled with "every species of sin and corruption, either under the most horrible forms imaginable, or represented by different kinds of dreadful torments." It is a place of "horror," a vast "temple of anguish and despair" in which there is no comfort and not a "consoling idea admitted." For those who are there for all eternity, the suffering is made worse by the "absorbing tremendous conviction" that the just and all-powerful God has given the damned what they deserve.[140]

Particularly striking was Emmerich's prophecy that Satan would be unchained for a time fifty or sixty years before the year of Christ 2000, and other demons let loose earlier still, paving the way for Lucifer's planned road of ruin. Emmerich's vision is published in *The Dolorous Passion of Our Lord Jesus Christ*. She stated of hell, "Many [demons] were chained down in a circle which was placed round other circles. In the center of Hell I saw a dark and horrible-looking abyss, and into this Lucifer was cast, after being first strongly secured with chains." The devil was surrounded by thick clouds of sulfurous black smoke.

Emmerich then related the frightful arrangement that had been made, permitted by the Almighty Himself: "God himself had decreed this; and I was likewise told, if I remember rightly, that he [Satan] will be unchained for a time fifty or sixty years before the year of Christ 2000. The dates of many other events were pointed out to me that I do not now remember, but a certain number of demons are to be let loose much earlier than Lucifer, in order to tempt men, and to serve as instruments of the divine vengeance. I should think that some must be loosened even in the present day, and others will be set free in a short time."[141]

Of course, that fifty to sixty years before the year 2000 would have been circa 1940–50. That would have been the time of the deadliest war in the history of humanity—World War II—with events like Pearl Harbor, the Holocaust, the start of the Cold War, and the spread of communism from Joseph Stalin's USSR and Mao Zedong's Red China (history's two most prolific killers) into Asia and Africa and elsewhere. Communism in the twentieth century killed over one hundred million people. It was also the time of the atomic age, followed by the upheavals of the sexual revolution, hundreds of millions of abortions, terrorism, and much more.

As for the demons let loose much earlier than Lucifer, in preparation for Lucifer's destructive role through the twentieth century, the timeline of destruction also seems to fit. This would have been precisely in the period (before Emmerich's death in 1824) that Karl Marx and Friedrich Engels were both born in Emmerich's native Germany (1818 and 1820, respectively). The two would coauthor the *Communist Manifesto* (published in 1848), their "Communist confession of faith," as Engels called it,[142] thereby unleashing a terrible ideology—one that the Catholic Church called "a Satanic scourge . . . orchestrated by the sons of darkness."[143] That "pernicious, diabolical" ideology, as the Church described it, would lead to the deaths of more people than any ideology in all of history.[144]

That preparatory nineteenth century was pockmarked by the birth of such men as Lenin, Stalin, and Trotsky, ultimately cementing the Bolshevik Revolution in 1917, which eventually led to the Cold War in the late 1940s (moreover, it was Stalin and Hitler together who launched World War II with the Hitler–Stalin Pact in August 1939). The evil of communism born in the mid-nineteenth century would not fully wreak its havoc until those fifty to sixty years before the year 2000, which was precisely the period when it killed the most people.

The ideology of Marx, Engels, Lenin, Stalin, Mao, Pol Pot, and Fidel Castro all certainly coincides with these visions of Anne Catherine. Adding to the weight, if not credibility, of her vision of hell was the vision of another female German mystic, the great St. Hildegard of Bingen (1098–1179).[145]

Bingen, a German Benedictine abbess and one of the most brilliant women in the history of Christianity, was a mystic, a visionary, a musician, a composer, and a doctor of the Church. She produced three volumes of visionary theology, the first of which is titled *Scivias*, completed around 1151 or 1152. It reports twenty-six of her visions, including those on hell and the devil.

Hildegard described the devil as a monstrous, horrible-looking worm. This creature was "amazingly huge and long," with the mouth and nose of a viper and the hands of a man and a grotesquely deadly tail. His presence "provoked a feeling of horror and fury beyond words." And then Hildegard noted this detail, which is eerily reminiscent of the description of Anne Catherine Emmerich many centuries later: "A chain was riveted around the neck of the worm, binding its hands and feet as well, and securely fastened to the rock in the abyss. In this way the monster was restrained so that it could not move around as its wicked will wished."[146] Thus, in this twelfth-century mystical vision that Hildegard had of the devil, Lucifer is chained. When was he unchained? Emmerich offered that answer.

Notably, it was Emmerich and Bingen's native Germany that produced so many men of destructive ideas, from Marx and Engels to the 1920s and 1930s Freudian-Marxism of the Frankfurt School to Hitler and more. Even today, the most rebellious clergy in the entirety of the Catholic Church remain in Germany with its dissident cardinals—the home of another mightily rebellious priest, Martin Luther.

Many might want to dismiss these hellacious visions by Emmerich and Hildegard as being outside the Scriptures. They might scoff at their visions of chaining and unchaining. Many might also contend that a loving God would never unleash Lucifer to wreak havoc on His people. And yet, what Emmerich and Hildegard of Bingen reported does not seem to be outside the bounds of the Scripture, or at least not a contradiction of it. Indeed, what is so intriguing about these two visions is how they seem to reconcile with the New Testament's closing book: the book of Revelation.

Revelation 20:1–3 states, "Then I saw an angel coming down from heaven, holding in his hand the key of the bottomless pit and a great chain. And he seized the dragon, that ancient serpent, who is the Devil and Satan, and bound him for a thousand years, and threw him into the pit, and shut it and sealed it over him, that he should deceive the nations no more, till the thousand years were ended. After that he must be loosed for a little while." And then, Revelation 20:7 states, "When the thousand years are ended, Satan will be loosed from his prison."

That is, of course, remarkably similar to the visions of Anne Catherine Emmerich and Hildegard of Bingen, right down to the thousand years and the devil being unchained for a short time. Of course, as the Scriptures say, we cannot know the exact time. Nonetheless, the Scriptures do point to a thousand-year period and then a short time that follows. If the period of the devil being bound had been, say, 940/50 to 1940/50, it would not be inaccurately represented by the claims of Emmerich and Bingen. That would also mean, yet again, that the Middle Ages, or Dark Ages, were not as dark as their secular detractors like to frame them. Sure, they were far from perfect, but the devil had not been loosened upon them as he has upon our age. In this way, too, looking forward and not just backward, Anne Catherine Emmerich gave us much to ponder, including about what might have been unchained in our time.

Visions of "Demolishers" and a "Counterfeit Church"

Anne Catherine Emmerich's prophetic visions also offer us much to ponder about our Church, and they most certainly had a purpose for the Catholic Church. As biographer Rev. Carl Schmöger noted, "They were not only prophetic pictures, but real, personal combats, fruitful in results inasmuch as they were a continued development of the great combat of the Church. . . . The sentiments and designs of the Church's enemies were made known to her, that she might oppose them by prayer."[147] Emmerich opposed them in prayer and through her suffering.

Of these prophetic visions of her Church in combat, one that particularly stands out is her revelation concerning what she described as a "counterfeit church," also variously translated as a "false church." She visualized a Catholic Church in crisis, attacked from without and within. And for Emmerich, this entailed some truly apocalyptic images, a word that she did not shy from.

The first of these related visions came on December 27, 1819. It was the feast day of St. John the Evangelist, and Sr. Emmerich suddenly beheld St. Peter's Basilica in Rome aglow, shining like the sun, emanating streams of light all over the world. "I was told," she said, "that this referred to St. John's Apocalypse. Various individuals would be enlightened by it and they would impart their knowledge to the whole world. I had a very distinct vision."[148] (The "it" here is not entirely clear, though it likely refers to the entire process of illumination, physical and spiritual, that she was describing.)

According to her biographer, Fr. Schmöger, throughout this Christmas octave running from the Nativity on December 25 through January 1, Emmerich had constant visions of the Church, even as she struggled to fully relate and connect them, which frustrated her.

Nonetheless, her images of St. Peter's Basilica remained impressed upon her mind. It was clear that this building, both symbolically and real, was under assault: "I saw St. Peter's," she related. "A great crowd of men were trying to pull it down while others constantly built it up again. Lines connected these men one with another and with others throughout the whole world. I was amazed at their perfect understanding."[149]

What she meant by "lines" was not explained, though it was unmistakable to the stigmatist that some were tasked with defending Mother Church while others were hellbent on taking the Church down. That was the central message being conveyed.

"The demolishers, mostly apostates and members of the different sects, broke off whole pieces and worked according to rules and instructions," said Emmerich of the conspirators. "They wore white aprons bound with blue riband. In them were pockets and they had trowels stuck in their belts. The costumes of the others were various. There were among the demolishers distinguished men wearing uniforms and crosses. They did not work themselves, but they marked out on the wall with a trowel where and how it should be torn down." Here, she paused to lament, "To my horror, I saw among them Catholic priests."[150]

These were apostates, including bad priests, enemies less at the gates than inside the gates. She saw how they deceived the pope. They were "false friends" working against him: "They worked quietly and confidently, but slyly, furtively, and warily. I saw the Pope praying, surrounded by false friends who often did the very opposite to what he had ordered."[151]

Sr. Emmerich said that she saw in this vision many clergy that she knew, some apparently doing harm while others worked to hold the edifice up. She also saw "a most majestic lady floating over the great square before the church. Her wide mantle fell over her arms as she arose gently on high, until she stood upon the cupola and spread it over all the church like golden rays. The destroyers were taking a short repose, and when they returned they could in no way approach the space covered by the mantle." On the majestic lady's side was a new pope, "younger and far sterner than his predecessor."[152]

Three days later, on December 30, Emmerich again saw St. Peter's, but this time standing atop the basilica was a fierce defender protecting it: St. Michael the Archangel. Michael had the support of a squadron of saints: "Numbers of saints hovered in the air over the combatants, pointing out what was to be done, making signs with the hand, etc., all different, but impelled by one spirit." And then came Jesus Christ Himself on the scene: "When the angel had descended, I beheld above him a great shining cross in the heavens. On it hung the Savior from whose wounds shot brilliant rays over the whole earth." Emmerich here described Jesus in almost St. Faustina–like Divine Mercy imagery: "Those glorious wounds were red like resplendent doorways, their center golden-yellow like the sun. He wore no crown of thorns, but from all the wounds of His head streamed rays. Those from His hands, feet, and side were fine as hair and shone with rainbow colors; sometimes they all united and fell upon villages, cities, and houses throughout the world."[153] Jesus's source of light gushed forth to cover the whole world.

This appeared to be an apocalyptic battle, one in which Jesus, His Blessed Mother, St. Michael the Archangel, the saints, and their Holy Mother Church prevailed. Emmerich assessed, "When the combat on earth was over, the church and the angel became bright and shining, and the latter disappeared; the cross also vanished and in its place stood a tall, resplendent lady extending over it her mantle of golden rays. . . . When I saw this reunion, I felt that the kingdom of God was near. I perceived a new splendor, a higher life in all nature, and a holy emotion in all mankind as at the time of the Savior's birth."[154]

This victory was followed by a great celebration: "Then I saw a great feast in St. Peter's which, after the victorious battle, shone like the sun. I saw numerous processions entering it. I saw a new Pope, earnest and energetic. I saw before the feast began a great many bad Bishops and pastors expelled by him. I saw the holy Apostles taking a leading part in the celebration. I saw the petition: 'Lord, Thy kingdom come,' being verified."[155]

Trying to discern the precise meaning of each of these visualizations will frustrate readers today. To her credit, Emmerich herself sensed just that; she admitted struggling to connect them herself. Moreover, Emmerich did not always receive these visions in a perfect chronological order. Nonetheless, they did continue to come to her because they were warnings of a great tribulation. Indeed, four months later, on April 12, 1820, Anne Catherine Emmerich declared, "I have had another vision on the great tribulation everywhere reigning."[156]

That tribulation involved the Catholic Church at the epicenter. Even as the precise symbols were not always clear in their exact meaning, what is indisputable is that the German nun foresaw major battles within and against her beloved Catholic Church.

That brings us to Anne Catherine Emmerich's specific vision of a "counterfeit church." That unsettling prophecy came on May 13, 1820. (Incidentally, May 13, 1917, a century later, would be the day of the appearance of Our Lady at Fatima, and ultimately the feast day of Our Lady of Fatima.) The transcription of that vision began with this statement from Emmerich: "Last night, from eleven to three, I had a most wonderful vision of two churches and two Popes and a variety of things, ancient and modern."[157]

This vision of two churches includes the counterfeit church. The two popes were well apart in time, "ancient and modern," as she put it. The ancient one, as she proceeded to assert, was Pope Boniface IV (550–615), whose papacy ran from 608–15.[158] The modern pope is less clear. To be sure, she does refer to the "present Pope and the dark church of his time in Rome."[159] On the one hand, one might assume that this was the modern pope of her day, who at the time would have been Pope Pius VII (1742–1823), who served a long papacy from 1800–1823, and was admired then and still today (in 2007, Pope Benedict XVI granted Pius VII the title servant of God). But on the other hand, Emmerich does not specify Pius VII by name (as she did with Boniface IV), and her prophetic visions usually concerned future events rather than those of the moment. Furthermore, in other papal prophecies, her details seem to more clearly apply to Pius VII.[160] Thus, she may well have been speaking of a future pope, perhaps even in our own day or yet to come.[161]

More importantly, whether this "dark church" existed in the time of Pius VII or not, Emmerich warns of the growth of a "counterfeit church." Perhaps it began growing at that time of Pius VII—or, if not under that pope, then maybe under a future pope. Either way, it was growing. She forecast:

I saw the fatal consequences of this counterfeit church; I saw it increase; I saw heretics of all kinds flocking to the city. I saw the ever-increasing tepidity of the clergy, the circle of darkness ever widening. And now the vision became more extended. I saw in all places Catholics oppressed, annoyed, restricted, and deprived of liberty, churches were closed, and great misery prevailed everywhere with war and bloodshed. I saw rude, ignorant people offering violent resistance, but this state of things lasted not long. Again I saw in vision St. Peter's undermined according to a plan devised by the secret sect while, at the same time, it was damaged by storms.[162]

To many modern Catholics, including not a few who have chimed in on various websites, the Emmerich vision, "I saw in all places Catholics oppressed, annoyed, restricted, and deprived of liberty, churches were closed, and great misery prevailed everywhere," could easily seem to apply to our time of COVID-19 and closed churches. Perhaps so. In fact, it is hard to imagine any other comparable moment in all of Catholic history in which churches were closed truly everywhere, in countries not only in certain regions or continents but all over the world, with parishioners being restricted and deprived of the liberty to even receive Holy Communion.

But at last, there was good news: that Church under siege would be "delivered at the moment of greatest distress." It would be restored, protected by the Blessed Mother herself and a vigilant new pope. Emmerich continued in the next line, "Again I saw the Blessed Virgin extending her mantle over it. In this last scene, I saw no longer the reigning Pope, but one of his successors, a mild, but very resolute man who knew how to attach his priests to himself and who drove far from him the bad. I saw all things renewed and a church which reached from earth to Heaven."[163]

If this vision was accurate, is it a vision that has come to fruition and is now in the past, or is it yet to come? Is today's Church still in crisis, still in counterfeit, still in combat and mired in darkness, and still waiting for that intervention by the mantle of the Blessed Mother and vigilance of that pope still to come? Does the vision apply to the

Catholic Church right now? Was COVID-19 a marker, with Pope Francis soon to be replaced by a more resolute successor? I certainly do not know these answers, and I am not trying to suggest or imply anything. Nonetheless, such were the visions, the statements, and these are merely some interpretations that some people no doubt have considered regarding times past, today's time, and the future.

Truly, only God knows. We mere mortals must wait and see.

✝

Anne Catherine Emmerich died on February 9, 1824. She went permanently to the other world from the same bed where she had received countless visions and visitations and lived on nothing but a little water and her small slice of Daily Bread—the Holy Eucharist. All along, she bore her sufferings and her stigmata. They and she spoke to us in profound ways.

The German stigmatist was beatified on October 3, 2004, the eve of the feast day of St. Francis, the great stigmatist, of whom she had among her many visions a blessed vision of *Il Poverello* receiving the wounds of Christ six centuries before she had. She was beatified that lovely, sunny autumn day in Rome by Pope St. John Paul II.

"Blessed Anne Catherine Emmerich told of the 'sorrowful passion of our Lord Jesus Christ,'" said the pope at the beatification ceremony, "and lived it in her body." The Polish pope, hobbled and bent over by the Parkinson's disease that in six months would take his own life, admired how Emmerich withstood "physical weakness [by] her strong character as well as her unshakable faith." These were spiritual traits that he himself was then displaying to the world. And still today, concluded the pontiff in his beatification statement, quoting 1 Peter 2:24, "she passes on to all the saving message: Through the wounds of Christ we have been saved."[164]

She passes on that and yet more to us today. Anne Catherine Emmerich also passes on profound glimpses into trying but triumphant times past and yet to come.

CHAPTER 5

SAINT GEMMA GALGANI (1878–1903)

St. Gemma Galgani was born on March 12, 1878, to two devout parents, Enrico Galgani and Aurelia Landi, in the village of Camigliano, Italy, near the city of Lucca in the Tuscany region. Her father was a chemist and a pharmacist, earning a decent income to provide a middle-class home to his wife and several children, though most of Gemma's siblings died young. Sadly, the parents would likewise die at young ages. Gemma lost her pious mother first—a woman described as "a saint and a most perfect model to all Catholic mothers"—to the scourge of tuberculosis when Gemma was only seven years old.[165]

The parents chose not a traditional Christian name or that of an Italian saint for the baby girl but Gemma, which in Italian means "Gem." They had been thus inspired by the priest at her baptism, who, upon gazing at the beautiful infant child, declared *"Una gemma del Paradiso"* (a gem from heaven).[166]

The infant girl was, in their eyes, a gem. And she would be so to the world as well. She may not have been given the name of a saint, but not long after her precious time in this world, the name Gemma would become the name of a saint, thanks to the extraordinary life lived by the girl.

The definitive go-to source on the life of St. Gemma of Galgani is the biography produced by her spiritual director, Fr. Germano di San

Stanislao (also known as Fr. Germanus of St. Stanislaus).[167] The highly respected Passionist father and scholar became her spiritual director in January 1900, a few years before her death at age twenty-five in April 1903.

The young Gemma was a smart student and a good writer. She produced a large number of letters, though most remain untranslated from the original Italian. At the command of her regular confessor, Msgr. John Volpi, the auxiliary bishop of Lucca, she began writing a diary, which was only recently published in English in 2022. That diary begins with a July 19, 1900, entry. In that same volume are portions of an autobiography that Gemma had started writing on February 17, 1901, in obedience to the request of Fr. Germano.[168]

Most remarkable about the existing manuscript of the autobiography, which today is on display at Sts. John and Paul Church in Rome, is that each page is marred by what appear to be burn marks. Gemma's lovely penmanship in the original handwritten notebook, which filled ninety-three pages, has the appearance of being burned on every page. Why? What caused this? The answer is the same demonic one that assaulted her throughout her life. According to Fr. Germano, once the manuscript was finished, it was hidden in a drawer by Gemma's adopted mother, Signora Cecilia Giannini, until it could be handed to Fr. Germano. Following this, Gemma saw a demon pass through the window of the room where the drawer was located, laughing and then disappearing into the air with the papers. He gnashed his teeth at her and snarled, "War, war, your book is in my hands."[169] This was symptomatic of the unholy war declared upon Gemma by the devil throughout her earthly pilgrimage.

In response, Fr. Germano went to work, seeking to exorcise the demon, and ordered it to bring back the manuscript. It was returned. "But in what a state!" recalled Fr. Germano. "The pages from top to bottom were all smoked, and parts burned, as if each one had been separately exposed over a strong fire. Yet they were not so badly burned as to destroy the writing. This document, having thus passed through a hell fire, is in my hands."[170]

As we shall see, this was just one of many examples of Gemma Galgani's countless battles with the underworld. Such was her unique mission of suffering. It was a form of earthly training for a greater glory to ultimately come.

Gemma's Supernatural Life and Gifts

Like another stigmatist in this book, Padre Pio, Gemma had a guardian angel with whom she communicated constantly as an aide in her battles. Like Padre Pio, she would need one most acutely. And, like Padre Pio, she was tormented by the devil not only spiritually but physically. Gemma could see this angel, who was a visible presence in her life at all times. He watched over her always, in direct interaction daily.[171] She also remained in very frequent communication and contact with the Lord Jesus and His Blessed Mother.

From her early days, Gemma showed remarkable signs of piety and was granted unusual spiritual favors. Most prominent among these was suffering. This was not wasted suffering but a sacrificial suffering offered up to Christ to unite to His own sacrifice on the Cross for the expiation for the sins of those in this world and especially for the souls in purgatory. "How long has it been since you last prayed for the souls in Purgatory?" Jesus once asked her. She asked Him a question in response: "Do bodily pains relieve the souls in Purgatory?" "Yes," answered Jesus, "yes, daughter: even the smallest suffering gives relief."[172]

This intensity of suffering was especially acute for Gemma with the death of her mother in September 1885, when Gemma was seven years old. The slow death of her mother that year had been torturous to the girl. That sorrowful event was followed by an ongoing sting of physical pain gifted to Gemma thereafter for the remainder of her earthly life. Each step of the way, one form of suffering seemed for Gemma a preparation for another form and level altogether, and always with a predesigned purpose. "I can say with truth that ever since the death of my mother," wrote Gemma later, "I have never spent a day without suffering some little thing for Jesus."[173]

To this end, Gemma had a singular theological-spiritual focus: the suffering of the Lord's passion. As Fr. Germano put it, this was for her a "favorite, and indeed almost constant, subject of thought and prayer."[174] All of this, in retrospect, conditioned her for the ultimate suffering to come during her final years: her sharing in Christ's passion through His wounds at Calvary.

Gemma often pleaded with Jesus to be permitted to share in His sufferings on the Cross, or at least to be able to feel physically some of what Christ experienced in the hours leading up to His death. This was ultimately granted to her, partly satisfied by her receiving the stigmata in her hands, feet, side, and head.[175]

That peak, that pinnacle of her pain, had been long in the making. Just prior to that, she had suffered a serious illness from 1898 to 1899, inflicted by an abscess on her spine that caused severe infection, probably what doctors today might diagnose as sepsis. She would be cured of this miraculously by Jesus, who had asked her on March 3, 1899, "Gemma, do you want to be cured?" Gemma said that she was so moved by the gracious offer of mercy that she could not answer. She need not. The grace was given, and she was cured.[176] Clearly, she had to be cured of this affliction in order for her body to recover for the decisive trial to come: the stigmata.

Thereafter, the marks were not long in coming. Merely three months after being cured from the abscess on her spine, Gemma received the stigmata. The phenomenon occurred on June 8, 1899. She later wrote of how she had been prepped for that moment:

> One evening when I was at prayer [in April 1899],[177] He [Jesus] came to bring peace to my soul. I felt myself entirely recollected, and I found myself a second time before Jesus Crucified. He said to me, "Look daughter, and learn how to love," and He showed me His five open wounds. "Do you see this Cross, these thorns, these nails, these bruises, these tears, these wounds, this blood? They are all works of love and of infinite love. Do you see how much I have loved you? Do you really want to love me? Then first learn to suffer. It is by suffering that one learns to love."[178]

There is obviously powerful spiritual insight in this passage. Jesus showed Gemma that learning how to love meant looking upon His suffering and His offering on the Cross. Those were works of infinite love. If Gemma really wanted to love, and to love Jesus, and to serve Jesus, then she—and presumably all of us followers of Christ—had to first learn to suffer. It is by suffering that we learn to love.

Of course, Christ told us in the New Testament that His followers must deny themselves, pick up their crosses, and follow him (see Mt 16:24–26). Unfortunately, this call to suffering is lost among so many Christians today, many of whom plead, "Why me?" and question or lose their faith when "bad things happen to good people." But this was not the understanding of Jesus nor of the stigmatists. They understood and experienced it like few others.

At that moment, Gemma, already locked in a customary state of ecstasy, fell faint on the floor for what she estimated was several hours. This was a heavier moment of anguish than usual, one that leveled her. And yet, she called it a "great consolation," one for which "I was not tired out." To the contrary, she was ready for more. Much more.

Gemma Galgani Receives the Stigmata

That altogether higher form of suffering transpired on June 8, 1899. On that day, Gemma Galgani was given the wounds of Jesus Christ. It was a Thursday evening, the time when the wounds thereafter would typically appear anew each week. Here is the full written statement from Gemma regarding what happened that day:

> On the eighth of June, after Communion, Jesus told me that, that evening, He would give me a very great grace. I went that same day to Confession, and I told Monsignor [Volpi] about it. He told me to be very attentive so that I could tell him about it afterward.
>
> Evening came, and all of a sudden, earlier than usual, I felt an interior sorrow for my sins far deeper than I had ever experienced before. In fact, it brought me very, very close to death. After this, all the powers of my soul became recollected. My intellect could think of nothing but my sins and the offense they gave to God. My memory recalled all my sins to mind and made me see all the torments that Jesus had suffered in order to save me. And my will made me detest them and promise to be willing to suffer anything in order to expiate them. My mind was flooded with thoughts, thoughts of sorrow, of love, of fear, of hope, and of comfort.[179]

This passage should give all of us great pause. One must stand in wonder and awe at how this saintly soul's sins could have been so vast. She had always been a pious young woman of virtue and humility, but such was her perfectly acute sense of sin during this higher state of spiritual illumination that Gemma was attuned to the realness of sin in a way others are not. We are apparently so far removed from that level of awareness that we cannot even relate to where Gemma stood at that moment. If the virtuous Gemma Galgani felt this sinful, imagine how we would feel in such a moment of illumination.

Interestingly, at this point in her description of receiving the stigmata, Gemma states that the Blessed Mother intervened, as did her guardian angel. It was as if heavenly helpers came to the scene for assistance in an obviously overwhelming moment:

> Following on this interior recollection, I was quickly rapt out of my senses, and I found myself before my heavenly Mother. At her right stood my Guardian Angel, who told me to make an act of contrition. When I had finished it, my blessed Mother said to me: "Daughter, in the name of Jesus all of your sins are forgiven." Then she added: "Jesus my Son loves you very much, and He wishes to give you a grace. Do you know how to make yourself worthy of it?" In my misery I did not know what to answer. She continued "I will be your Mother. Will you be a true daughter?" She spread her mantle and covered me with it.
>
> At that moment, Jesus appeared with all His wounds open. But blood no longer came out of those wounds. Rather, flames of fire issued forth from them, and in a moment, those flames came to touch my hands, feet, and heart. I felt as if I would die. I fell to the floor. But my Mother supported me, keeping me covered with her mantle. I had to remain several hours in that position. Then the Blessed Mother kissed me on the forehead, and it all disappeared, and I found myself kneeling on the floor. But I still felt an intense pain in my hands, feet, and heart.
>
> I arose to lie down on the bed, and I noticed that blood was flowing from those places where I felt pain. I covered these

parts as best as I could, and then, with the help of my angel, I was able to get in bed. These sufferings and pains, although they afflicted me, filled me with perfect peace. The next morning, I was able to go to Communion only with great difficulty, and I put on a pair of gloves in order to hide my hands. I could hardly stand on my feet, and I thought I would die any minute. The sufferings continued until three o'clock Friday afternoon, the solemnity of the Sacred Heart of Jesus.[180]

In her next entry in her autobiography, Gemma says that after "some time passed," namely, six days, every Thursday "about eight o'clock," she began to once again feel these same wounds repeated.[181] This would continue every week thereafter.

On July 19, 1900, some thirteen months after this initial experience, the stigmata that began in Gemma's hands and feet were now implanted on her head as well. On that Thursday, after her "six days of absence of Jesus," she once again found herself joined in his suffering, but this time in a heightened way: "He approached me, took from His head the crown of thorns, and placed it upon mine and then went aside."[182] Now, she also bore the wounds of Christ on her head.

Particularly elegant is a passage from Gemma's diary two months later, on Friday, August 17, when she describes a glorious moment when Jesus removed (as became His custom with her) the crown after another Friday of suffering. Gemma said that Jesus always blessed her after removing the crown. When He did so this time, "He lifted His right hand; from that hand I then saw a ray of light shine forth, much stronger than a lamp. He kept His hand raised; I remained fixed in watching it." She said that this "light that shone from His wounds . . . showered an abundance of graces."[183]

Some readers will recognize here a striking parallel to another stigmatist of the early twentieth century, St. Faustina Kowalska, and her Divine Mercy image of Jesus with rays of light emanating from His wounded heart of mercy.

Fr. Germano's Testimony

A keen, authoritative witness to Gemma's share in Jesus's passion and weekly sufferings of the gift of the stigmata was Fr. Germano, her spiritual director and biographer, and (as noted) a highly respected theologian. At great length, he detailed the phenomena that he and others witnessed constantly throughout the final four years of Gemma Galgani's remarkable life.

"These wounds opened and poured forth copious streams of blood every week for some years, during the period between each Thursday to Friday night," Fr. Germano attested. "They then closed of themselves in such a way that by Saturday, all trace of anything beyond a white mark in the flesh had disappeared."[184]

In addition to these marks of the Crucifixion, added Fr. Germano, at various times, Gemma received "other tokens of her participation in the torments which Our Lord endured." For instance, on July 19, 1900, while in an ecstasy, the vision of Christ wounded and bleeding came so clearly to her, standing in front of her, that Gemma begged Jesus to let her suffer yet more, sharing still more in His agony and the bodily pain that He felt. What could that entail? At that moment, according to Fr. Germano, Christ took the crown of thorns from His head and pressed it upon Gemma's head. From that time, every Friday, she also bore the marks of the thorns. Fr. Germano states, "Her forehead was frequently seen by many witnesses to be encircled with punctures such as the actual thorns would have made, and more strangely still, the whole of her head was found to be pierced in various places as it would have been had the crown been made in the shape of an entire cap, as the revelations of some Saints have indeed described it."[185] Again, we see the stigmata in the form of a crown of thorns—here affirmed by an eyewitness testimony.

In addition to these signs of Christ's passion, the Lord also permitted Gemma to suffer on many occasions a sweat of blood as He did during His agony in the Garden of Gethsemane. And here, too, there were witnesses: "This phenomenon," noted Fr. Germano, "which naturally could not be hidden from those who lived with her, is testified to by many witnesses, and the fact cannot reasonably be called in question."[186]

There were also marks that Gemma received that not all stigmatists bore. For instance, her left shoulder was marred by a chronic open wound, which, as noted by Fr. Germano, "according to some revelations, although it is not recorded in Holy Scripture, Our Blessed Lord received from carrying the Cross to Calvary. With this also came the bruised knees, which must have been caused by His repeated falls."[187]

That is not difficult to imagine. No doubt, whether recorded in Scripture or not, Jesus certainly bore a shoulder wound from carrying the Cross that repeatedly felled Him, so much so that Simon was tasked to help Him carry it. As noted in this book, other stigmatists likewise displayed that shoulder wound.

And still more, in what Fr. Germano described as "perhaps the most extraordinary marks of Our Lord's sufferings which the saintly girl bore on her flesh," were marks from the brutal scourging at the pillar. To the eyewitnesses, said Fr. Germano, these were especially fearful to behold, as "great gashes appeared in the flesh of her body, on her legs and arms, as if they had really been torn open, in places even to the very bone, by the loaded whips of the soldiers, as in the case of Our Lord."[188] Christ's young suffering servant in Lucca was being spared little.

Added Authoritative Testimonies to Gemma's Stigmata

Adding to the ecclesiastical testimony and authority of Fr. Germano were other prominent clergy who likewise saw these phenomena with their own eyes. One of the Passionist priests, Fr. Cajetan of the Child Jesus, submitted this formal testimonial:

> I the undersigned hereby testify and declare that in July, 1899, I saw certain extraordinary wounds on the hands of the young girl Gemma Galgani. In the inside, that is, in the palms there was seen a raised piece of flesh like the head of a nail, about as large as a half-penny. At the back of each hand there was a somewhat deep laceration that seemed to have been caused by a blunt nail forced through the hand from the opposite side.
>
> I, and those who were with me, had no hesitation in saying that those were Stigmata which could not have come from any

natural cause. In fact, we saw her hands on Thursday free from any marks. On Friday morning we found them as we have described. We examined them again on Saturday and found no mark except a small reddish cicatrix [scar].[189]

Another major Church authority who served as a witness, perhaps with more testimonials than any figure other than Fr. Germano, was Fr. Peter Paul of the Immaculate Passionist Provincial, better known as Msgr. Camillo Moreschini, the highly respected archbishop of Camerino. He had been superior general of the Passionists. After that position, Pope St. Pius X employed him in the role of apostolic visitor for twelve different dioceses before raising him to the level of archbishopric of Camerino. One of his many testimonials on Gemma merits quoting at length:

> Having heard others speaking of this young girl and relating strange things about her, while suspecting that it was a matter of mere feminine delusions, I thought I would make sure of it with my own eyes. I went to her house, it was Tuesday, and saw the child. I felt inspired to ask Our Lord to deign to give me a palpable sign if He were truly the Author of those marvelous things. Then mentally, without speaking of it to anyone, I thought of two things: the sweat of blood and the manifestation of the stigmata. When it was Vespers time she withdrew quite alone to say her usual prayers before the crucifix. In a few minutes she was in full ecstasy. I entered, and with my own eyes beheld her totally transfigured so that she looked like an angel, although torn by terrible pain. From her face, head and hands there flowed fresh blood, and I suppose it was the same all over her body. That flow of blood lasted for about half an hour, but did not reach the ground, because it dried quickly while flowing. I withdrew, greatly moved, and Gemma, coming out of the ecstasy, being alone with her aunt, said: "The Father has asked for signs from Jesus, and Jesus has told me that He has already given him one of them and will also give him the other. Oh, what do these signs mean? Does

He say it?" In the evening the lady just mentioned asked me quite anxiously: "But, Father, would the other sign you have asked for be that of the Stigmata?" I was astounded, and she continued: "I ask this because if it was so, Gemma has them already opened, come and see." I went, and found that blessed creature in ecstasy the same as the first time, with her hands pierced (I say pierced) through and through by a large freshly opened wound from which blood flowed in abundance. The affecting spectacle lasted about five minutes.[190]

According to this account, Fr. Peter Paul was uniquely treated by the Lord to a sample of Gemma's stigmatic suffering on a Tuesday, prior to the full sequence that customarily commenced from Thursday evening through Friday afternoon. This was an exception, apparently granted to the priest in answer to a silent prayer. Both the Lord and his suffering servant obliged.

Here, at this point, Fr. Peter Paul's testimony went into further detail, most of which was excluded by Fr. Germano for purposes of brevity. Fr. Germano paused to note, however, that those further details, provided by Fr. Peter Paul in "minute description," coincided "in every respect" with what Fr. Germano described in his biography. Fr. Germano did, however, include Fr. Peter Paul's closing paragraph:

With the cessation of the ecstasy the wounds closed, the blood ceased to flow and the torn skin returned at once to its natural state, so perfectly that nothing more was needed but to wash her hands in order to find that every vestige of what had happened was gone. Jesus had heard me, and thanking Him I laid aside every doubt, established in my belief that *digitus Dei est hic* [the finger of God is here].[191]

Fr. Peter Paul also at this time wrote to Msgr. Volpi, auxiliary bishop of Lucca, who became Gemma's ordinary confessor. He wanted to ensure that Volpi had a written account of what he had witnessed. He wrote:

> Rt. Rev. Monsignor: I make it my duty to inform you of what I
> witnessed in Gemma Galgani on Tuesday the 29th of August. I
> saw with my own eyes the wounds on both sides of her hands,
> and that they were truly torn open. When the ecstasy ended
> everything healed up, the cicatrices alone remaining. How
> could such a wound heal thus instantaneously by natural
> means? My opinion is that it is the work of God.[192]

Not surprisingly, Msgr. Volpi, not yet her confessor, wanted to see
this for himself. And he did. As Fr. Germano related, at about 2:00
p.m. on Friday, September 8, 1899, Msgr. Volpi came to the house
with a physician. Gemma's caretaker, Signora Cecilia, ran to meet
them, saying, "Come, come, it is just the right time." She brought
them into the room. They witnessed the bleeding right up until the
normal cessation time of 3:00. The doctor took a wet towel and wiped
the blood from Gemma's hands and forehead. He was struck when the
blood immediately disappeared, and the skin showed no signs of punctures, scratches, or any laceration. The doctor saw the same pattern of
bleeding and then cessation of bleeding in Gemma's feet and side.[193]

Fr. Germano's biography contains many accounts like this. He also
offers this from Fr. Peter Paul on Gemma's supernatural composure
during these moments of agony. Here again is his testimonial, quoted
at length:

> According to the opportunities offered me, I often conferred
> with Gemma. I heard her General Confession which she
> wished to finish at three intervals, and I had then the oppor-
> tunity of knowing that she had preserved her baptismal inno-
> cence. I have seen her several times in ecstasy. When she set
> herself to pray or was spoken to of spiritual things, especially
> of Our Lord's Passion, she went into ecstasy. Then she seemed
> to be transfigured, with her eyes open and fixed on one point,
> remaining immovable in her person although her limbs were
> quite flexible. She was during ecstasy insensible to any noise
> that was made near her, or to the puncture of a pin, or to
> burning with a taper. But although so dead to sense during

the ecstasy, she was all alive to heavenly things and was heard to give vent in fervent expressions to her love of God: "Yes, I love Thee, my Jesus; I will be all Thine. I will suffer all I can for Thee." Her bearing during those moments was truly angelic, and her countenance was resplendent with beauty joined with a marvelous majesty.

I have been able to notice in her an angelic purity. Not only did she preserve her baptismal innocence but, as far as I could ascertain, she never committed a deliberate defect during her whole life. Her humility was most profound. She was devoid of self-esteem, desiring to be humbled and corrected; and having been despised and mortified without measure, she gave no sign of the least displeasure or resentment. On the contrary, in her countenance she showed that she was more pleased than otherwise. Her obedience was singular and admirable. She never gave any opposition, even to the least hint or desire of others.[194]

Fr. Peter Paul also addressed the matter of Gemma's lack of food—that spiritual inedia so common to stigmatists. She lived off very little food, consuming mainly only the Eucharist, and she slept very little. All these mortifications, heaped upon the stigmata, surely would have been so physically overwhelming as to kill a normal person not being sustained by supernatural means:

Her mortification of her senses was continuous and most severe. She took very little food, so that it seemed a miracle how she lived. And if she had not been restrained by obedience she would have deprived herself of that little; for, as she said, she felt satisfied by the Bread of Angels, which she received every morning. With her everything was good, everything was equal. In her attire she never had any ambition and never asked for any special garment. Nor did she ever seek any amusement or recreation, nor complain of cold or heat, as though she were insensible to everything. A love of suffering was with her almost characteristic. No one ever heard her utter a complaint

even in the midst of the terrible pains she underwent during
her long sickness, or from the violent assaults of the devil.[195]

As we shall see, her battles with the devil were especially intense.
How could she take on that ordeal as well? Once again, the key was
the supernatural infusion of grace from her Lord and Savior. Fr. Peter
Paul continued:

> Her constant remembrance of Jesus Crucified stimulated her
> to suffer always, so that she desired nothing more than suf-
> fering, and whatever she suffered seemed little. This perfect
> creature had offered herself a victim to the Sacred Heart of
> Jesus for the conversion of poor sinners, and for this end she
> willingly offered every suffering. For the same end, and still
> more through love, she desired continually to suffer with Jesus
> on the Cross, to live always on the Cross, and to die with Him
> on the Cross. And in this it would appear that her Divine
> Spouse satisfied her, because in life and in death she suffered
> always a cruel martyrdom of body and soul. What shall I say of
> her union with God? I can certify that this was unceasing. Even
> in the midst of the most distracting occupations she was always
> recollected and in mind and heart united to God. On account
> of this habitual and profound recollection her voice was never
> heard. She answered briefly the questions that were asked her
> and then resumed her silence. Indeed, so intimate was her
> union with God that she seemed more a celestial being than
> a creature of earth. Behold these are, put briefly, the virtues
> which Gemma practiced always, and which go to show that she
> was full of the love of God. Hence I hold that the wonderful
> phenomena which we have admired in her are the work of that
> God, whom she loved so much and served so well.[196]

And in this regard, the comportment of this special stigmatist,
Gemma Galgani, was likewise saintly.

Knowledge of Future Events and Death

Gemma was also gifted with foreknowledge of earthly events.[197] This began early for her, namely, with the death of her mother—of which Jesus gave her a warning ahead of time. He also, customarily for Gemma, made that moment an opportunity for the girl's consent to sacrificial suffering.

Gemma, not surprisingly, remembered the moment well, writing about it years later in her autobiography. She said it was May 26, 1885. Gemma was seven years old and had just received Confirmation but did so weeping. Her joy upon entering into this holy sacrament was tempered by her anxiety that her very ill mother was at home dying, and she would not see her in this world again. She wanted to dash home to be with her.

The girl also wanted her mother to take her with her to heaven. Gemma herself had always suffered from physical ailments—ever racked with pain and getting no relief from one failed operation after another.[198] Doctors were futile in helping her, whether from a diseased foot or infected spine or some other condition, no doubt because these ailments were part of the Lord's plan for her. Her own health was always a concern to her parents, who constantly thought that Gemma's own life was in peril. That was fine with Gemma, who desired eternity with Jesus. Hence, she wanted to die with her mother. If God was going to take up her mother, why not go with her? But that was not the plan of the Master of the Universe.[199]

Gemma assisted at the Mass that followed her May 26 confirmation, all the while praying for her mother and struck with sadness. Then, all of a sudden, she heard a "voice in my heart" saying to her, "Are you willing to give your mother to me?" She answered, "Yes, if you will take me, too." The voice replied, "No, give me your mother willingly. But you must remain with your father for the present. I will take your mother to Heaven, understand? Do you give her to me willingly?"[200]

Gemma, in her autobiography, did not list her exact reply, recording only that she gave her consent. When the Mass was over, she hurried home. She looked at her mother—still alive—and wept. She simply could not contain herself at the thought of losing her mother.[201]

Over the next two months, the girl never left her mother's side. She was forcibly separated from her by her father, who evidently felt that the trauma of Gemma watching her mother ebb away was making Gemma's own physical challenges worse. He feared losing his daughter before his wife. He sent her to Lucca to live at the home of her mother's brother. The girl later described that separation from her mother as "a torture." Alas, she was not with her mother when the beleaguered woman died on September 17, 1885.[202]

Some eighteen years later, in 1903, Gemma was given foreknowledge of her own death. Up until that point, Gemma, like many young women gifted with such unusual piety, had thought of becoming a religious, but that changed as she was made aware that her time on earth was coming to an end, as the Lord had special plans for her as a servant in the next world. According to Fr. Germano, she ceased to speak of the idea of joining a religious order and instead occupied herself solely with preparations for death, which would come "as she had foretold, in six months." Said Fr. Germano, "God was satisfied with His faithful servant's desire and with the merit of the sacrifice she had so generously made. She had already, as an act of private devotion, made the vows of religious profession. She was a religious and Passionist in mind and spirit and bore the stigmata of His Passion on her body. She was then fit to leave this world, well satisfied and full of joy at having perfectly attained the end for which God placed her in it."[203] That moment came, according to divine schedule.

Fr. Germano visited Gemma as she weakened terribly and was approaching death. This was not her usual suffering. She was dying. Sitting at her bedside, he gently asked, "Well, Gemma, what are we to do?" The young woman answered with confident serenity, "Go to Jesus, Father." Fr. Germano later noted that she had said this in a tone of inexpressible joy. "But really?" he added. "Yes, Father, this time Jesus has told me clearly, so clearly. To Heaven, my Father, to Jesus, with Jesus in Heaven!" "But," pleaded her priestly spiritual director and friend, "I do not wish you to die yet." She replied to him with an expression of what Fr. Germano called "characteristic vivacity," saying,

"And should Jesus wish it, what then?"[204] The priest was not going to question that.

Fr. Germano said that Gemma then "went into the most minute particulars about her death," from how the last sacraments would be administered to how her body would be clothed to how she should be placed on the bier and carried to the cemetery. He said she spoke of these things with an "admirable indifference," almost as if they were discussing changing the sheets of her bed or rearranging the furniture in the room: "She listened and answered with brightness and grace."[205]

Fittingly, the final days of this girl bearing the wounds of Christ's passion arrived on Easter 1903. And quite fascinatingly, like Jesus in his final days, from His agony in the Garden to His feeling of abandonment on His way to Calvary,[206] Gemma battled the devil as well as the anguish of abandonment by her closest friends, the latter of which happened almost inexplicably. It made sense only from a spiritual perspective—from the view that God had so ordained it. And she seemed to know it.

One of the nurses at the girl's bedside winced at the diabolical attacks commencing before her, writing to Gemma's spiritual director, "That abominable beast will be the end of our dear Gemma—deafening blows, forms of ferocious animals, etc.—I came away from her in tears because the demon is wearing her out, and there is no remedy for what the wretch will surely do to her. We help her by sprinkling holy water in the room. Then the disturbance ceases, but only to begin soon again worse than before."[207]

The beast tormented her soul and her body. "Horrible and fetid animals, whether real or imaginary, came into her bed," recorded Fr. Germano, "crept over her limbs and tormented her in various ways so that the dear child had no means of relief. More than once, full of terror, she said to the sister in attendance that she felt a serpent winding around her from head to foot and striving to crush her. In order to be relieved, she repeatedly asked with great earnestness to be exorcised." She even tried to do an exorcism herself, sternly stating in a resolute voice to whatever was attacking her, "Wicked spirit, I command you to depart from here to the place that is destined for you. If not, I will accuse you before my God." Then, turning to the heavenly Mother, she exclaimed, "O Mother, I am in the hands of the devil who labors, strikes, torments me in order to drag me from the hands of Jesus. No, no, Jesus! Do not abandon me, Mother, I will be good. Pray to Jesus for me. I am alone at night, full of terror, oppressed."[208]

Naturally, this wore down Gemma Galgani. She was nearing the end, once again suffering at another heightened level that must have been preparation for her yet more extraordinary role in the next world.

"The cruel malady had run its course," wrote Fr. Germano. "Gemma had nothing more left than a breath of life. Her whole body was in agony, the pallor of death was depicted on her countenance, she was stretched motionless on her bed in aspect so pitiable that one saw in her an image of Jesus expiring on the Cross." As for the oppressive presence of the devil, Fr. Germano had this to say: "Four or five days before she died, she became so heavy that three strong persons—even the workmen of the establishment—could scarcely lift her, although she was reduced to skin and bone and so slight in figure that a baby might have moved her." She could not have weighed more than one hundred pounds, and yet, even groups of three men could barely lift her. One of the nuns present to assist said, "We have managed a great many sick people, but never have we met anything like this." Gemma explained to them what was pressing her down—what was oppressing her: "It is not I, you know, that weighs so." She and they concluded that it was the devil himself holding her down.[209]

Throughout her death spiral, others could not see the devil, but Gemma could. The others certainly felt a presence. And, in fact, as soon as she expired, they were able to lift her with ease, as if she returned to her natural weight. The earthly ordeal was over.[210]

The devil was there, tormenting Gemma in her final hours. Like Christ, Gemma felt abandoned by those closest to her in her hour of need. But she accepted this and other Christ-like sacrifices. Consider this example.

On Holy Thursday, Gemma had refused water, as Christ would, saying she would happily bear the burning thirst. On Good Friday, around 10:00 a.m., when a lady friend at her bedside said she was going home to her house nearby to rest a little, Gemma requested, "Don't leave me until I am nailed to the Cross. I have to be crucified with Jesus. He has said to me that His children have to be crucified." This seemed almost literally true. One of the witnesses later said, "Look at Jesus dying on the Cross; that was the appearance of Gemma in those moments."[211]

But most troubling was the sense of Christ-like abandonment that Gemma received during those final hours. "Add that abandonment, too truly real, by men," noted Fr. Germano. "Of all this He Himself complained from the Cross, and Gemma in this also had to be like Him. It would naturally be asked with some surprise why our dying saint in her moments of greatest need was abandoned by her confessors, directors and spiritual guides, and that only a few pious women stood by her, moved rather by charitable sympathy at the sight of so much suffering than by the desire to be of assistance to her." But nonetheless, it was so, "because God so willed in order to put a climax to the martyrdom and merits of His faithful servant."[212]

As examples of this abandonment, Fr. Germano noted that the priest of a nearby church brought Gemma the Viaticum and then quickly disappeared. The curate of the parish gave her a rapid anointing and then took off, returning only at the last moment to "read the recommendation of her soul." The extraordinary confessor, whom she had called for explicitly, dropped in, heard her confession for an instant, and then bolted. Fr. Germano noted that the poor girl's "ordinary confessor who, alone having directed her from her infancy, knew thoroughly all the mysteries of her life and would have been able to help and console her in the midst of such pains, temptations and battles, only showed himself for a few moments, although the poor soul had asked him several times to come and see her." And where was Fr. Germano? He reluctantly conceded later, "I myself being at a great distance, knowing nothing of her imminent danger and great need, neither thought of going or of writing a consoling letter to her. Thus Gemma was left alone to suffer with Jesus only."[213] Just as Jesus was left alone with His Father at Gethsemane and Calvary.

And akin to the words of the Son to His Father during His final gasps, here were Gemma's last words: "Now it is indeed true that nothing more remains to me, Jesus. I recommend my poor soul to Thee . . . Jesus!" As Fr. Germano put it, "It was the *Consummatum est* ("It is consummated") and the *In manus tuas* ("Into Thy hands") of Our Savior dying on the Cross. These were Gemma's last words."[214]

The last words were uttered on April 11, 1903, an hour after midday on Holy Saturday. Gemma had once told her aunt, "I have asked Jesus to let me die on a great solemnity. What a delightful thing to die on a great Feast!" As Fr. Germano put it, "Yes, what a charming thing to die on the Solemnity of Our Lord's Resurrection, after having kept Good Friday on the Cross with Him, sharing in all His agony!"[215] It was a final earthly gift of sacrificial sharing from the Lord to His beautiful gem of a servant.

Fighting the Devil—Today

So ended the earthly life of Gemma Galgani. And yet, her heavenly life had just begun. She had been prepared, steeled, in a truly phenomenal way. She fought the devil and his legions in this world, and now she was ready to engage them in immortal combat in the next. That step took a giant leap forward with her beatification by Pope Pius XI on May 14, 1933, and canonization by Pope Pius XII on May 2, 1940. "She bore in her flesh the wounds of Christ," stated Pius XI. At her canonization, Pius XII affirmed that among her "divine favors was the very special one of manifesting in her virginal flesh the living image of Christ and mysteriously sharing in the various sufferings of His passion."[216]

As these dates of her beatification and canonization suggest, it did not take the Church long to affirm Gemma Galgani's sainthood. It almost seemed as if the popes knew that the modern world would need her, especially the Church Militant in her battles against seemingly ever-escalating evil.

Gemma's personal writings and those of Fr. Germano are filled with chilling references to her encounters with the dark realm. When Gemma spoke of "the devil," it seemed that she was often referring to a demon of some sort and not necessarily Lucifer himself, though the distinction was not always made. As for Fr. Germano, he stated that it was a "furious" Satan himself who "threw off" his mask and waged "open war" against the girl: "He appeared to her repeatedly in horrible forms: at one time as a savage dog, at another as a hideous monster, again as a man in a fury. He used to begin by terrifying her with his horrible and threatening appearance. Then he rushed on her, beat her, tore her with his teeth, threw her down, dragged her by the hair and in other innumerable ways tortured her innocent body."[217] Whether Satan himself or his minions, Lucifer was in command of this pernicious militia.

As Fr. Germano noted, no one should attribute these incidents to something akin to hallucinations, "for their effects were but too real—her hair scattered about the room, the bruises and livid marks that remained for days, the excessive pains she felt in all her members, etc. So also were but too real the noises that were heard of blows and of the shaking of her bed, lifted and then thrown down, as remained to be seen. Nor were these assaults and annoyances things of a few moments. They lasted for hours together without cessation, and even during the whole night."[218] Fr. Germano quoted this unsettling letter from Gemma regarding the attacks of this beast:

> Today I thought I was to be entirely free from that nauseous animal, and instead he has knocked me about greatly. I had gone to bed with a full intention of sleeping, but it turned out otherwise. He began with certain blows that made me fear I should die. He was in the shape of a big black dog and put his paws on my shoulders, hurting me greatly. I felt it so much in all my bones that sometimes I thought they were broken. Also, when I was taking holy water he wrenched my arm so violently that I fell from the pain. The bone was dislocated, but went back because Jesus touched it for me, and all was remedied.[219]

And here is another written account from Gemma to her spiritual director, with yet another occasion of the cruel beast doing direct physical damage to the innocent girl:

Yesterday, too, the devil knocked me about. Aunt told me to draw a bucket of water with which I was to fill the room jugs. When passing with jugs in my hands before the image of the Heart of Jesus, to whom I offered fervent acts of love, I got such a strong blow of a stick on my left shoulder that I fell, but nothing was broken. Even today I feel very unwell and everything I do seems to give me pain.[220]

And here is an especially alarming letter shared by Fr. Germano, in which "the demon" tried to sow spiritual doubts in the girl about Christ's salvation in addition to thrashing her:

Once more I have passed a bad night. The demon came before me as a giant of great height. He beat me fiercely all night, and kept saying to me: "For thee there is no more hope of salvation. Thou art in my hands." I replied that God is merciful, and that therefore I feared nothing. Then giving me a hard blow on the head he said in a rage, "Accursed be thou!" and disappeared. I went to my room to rest a little, and there I found him. He began again to strike me with a knotted rope, and kept on because he wanted me to listen to him while he suggested wickedness. I said no, and he struck harder, and knocked my head violently against the ground. At a certain moment it came to my mind to invoke Jesus' Holy Papa [thus she used to name the Eternal Father]. I called aloud: "Eternal Father, through the most Precious Blood, free me!" I don't quite know what happened. That contemptible beast dragged me violently from my bed and threw me, dashing my head against the floor with such force that it pains me still. I became senseless and remained lying there until I came to myself a long time afterwards. Jesus be thanked![221]

These brutal attacks were frequent, as they would be for Padre Pio. Indeed, Fr. Germano attested, "It would take too long to recount all these painful scenes. They happened very often and sometimes continued for days." They happened so often that "the poor victim had become in a certain sense inured to them," actually ceasing to be alarmed by them: "She regarded the hellish monster with a serenity like that of a dove looking at any unclean animal."[222]

She really had become almost inured to them. In fact, she would occasionally answer the devil contemptuously, even laughing at him as if he were downright silly. She told Fr. Germano, "If you had but seen him, Father, how he ran, and how often he tripped as he fled, and gave vent to his rage, you too would have laughed at him. My God! How fetid he is, and how horrible to look at! But Jesus has told me not to fear him."[223] Fear not, perhaps. But nonetheless, Fr. Germano forbade her thereafter to mock the devil. He certainly was not calm. He was afraid.

On one occasion, a demon was in the room with Fr. Germano and Gemma, terribly unsettling the priest. The girl tried to buck up the priest: "Don't be afraid, Father, it is that vile demon who wants to annoy me. But don't fear, as he will not do you any harm." Fr. Germano approached her trembling, with holy water, which he sprinkled across her bed. The demon vanished, said Germano, leaving the girl "in perfect serenity as if nothing had happened."[224]

Again, the examples of the attacks are legion. Here are just three examples of Gemma being attacked by the devil in the month of August 1900, which she shared in her diary.

One incident occurred on the evening of August 3, 1900, a Friday, meaning a day when Gemma was exhausted from her customary two-day period of stigmatic suffering. The devil was no gentleman and certainly had no care. He always attacked, especially during someone's weakest point. The girl longed to get some sleep but was tormented when a "tiny, tiny man appeared, all covered in black hair," at her bed. "What a fright!" she wrote. "He put his hands on my bed and I thought he wanted to hit me." She clutched her crucifix and called on Jesus and her guardian angel for assistance, which made the demon furious. "He rolled around on the floor, cursing; he made one last effort to take away the cross I had with me, but then he instantly fell backward."

At that moment, her guardian angel opened his wings and "alighted" next to her, blessed her, and the "bad devil" bolted. She learned the next morning (presumably from her guardian angel) that at the very moment that this devil was rising in fury, the scapular of Our Lady of Sorrows had been placed on her (she does not specify by whom). She recalled that the diabolical figure had been trying to take something off of her and realized "it could be nothing but that."[225]

A few weeks later, on August 20, the devil attacked her in bed again, this time physically striking her. The devil gave her such a strong shove that she fell off the bed and banged her head on the floor "with such great force that [she] felt a sharp pain." She went unconscious and lay on the ground for what she estimated had been a long time.[226]

Five days after this incident, on August 25, the devil visited and harassed her about going to confession. "When are you going to Confession?" he asked her. "This evening," she replied. "And why?" he pressed. "Why do you go so often? Don't know you know that your confessor is a swindler?" She made the Sign of the Cross several times, prompting the demonic figure to strike her so severely that she shook.[227]

These physical blows endured by the girl are astonishing to read about. While they are difficult to bear when reading about Padre Pio, a male stigmatist, they seem even harder to imagine in the case of a young girl being so viciously assaulted. The Lord and His guardian angels apparently permitted this to an extent, clearly for purposes of preparation.

Saint Gemma Galgani—A New Terror of Demons

Upon her death in April 1903, Gemma's battles with demons took a dramatic upward turn. The next time she confronted them in the supernatural arena, Gemma Galgani—ultimately, St. Gemma Galgani—would have the upper hand.

No, there are no demons in heaven. She was free of them there. As the Blessed Mother told her after one of Gemma's bouts with a demon, "In Heaven there is no more suffering."[228] But it appears that Gemma Galgani was being primed on earth to fight demons as an intercessor in heaven, one who could appear on earth when invoked to fight them.

That seems to have been the divine plan all along. Jesus had told Gemma, "Remember that I have created you for Heaven; you have nothing to do with the earth."[229] Her earthly suffering need not have been viewed in awe by people of this world sitting at her bedside, marveling at her bleeding hands and head. Her purpose in this world was to suffer in anticipation of her duties in the next. On earth, she was getting spiritually equipped. In fact, there is today, a century after her death, much testimony from modern exorcists about how St. Gemma's intercession has helped them in exorcising demons.

Journalist Matt Baglio's book *The Rite: The Making of a Modern Exorcist*, published by Doubleday, chronicles the work of California priest Fr. Gary Thomas, trained in Rome in the rite of exorcism. The book describes the exorcism of a thirty-five-year-old Italian woman named Anna in 2005.

"The exorcism had been going on for the better part of an hour, and the strain was beginning to show on everyone," Baglio recorded. "Should he [the priest] continue?" Just then, the possessed woman's head turned, her eyes fixating on a spot near the far wall. "No!" roared the demon in a guttural voice emanating deep from within this poor woman. "The one in black is here, the jinx!" Baglio wrote that the exorcist suddenly felt a ray of hope, knowing from past exorcisms that this was the demon's name for St. Gemma Galgani, who was dressed in her traditional black and looked just as she did as a young woman in her early twenties. "Let us thank Gemma Galgani," announced the grateful exorcist, "for being here with us today."[230]

Notably, the exorcist here also thanked St. Mother Teresa of Calcutta, who joined Gemma in the exorcism. The two women, both appearing in their twenties (only the demon could see them), warmly greeted and embraced one another, prompting the raging demon to fume, "Oh, look at them. Look at them! They are hugging and greeting each other! Disgusting! Disgusting!"

It is apparently not unusual in these exorcisms for St. Gemma to be joined by other saints helping to purge the possessed. A 2012 Italian book, *La mia Possessione* (My Possession) by Francesco Vaiasuso, details a difficult exorcism of a man possessed since he was four years old. On this occasion, St. Gemma was joined by Pope St. John Paul II and by fellow stigmatists Sts. Padre Pio and Faustina Kowalska, who assisted at the exorcism.[231] This was a powerful squad of saintly warriors coming upon the scene.

Catholic author Glenn Dallaire, who runs the website Mystics of the Church, has collected a number of first-person accounts from exorcists that he has interviewed. They told Dallaire candidly about how St. Gemma Galgani has aided them in their work.

Dallaire interviewed Padre Alfredo Pallotta, CP, a Passionist priest and longtime exorcist who served as chaplain at the Monastero-Santuario di Santa Gemma Galgani (Monastery-Sanctuary of St. Gemma Galgani) in Lucca, Italy. Padre Alfredo, who died in July 2012, was an official exorcist and wrote about these exorcisms in articles and books, including his 2005 work *Un esorcista si confessa* (An Exorcist Confesses). Dallaire shared images and translations of letters from Fr. Alfredo on his website, which is available for public viewing. In a March 4, 2010, letter to Dallaire, Fr. Alfredo said of St. Gemma, "She has often been near me in the exorcisms, above all when I carried them out in her Sanctuary."[232]

Fr. Alfredo told Dallaire of a particularly bracing example of a possessed person who was levitated by a demon (he also wrote about this incident in his book). This incident occurred on June 17, 2007, and St. Gemma was there to help: "She was present to help me in fighting the Fiend who had so often appeared to her in life. The demon often informed me of her presence, calling her the 'stigmatized.'" Think about that: this demon referred to St. Gemma Galgani as the "stigmatized" one.

There are many reported examples like this with Gemma, related by mainstream Catholic sources and reputable newspapers and book publishers. The *National Catholic Register* in December 2019 did a fascinating exclusive about a New York mother named Terese Piccola who suffered from demonic possession. She, too, had extraordinary assistance from St. Gemma Galgani. "St. Gemma Galgani came as well," said Piccola. "I never knew her before these sessions, but she was insistent on being friends. The demons hated her and would spit at pictures of her, as well as [those of] St. Gabriel Possenti. She became a spiritual sister to me, remaining with me to the very end, always prompting me in small ways."[233]

Still another example comes from Msgr. Stephen Rossetti, an American exorcist who has likewise written a book about his experiences, titled *Diary of an American Exorcist* (Sophia Institute Press, 2021). He states flatly that "demons hate Gemma." Fr. Rossetti writes of a woman named Valerie who spent years mired in the occult and ultimately counted on St. Gemma to help pull her out. Valerie said that whenever she presents a picture of Gemma and prays for her help, the demons wince. She said they "hate" her with "pure disgust" and feel like "vomiting" whenever St. Gemma is invoked. They screech, "Keep that woman away from me!"[234]

Again, there are many examples like this that have been published.[235] Clearly, St. Gemma Galgani's sufferings and battles against the devil during her actual lifetime had a divine objective that made her eternally stronger in her next life, her heavenly one, and has made her a powerful servant to those of us still here in this realm.

St. Joseph, the foster father of Jesus, is known as the Terror of Demons. But it looks as though St. Gemma Galgani is meeting that purpose as well. St. Gemma Galgani's feast day is April 11, but she is available to us for assistance 365 days per year. Here was a stigmatist with a special purpose that continues for eternity.

CHAPTER 6

SAINT PADRE PIO
(1887–1968)

With the possible exception of St. Francis of Assisi, no other stigmatist is as widely known and celebrated as Padre Pio. And few have been so beloved, whether as stigmatist, priest, or a figure of any sort in the long history of the Catholic Church. Over the last one hundred years, his only rivals are Pope St. John Paul II, St. Mother Teresa, and (certainly in the United States) Ven. Bishop Fulton Sheen.[236] In his native Italy, in particular, he is revered with everything from prayer cards to framed photos abounding in chapels, homes, and shops.

Born May 25, 1887, in the little town of Pietrelcina, just six miles from the city of Benevento, the capital of the province by the same name, this future Capuchin priest was given the name Francis. Francesco Forgione was born to Maria Giuseppa Di Nunzio (1859–1929) and Grazio Mario Forgione (1860–1946), two peasant farmers from the Southern Italian region of Campania. They had at least seven children in all, two of whom died in infancy, and some reports claim there were eight children. There may well have been eight, perhaps inspiring Fr. Pio's common blessing to couples that he wed wishing them the gift of *otto bambini* (eight children) as parents in the years ahead.[237]

Padre Pio's parents were very devout and dedicated to their children, giving their lives wholly to them. At the turn of the century, circa 1899–1901, Francesco's father, although he spoke no English, went so far as to go alone to the United States for a time to earn money to send his second son to seminary. He worked in the little Mahoningtown neighborhood of the small city of New Castle, Pennsylvania.[238] It was the kind of sacrifice that the parents made for their *bambini*. Francesco badly wanted to be a priest, and so his father and mother wished this for him as well.

Grazio and Giuseppa had seen immediately in Francesco striking spiritual gifts. Those gifts and the sacrifices of Grazio and Giuseppa would eventually bring Francesco to a Franciscan seminary. He would find a new spiritual home at Our Lady of Grace friary in the town of San Giovanni Rotondo, located in the province of Foggia in the region of Apulia in the beautiful Gargano mountains.

San Giovanni Rotondo would be made famous by the new friar. He would transform it as he himself would be transformed. It was there that Francesco Forgione became the Padre Pio of history.

Pio's Extraordinary Spiritual Gifts

From his earliest days, Padre Pio was in touch with the other world. This was a unique contact that brought many blessings but also heavy trials. In the negative, it entailed terrible torment by the devil and his legions. Pio later recalled that from his earliest childhood days he was "surrounded by frightening monsters."[239] As he grew into his teens, and especially as he pursued the priesthood, the harassment became physical as the young man was constantly assaulted by demons. Fellow seminarians and later friars heard in horror the banging, pounding, and screams that emanated from Pio's cell late at night. Padre Pio may well have been the single most assaulted priest in the history of the Church. And, as we shall see, he suffered not only from demons but from clergy who misunderstood him and his gifts.

On the positive side, from his earliest days, Padre Pio had contact with Jesus Christ, the Virgin Mary, and—especially helpful in with-standing the attacks of demons—his guardian angel. These visits were so common, so routine to his daily existence, that the young Pio was mystified when learning from fellow seminarians that they did not have such encounters. "Don't you see the Madonna?" he asked a fellow friar who became one of his closest friends and confessors, Padre Agostino. When a shocked Agostino replied no, Pio retorted, "Surely, you're saying that out of humility." Pio explained to another priest, "I see my guardian angel just like I see you."[240] He assumed that everyone saw and spoke to these heavenly forces.

Among them, Pio's relationship with his guardian angel is worthy of us learning about and internalizing in our own lives. He often asserted that he had an especially powerful guardian angel who was a stalwart protector. He counted on the angel. He talked to the angel, joked with the angel, and even, at times, reprimanded the angel for not coming to his aid during certain diabolical attacks. He would ask his guardian angel in frustration after a night of beatings, "So where were you last night?"[241] We can perhaps assume that the Lord, in those instances, meant for Pio to withstand certain assaults on his own, for whatever penitential purpose or preparation.

Padre Pio was vigilant in telling people to be mindful of their guardian angels. In June 1915, he wrote a letter to one of his spiritual daughters, Anita Rodote, about the power of these spiritual beings and how and why we must remember them and look to them always:

> Have great devotion, Anita, to this beneficent angel. How consoling it is to know that we have a spirit who, from the womb to the tomb, never leaves us even for an instant, not even when we dare to sin. And this heavenly spirit guides and protects us like a friend, a brother.
>
> But it is very consoling to know that this angel prays unceasingly for us, and offers God all of our good actions, our thoughts, and our desires, if they are pure.
>
> Oh! For goodness' sake, don't forget this invisible companion, ever present, ever disposed to listen to us and even more ready to console us. Oh, wonderful intimacy! Oh, blessed companionship! If only we could understand it! Keep him always before your mind's eye. Remember this angel's presence often, thank him, pray to him, always keep up a good relationship. Open yourself up to him and confide your suffering

to him. Be always afraid of offending the purity of his gaze. Know this, and keep it well present in your mind. He is easily offended, very sensitive. Turn to him in moments of supreme anguish and you will experience his beneficent help.

Never say that you are alone in the battle against your enemies; never say that you have no one to whom you can open your heart and confide. It would be a grave injustice to this heavenly messenger.[242]

This is a message about our heavenly protectors that we all should be mindful of at all times.

Padre Pio was gifted with all sorts of extraordinary spiritual gifts, from bilocation to miraculous healings to reading sinners' hearts and souls and knowing their pasts—which he would relate to them during confessions, to the astonishment of the sinner. He often had foreknowledge of when certain people would die. As for loved ones who had passed, he sometimes knew their place after death, whether it be heaven, hell, or purgatory.

Numerous books have been written about these extraordinary instances in the life of Padre Pio. This book is not the place to share the many examples that would fill these pages.[243] One example worth noting, however, is a well-documented case, which, if it did not have supporting testimony, would strike most as inconceivable on its face: the reported appearance of Padre Pio appearing in the sky during World War II to prevent a bombing.

Two authoritative modern biographies that document the episode are C. Bernard Ruffin's *Padre Pio: The True Story* (Ruffin, a Lutheran pastor, released an updated third edition of the biography in 2018) and Renzo Allegri's *Padre Pio: Man of Hope*. Allegri, a respected Italian journalist, interviewed people who interacted with Pio. In the case of Pio appearing in the sky, Allegri tracked down Dr. Bernardo Rosini, a general in the Italian Air Force. Rosini testified:

After the war, I was serving in Bari at the United Air Command, which was responsible for all the new units that were created after Italy's defeat and that operated side by side with the Air Force.

The General Command for the U.S. Air Force was also in Bari. I got to know several officers who told me that Padre Pio had saved them during one of their operations. Even the commanding general played a role in this incident, which was widely discussed. One day he himself wanted to pilot a squadron of bombers on a mission to destroy a German munitions dump that was located near San Giovanni Rotondo. The general said that when he and his pilots were in the vicinity of the target, they saw the figure of a monk with upraised hands appear in the sky. The bombs broke loose from the plane on their own, and fell in the woods, destroying the target without the pilots intervening.

That evening this episode was the main topic of conversation among the pilots and their officers.[244]

The witnesses could not stop talking about it, and the story became legendary. Rosini continued:

Everyone wanted to know who the monk was. Someone told the commanding general that there was a monk who worked miracles living in San Giovanni Rotondo. He decided to go to San Giovanni Rotondo as soon as the country was liberated to see if it was the same monk that he had seen in the sky. After the war the general, accompanied by some of the pilots, went to the Capuchin monastery there. As soon as they entered the sacristy, they saw several monks and immediately recognized Padre Pio as the one they had seen in their planes. Padre Pio introduced himself and, putting his hand on the general's shoulder, said, "So, you're the one who wanted to destroy everything." Overwhelmed by the monk's look and his words, the general knelt down in front of him. Padre Pio had spoken, as usual, in his dialect, but the general was convinced that the monk had spoken to him in English. The two became friends. The general, who was Protestant, later converted to Catholicism.

C. Bernard Ruffin also documents the story, citing Fr. Dominic Meyer (1892–1966), the American Capuchin priest who was close to Padre Pio, serving as the friar's secretary for all English and German correspondence. He was also a man of credentials and seriousness who tended to downplay claims of the miraculous in the case of Pio, responding to many of them as fantasies not to be taken seriously. Fr. Meyer was told about the incident from Dr. Guglielmo Sanguinetti, a medical doctor and convert to the faith who became Pio's right-hand man at the hospital that the friar established, the Casa Sollievo della Sofferenza. Ruffin documents other cases of biographers reporting the incident, including Fr. Charles Mortimer Carty in his seminal English biography of Padre Pio, published in 1952.[245] The extensive documentation of this story indicates that it is no mere fable. As with so many accounts involving Pio, it can be chalked up to the category of otherworldly.

Gift of Prophecy

Also documented was Padre Pio's ability, in certain cases, to have prior knowledge of pivotal moments in people's lives. As noted, he, at times, seemed to know how many years certain individuals would live. For Pio, the purpose was nothing sensational but rather to issue vital warnings to individuals to get their spiritual acts together and be prepared for the next world before it was too late. Here again, books on Pio are replete with examples. Interestingly, he, unlike certain other stigmatists, did not make dire predictions about major future cataclysmic events. His charism seemed to be directed at individuals and the spiritual state of their lives and souls.

One intriguing case relates to the life of Pope John Paul II. During Easter 1947, a newly ordained young Polish priest named Karol Wojtyla paid a visit to San Giovanni Rotondo, drawn by what he had heard about this holy friar. He went to confession with Padre Pio. He also went to Mass, where he was struck at how the mystical stigmatist "physically suffered." He came away very impressed.[246]

Wojtyla never doubted Pio's unique connection to God. At one point, facing a grave situation with a friend, he would call upon it. In

1962, Bishop Wojtyla was anguished over the deteriorating health of a dear friend, a Polish colleague and psychiatrist named Dr. Wanda Póltawska, who was dying from cancer. There was little hope for Póltawska, and she and her doctors were resigned to her impending death. They estimated less than a 5 percent chance of her survival and were preparing for a final last-chance surgery. Wojtyla took an unusual step. For the first time, he wrote a letter to Padre Pio asking for the friar's prayers.

The letter, dated November 18, 1962, was written in Latin. Wojtyla sent it to Msgr. Angelo Battisti, the administrator of Padre Pio's hospital. When Pio received the letter, he reportedly looked at Battisti and said of the sender, "It's impossible to refuse this man."[247] That statement, well-known by Padre Pio aficionados, has been interpreted by some as a prophecy of the specialness of Wojtyla and his ultimate vocation and destination. Was it a prophecy that Wojtyla would one day become pope? Some have taken that interpretation. Indeed, why would Pio say that "this man" was "impossible to refuse"? Surely, that meant that he perceived or foresaw something particularly special about *this man*.

In his heartfelt letter on behalf of his friend, Wojtyla begged Pio's prayers for God's mercy for this "forty-year-old mother of four little girls in Krakow, Poland (who during the last war spent five years in a concentration camp), who now is in very grave danger . . . and possibly may die because of cancer."[248]

Not long after, when Póltawska was scheduled for an X-ray for a final look at the cancerous mass before surgery, her doctors were shocked to find that the thirteen-centimeter tumor had vanished. Póltawska was amazed at how it "had disappeared."[249] She was cancer free. Once near death's door, the mother of four was suddenly healed. Wojtyla was convinced that Padre Pio's intercession had wrought a miracle.[250]

Just eleven days after his first letter, on November 29, Wojtyla jubilantly wrote back to the Capuchin friar with great news that this "mother of four girls, on November 21, just before a surgical operation, suddenly recovered her health. Thanks be to God. Also to you, Venerable Father, I give the greatest thanks in the name of the husband and all the family."[251]

Returning to the question of whether Pio had a prophetic vision of a future pope, Wojtyla's biographer, George Weigel, considered the question, albeit very briefly and without giving it serious time, devoting a mere endnote to it in his lengthy work.[252] Pio biographer C. Bernard Ruffin likewise did not endorse the claim.[253] Oddly, however, neither Weigel nor Ruffin provide evidence or statements from Pio, Wojtyla, or their colleagues affirming that the prediction never took place. They simply dismissed the very notion rather curtly. Neither Weigel nor Ruffin dealt with it in any careful detail nor with consistency among their two accounts. Weigel anchors the alleged prophetic moment in Easter 1947, during Wojtyla's confession with Pio, whereas Ruffin goes to both Easter 1947 as well as the November 1962 letter as potential moments.[254]

And yet, there is, in fact, a source for the prediction. Austrian cardinal Alfons Stickler (1910–2007) made a statement that was reported in a major biography (754 pages in length) by veteran journalist Jonathan Kwitny, titled *Man of the Century: The Life and Times of Pope John Paul II*, published in 1997 by Henry Holt and Company. Kwitny, who was a reporter for the *Wall Street Journal* and hosted an award-winning PBS investigative television series, interviewed Cardinal Stickler. Perhaps adding to his credibility in this case, Kwitny harbored a very negative view of Padre Pio. Nonetheless, he quoted Stickler, who said that Wojtyla had once confided to him, "Padre Pio told him he would gain the highest post in the Church."[255] According to Kwitny's account, Pio said this to Wojtyla during that Easter 1947 meeting.[256]

Did Padre Pio indeed foresee that Karol Wojtyla would one day become pope? It would not have been out of character for Pio to have been able to foreknow the future of this unique man that he could not refuse.

Receiving the Stigmata

Of course, one extraordinary trait of Padre Pio not disputed by biographers nor by anyone with eyes to see was the gift of the wounds of Christ. Padre Pio received the stigmata on September 20, 1918, while alone in front of a crucifix of the suffering Christ in Our Lady of Grace chapel, the church of the friars at San Giovanni Rotondo.[257] Under order of obedience, Pio later spoke about the moment in a formal deposition at 5:00 p.m. on June 15, 1921, during the Vatican's official investigation. He said this to the Holy See's official apostolic visitor, who filed this verbatim written transcript:

> On September 20, 1918, after celebrating the Mass, I stayed in the choir for the due thanksgiving prayer, when suddenly I was overtaken by a powerful trembling, then calm followed, and I saw our Lord in the posture of someone who is on a cross (but it didn't strike me whether he had the Cross), lamenting the ingratitude of men, especially those consecrated to him and by him most favored. This revealed his suffering and his desire to unite souls with his Passion. He invited me to partake of his sorrows and to meditate on them: At the same time he urged me to work for my brothers' salvation. I felt then full of compassion for the Lord's sorrows, and I asked him what I could do. I heard this voice: "I unite you with my Passion." Once the vision disappeared, I came to, I returned to my senses, and I saw these signs there [Pio's stigmata], which were dripping blood. I didn't have anything [markings] before.[258]

The Lord had chosen an intimate moment when the young friar was alone. Fr. Benedetto, the superior, had departed for several days for a mission trip. Br. Nicola, a mendicant friar, was out making his rounds. Students at the friary were outside in the courtyard. It was just God and man alone in that sanctuary.[259]

The choir section where Pio was positioned inside the chapel was an elevated platform in front of the main altar. It was there that Pio was seated in the middle of the last row. Later, kneeling in front of a large crucifix made of cypress by an unknown seventh-century sculptor, which was hoisted up on a balustrade, he looked upward and was transfixed by the image speaking to him from the cross.[260]

Here one is struck by parallels to Pio's namesake, the founder of his religious order: St. Francis had likewise gazed upon a cross that literally spoke to him. Francis's crucifix at San Damiano had also been made by an unknown sculptor (believed to have been carved in the eleventh century). Today, this cross, the San Damiano cross, can be visited by pilgrims, hung in the chapel of St. Claire in Assisi; likewise, the cross that spoke to Padre Pio is also still visible today for pilgrims at the Capuchin chapel in San Giovanni Rotondo.

There are, however, notable differences between the two crucifixes. The contrasts might be seen as signaling the much longer period of suffering by Pio as well as the worse torments he would face, particularly from clergy in the half century ahead. The Christ on the cross at Pio's chapel is in agony, His mouth agape in pain, as opposed to the San Damiano cross, in which the Lord's mouth is closed and His expression not tortured. The San Damiano cross shows Christ's four nail marks in the feet and hands, but the blood is not dripping as it is in the cross that Pio gazed upon, nor is blood flowing from the Christ figure's head in the San Damiano image, as it is with the corpus at Pio's chapel.

The copious bleeding from the Christ figure in Pio's chapel turned out to be immediately symptomatic in his case, as the markings the Capuchin friar received at that moment started to bleed profusely. Pio struggled to drag himself back to his cell, with no one seeing him, though his fellow brothers were soon alarmed by the sight of a trail of blood from the choir through the corridor, leading to Pio's closed door. There inside, in pain and weeping with mixed emotions of joy and horror and shock, he frantically and futilely nursed his wounds, wrapping them in whatever makeshift bandages he could pull together. He tried to stop the hemorrhaging but instead merely soaked the handkerchiefs he applied to his marks. The friars, as well as Pio's superiors, soon saw the bloodied clothing. Pio had begged the Lord to hide his wounds, but that was not God's plan for him. Soon enough, the world would know.

A crucial element unfolding at this moment, the month of September 1918, was something much larger beyond that one friar and monastery: raging at that time was the most horrific war in the history of the world up until that point. That war, at the time called the "Great War," was a great catastrophe unlike any seen in the history of man.

The intellectual philosopher Sidney Hook dubbed World War I "the second fall of man."[261] It broke out in August 1914, with two popes trying to stop it, both Pius X (1903–14) and Benedict XV (1914–22), the latter of whom called it "the collective suicide of civilized Europe." Benedict was aghast at how men of science, reason, and compassion could channel their marvelous ingenuity into modern machines of warfare employed to annihilate a whole generation of their young men. Benedict rightly labeled it an unjust war, given that the combatants had no compelling reason for engaging in this unprecedented mass slaughter of Europe and beyond. The war was based on no overriding moral issues justifying such a scale of death.

And yet, the conflict not only produced over ten million dead young men but would lead to World War II and the Cold War. World War II would subsequently dwarf World War I in deaths, and the Soviet global communist ideology undergirding the Cold War killed still more. Moreover, by 1918, with the war into its fourth ghastly year, something else was being unleashed: the vast influenza epidemic that would kill tens of millions more, even more than the gruesome war.

A poignant symbol of the suffering was erected on the Western Front. Titled *O Cristo das Trincheiras*, "The Christ of the Trenches," it was a life-size statue of Jesus Christ hung with arms outstretched on a tall wooden cross. Soiled and bullet-scarred, it was given by the French to the government of Portugal to memorialize the thousands of Portuguese decimated at the Battle of Flanders. Today, the Christ of the Trenches looks down upon the Tomb of the Portuguese Unknown Soldier at the Priory of Santa Maria da Vitoria (St. Mary of Victory) in Batalha, Portugal.[262]

But Portugal would also become the place of a truly divine moment related to the war. The situation on the battlefields of Europe was so awful that it precipitated the greatest miracle of the young century: Our Lady of Fatima and her Miracle of the Sun in October 1917. She, too, was aching for an end to this bloody disaster.[263] And so was Padre Pio.

That brings us back to that scene inside the chapel at San Giovanni Rotondo on September 20, 1918. Pio had offered himself to the Lord as a victim, a living sacrifice, to end the war and the epidemic.[264] Something had to be done. The Capuchin offered himself fully.

Were these stigmata granted to Pio by the Lord as an expiation for those horrors of war and epidemic? It must be conceded that this conflict that had raged with seemingly no end in sight for four years would now, finally, come to a close. It lasted only several more weeks. Pio received his wounds on September 20, 1918, and the wound of what had been the worst war in world history at last closed on November 11, 1918. Was the former related to the latter?

Only in the annals of heaven are these answers known. But for now, what was known, and that no one with eyes to see could dispute, were the bleeding wounds of Christ on the body of this humble and holy friar at San Giovanni Rotondo. The Lord had left His mark on him.

Father Charles Mortimer Carty's Eyewitness

Of all the stigmatists in this book, Padre Pio's wounds are the most well-documented. Virtually everyone who knows of Pio knows of him as the famous Italian priest who had stigmata. The marks are effectively synonymous with the friar. The photographs of Pio wearing gloves, as well as early pictures of him with holes in his palms, are world-renowned and widely available for viewing.

So accepted are Pio's stigmata that this chapter could probably skip altogether eyewitness descriptions, medical reports, and ecclesiastical investigations and focus on other key elements of Pio's life and sacrificial suffering that related to the stigmata and more. But we should pause to consider a few testimonies for the purpose of understanding precisely the nature of those marks.

A particularly valuable eyewitness to Pio and his stigmata was Fr. Charles Mortimer Carty, a respected, influential, and prolific twentieth-century American priest. Born in 1897, Carty was a popular clergyman, establishing with his friend and colleague Fr. Leslie Rumble a media-apologetics apostolate called Radio Replies Press, based in St. Paul, Minnesota, through which they distributed thousands of Catholic books and pamphlets, including on the subject of stigmata.

Among this prolific output of writings, Carty's most popular work was his landmark biography, *Padre Pio: The Stigmatist*, which was first published by Radio Replies Press. It was the earliest English biography of Padre Pio, and it put Fr. Carty in demand all around the country as a lecturer on the Italian Capuchin. He died during one of those tours on May 22, 1964, in Erie, Pennsylvania.

The book was enormously popular. TAN Books eventually picked up the work, which by its 1989 edition (the one cited in this chapter) was into its forty-first printing. The 1989 edition included Fr. Carty's prefaces from the tenth and twenty-fifth editions, where he explained what had led him to write this seminal work on Pio. What had prompted him was a life-changing visit.

Carty had been inspired by several trips to San Giovanni Rotondo in April 1950 and June–July 1952, which included personal visits with Padre Pio. He was "spellbound" by the first Pio Mass that he observed in April 1950, deciding "then and there" to write what he called "the first English book on this first priest to be stigmatized." He would write in the preface to his twenty-fifth edition, "I was present at several of his Masses to study the changing expressions of his face in his prolonged minutes of either contemplation or ecstasy. I marveled at his wit in recreation and rejoiced at his human gruffness as he shouted, with his booming voice, commands to the noisy congregation to keep silence and to kneel for the prayers at the beginning of Mass." Fr. Carty not only watched Pio but was embraced by him, having "the privilege of being embraced by him on three occasions in the Franciscan and European custom of cheek to cheek."[265]

The full Carty book is worth reading, but especially valuable are the words he used in describing what he personally saw, studied, and felt as he made physical contact with Pio. His careful notes on the stigmata are worth quoting here at length, coming irreplaceably from a priestly eyewitness:

Padre Pio's hands, which the faithful could see while he celebrated Mass, were covered with blood, and the wounds seemed
bigger than they were in reality. Washing them with water, the
stigmata appeared as circular wounds, about two centimeters
in diameter, in the center of the palm. Equal wounds were
found on the back of the hands in such a position that they
gave the impression that the wounds met each other and the
hands were pierced through and through or transfixed, so that
a bright light should be seen through the stigmata.[266]

The holes went all the way through the hands of Pio, as nails driven
into and through a person's palms would.

Here, integrating his knowledge of other twentieth-century stigmatists, Fr. Carty added, "It is properly on account of the depth of the
wounds, transfixed from back to front, that Padre Pio could not completely close his hands. Theresa Neumann wrote with great difficulty,
as did Padre Pio." Carty said that "visually, one could not see the depth
of Pio's wounds on account of the soft skin which covered the surface.
The skin every so often fell off to give place for the formation of new
skin." Here, he made a comparison to yet another twentieth-century
stigmatist: "As St. Gemma Galgani sought to hide her stigmata, so also
Padre Pio immediately sought to hide his stigmata."[267]

Carty conveyed the various guidelines that Pio's superiors had laid
out for the priest in attempting to keep his wounds discreet: "The reg-
ulation for wearing gloves was made by the Superiors General, after
they were satisfied with the various examinations and reports. Padre
Pio was required to wear gloves except at Mass. He was forbidden by his
superiors to show his hands to anyone. Even when celebrating Mass,
he tried to cover his hands with the long sleeve of the alb."[268]

Carty noted that when Pio first received the wounds, he applied
iodine to them twice a week in the hopes that doing so might slow the
copious flow of blood. After a visit from one of the first medical experts
to examine him, Dr. Amico Bignami, the Franciscan gave up on that
procedure. (Quite astonishingly, Dr. Bignami, a respected professor
of pathology at the University of Rome, who studied Pio's wounds for
several days in July 1919, confirmed the existence of the stigmata but

implied that they resulted from "autosuggestion."[269] It is a grand mystery how the good professor imagined that Pio could accomplish such an alleged feat by powers of imagination.) Neither iodine nor another salve or treatment made any difference. After all, these wounds were not of natural origin but of supernatural.

Fr. Carty proceeded to detail the other stigmata he saw on the friar:

> The wounds on his feet presented the same characteristics as the hands. A wound on top of the foot corresponded with a wound on the bottom of his foot. The stockings were always stained with blood on the top and the bottom. Different from the other Capuchins who wear sandals, Padre Pio wore shoes, but special shoes that were flexible, soft and partially made of cloth. They were sent to him as a gift from Switzerland. In descending the altar steps to give Communion to the faithful he appeared to me to step down backwards because of the intense pain in his feet. His gait was always uncertain, slow, and hesitating.
>
> The stigma on his side was the strangest of all, because it emitted a greater quantity of blood even though the wound seemed more superficial. He lost about a cup of blood each day from the wound in his left side. Once Dr. [Giorgio] Festa applied a clean white handkerchief to the left side of Padre Pio at nine in the evening. After ten hours, at seven the next morning, Dr. Festa found completely saturated with blood and serum not only that handkerchief but also another cloth of equal size which Padre Pio had applied above the handkerchief during the night.[270]

Fr. Carty learned that Pio's fellow Capuchins at the monastery never threw away his clothes that were saturated in blood but instead "jealously stored them away." The Holy Office at the Vatican had forbidden them to give away gloves or anything worn by Padre Pio. According to Fr. Carty, one such glove that had been applied to the body of the dying Mother Teresa Salvadores, who was superiora dell'Escuela Taller

Medala Milagrosa of Montevideo, was said to have immediately and miraculously cured her from cancer.

This healing reportedly had occurred in November 1921: "She was dying from a double disease, cancer of the stomach and lesion of the aorta." The woman was on her deathbed. Just then, Msgr. Fernando Damiani, vicar-general of Salto, Uruguay (and the brother of the famous opera tenor), went to San Giovanni Rotondo seeking to obtain a glove of Padre Pio, which he managed to secure. Upon returning to the nun's side at Montevideo, he applied the blood-soaked glove to her stomach and her throat: "Immediately the dying nun fell asleep and when she awoke she was cured," reported Fr. Carty. "She narrated that while asleep Padre Pio touched her side, then breathed on her while saying heavenly words."[271]

As for Pio's own health, Fr. Carty paused to make a notable observation, which he received from the original medical reports of Dr. Festa: "All of Padre Pio's organs, the lungs, the heart, the kidneys, and the spleen were perfectly healthy. His lungs, once diseased with tuberculosis, were sound and normal. After a surgical operation in 1925 for hernia, and in 1927 for a cyst on the neck, the healing of the surgical wounds was quick and without any sort of complication." That good health was more remarkable because of the nonstop bleeding and pain of Pio's stigmata: "The duration of the stigmata of Padre Pio is the longest which is recorded in the long list of stigmatics," Carty estimated. "At the time this book was written [1963], it was the 45th year since the visible stigmata appeared on his body, September 20, 1918. This long duration is more remarkable because his stigmata did not appear only on Thursdays or Fridays, as in many other stigmatics, but for 45 years without interruption he carried them night and day on all the days of the week."[272]

It was indeed astonishing that the man could still rise before dawn every day and offer Mass, oftentimes marathon Masses in duration, as parishioners watched in awe as this holy priest seemed frozen in time as he slowly, painstakingly consecrated the Eucharist and held the Lord Jesus in his hands, as if transported to another place. (And with his gift of bilocation, precisely that sometimes happened at those moments, as Pio was present in more than one location at the time.) And more still, he would walk from Mass to the confessional and spend endless hours hearing people's sins and absolving them, doing so for incredibly long periods that would have worn out not only the youngest of priests but surely a few athletes as well. But the bleeding priest was more than up for the task. He was supernaturally energized.

These were things that Fr. Carty directly observed. He next went into verbatim details from Dr. Festa's report:

> In the palm of the left hand, corresponding to half of the third metacarpus (bone from the carpus to the fingers) there was an anatomic lesion of the tissues in circular form with clear margins, about four-fifths of an inch in diameter. Dr. Festa found no change in July, 1920, from the time of his first examination in October, 1919. This lesion was covered with a reddish-brown scab. Padre Pio affirmed that from time to time this scab detached itself first at the edges then little by little toward the center until it fell off completely. Then the lesion appeared in all its detail with dark red color and always bleeding. Because of the presence of this scab it was not easy to judge the profundity of the wound. The Provincial Superior, who visited him shortly after the stigmatization[,] had the clear impression that the wounds observed on the palms of each hand went right through to meet or join the wound on the back of the hand.[273]

Here, Fr. Carty quoted Dr. Festa from an interview that he personally conducted with the physician: "If I were interrogated by superior authorities on this particular question, I would have to answer and confirm under oath, so much is the certitude of the impression received, that, if one fixed one's glance on the wounds in the palms of his hands, it would be easy to recognize in its detail written matter or an object previously placed in the side opposite or back of the hands." Fr. Carty continued, this time picking up from Dr. Festa's written report on the patient:

> The edges of the palm wounds had a limit of demarcation that was so clear, that the skin immediately surrounding, even

observed with a magnifying glass, presented neither swelling, redness, infiltration, nor even a single trace of inflammatory reaction.

In the back of the left hand a little nearer to the joint of the third finger, and therefore not in exact correspondence to the palm, there was another lesion, analogous to the first in form and character, but the edges were more confined and with an apparently more superficial scab. With equal characteristics one could describe the lesions existing on the back and in the palms of the right hand.[274]

As Dr. Festa examined the priest's palms, small and continuous drops of blood fell from their edges. When asked by the doctor to close his fist, Pio could not do so. Fr. Carty himself noticed that while Pio was vesting for Mass, he held the cincture loosely and tied it slowly because he plainly could not close his hand firmly around the cincture. He could not adequately grab the cord used to tie up the long, white alb that priests wear during Mass.[275]

Fr. Carty questioned Dr. Festa about the priest's struggles to make these simple motions, hindered as they were by the painful, ever-bleeding wounds. Festa told Carty:

> During my examination, in order to be able to study also the lesions of his feet, I myself helped him remove his stockings, which I immediately observed were abundantly stained with bloody serum. On top of both feet, and precisely corresponding with the second metatarsus (part of the foot between the tarsus and the toes), I found here also a circular lesion, of reddish-brown color covered with a soft scab, which duplicated exactly the origin and characteristics of those described in the hands; perhaps these were a little smaller and more superficial. There was perfect completeness of the metatarsus bone lying under with full length; there was no trace of infiltration, no swelling, no inflammatory reaction in the skin which surrounded it; also here there was light but continuous drops of bloody serum.

On the bottom of the feet and at a point corresponding to the top of the feet, there appeared at my observation two other lesions; one in each sole of the foot, well outlined in their edges, perfectly identical to the top wounds, and bleeding.

Direct pressing of any of the wounds caused very intense pain and the mere touching of the tissues that surrounded the wounds gave pain, but less pain.[276]

Fr. Carty next described a wound of Padre Pio that many biographers neglect to mention: what Carty called Pio's "heart wound." Again, going from Dr. Festa's examination, Carty reported:

In the anterior region of the left side, about two fingers under the nipple there was another lesion in the form of an inverted cross.

The length of this measured about seven centimeters or two and three-fourths inches. The width of the short arm of the cross was four centimeters or one and one-half inches. They intersected at right angles.

This figure of a cross was very superficial. The width of the wound in both the short and the long arms of the cross was about one-third of an inch. The color was the same as the hands and feet. A soft and small scab covered the central part, and not even here did the surrounding tissues offer traces of reddishness, infiltration or swelling. The painful sensitiveness caused by touching it was far greater and more extended than in the normal tissues of the other wounds.

Although so superficial, it bled much more freely than the other wounds. Padre Pio said he lost one cup of blood each day. Dr. Festa held that there is absolutely nothing in science that can give reason for this phenomenon.[277]

No, there most certainly was not. Carty said that Pio's wounds came "visibly upon his body all at once," not one by one in isolated occurrences as they had with Therese Neumann: "After 45 years, the longest record for any stigmatist, the wounds were the very same in character as when they appeared on his body, September 20, 1918." And, in each instance, down through the years, a soft scab would form, detach itself from the edges, and then fall off completely to make way for more bleeding and the formation of a new scab. This had been the repeated process daily and hourly for forty-five years thus far, with no cessation nor permanent healing. There remained the entire time the same five wounds, with the same reddish-brown hue as when they first appeared on his body, and bleeding the exact amount each time, with the blood and serum issuing in the same amount every day. The discomfort and "extreme sensitiveness" he had in the beginning never went away.[278]

Padre Pio's Vicious Doubters

Such was what Fr. Carty witnessed, as did so many who lived with or spent time with Padre Pio. Since the appearance of Carty's book in English, released while Padre Pio was still alive, numerous other works have been published, filled with reports from medical examiners like Drs. Amico Bignami, Giorgio Festa, Luigi Romanelli, and others. The holy friar's doctors saw the same astounding phenomena from the beginning, whether they were believers or atheists. Many of these men of science never hesitated to inform anyone that what they were witnessing was undeniably not natural.

And yet, this suffering, pious friar, beloved by so many as a modern spiritual superman, a bona fide miracle worker walking among them—a saint—nonetheless had some hellacious doubters. The worst of these, ironically, came not from the medical or scientific or secular world but from the clergy. The markedly unfair treatment heaped upon the holy priest by fellow priests may well have caused him more suffering, spiritually speaking, than the stigmata or even the physical attacks from the devil. It certainly dispirited him more. It was so hurtful because it came from fellow men of the cloth.

Arguably, the best modern English account of that ordeal by Pio is the excellent biography by Lutheran pastor C. Bernard Ruffin, who seemed much more willing to write about this treatment of the Capuchin priest by other priests than Fr. Carty had, perhaps because for Carty it was harder to accept (and in turn report) coming from fellow Catholic priests. Moreover, through his research published in the most updated (2018) edition of his biography, Ruffin learned more about this mistreatment than Fr. Carty probably knew. This chapter cannot do justice to what that ordeal was like. It is difficult to read about it as an outsider a century later, let alone from the vantage of what Pio himself experienced.

The clergy detractors included the likes of Padre Agostino Gemelli, Archbishop Pasquale Gagliardi (who was protected in his mistreatment of Pio by Cardinal Gaetano de Lai), Fr. Giovanni Miscio, Bishop Alessandro Macchi, Msgr. Umberto Terenzi, Fr. Giustino Gaballo of Lecce, Archpriest Fr. Michele De Nittis, Fr. Domenico Palladino, the Dominican Fr. Paul-Pierre Philippe, and the duo of Msgr. Carlo Maccari and Giovanni Barberini, the latter two of whom gave Gemelli and Gagliardi a run for their money as the cruelest of them all.

We can start with Padre Agostino Gemelli, a prominent Church official, physician, and psychologist from Milan and a founder of the Catholic University of Milan. He was learned, highly educated, very wealthy, hailing from an esteemed family in northern Italy, and insufferably conceited. He visited Pio on April 18, 1920, bringing with him his considerably inflated pride and prejudice.

Pio could feel the arrogance oozing from Gemelli's cold countenance the instant they first saw one another. Among Pio's charisms was his ability to read hearts, which no doubt made him more painfully aware of the vituperation exuding from the thirty-two-year-old Gemelli. The meeting ended with Gemelli (in the words of one witness) "looking furious" and shouting at the friar, "All right, Padre Pio, we'll meet again."[279]

Gemelli wasted no time marshaling his predisposed dislike of the priest into an immediate campaign against him, one that had been essentially premeditated before Gemelli even met Pio. The very next day, Gemelli smoked off a letter to the Holy Office, in which he asserted that psychologists—such as himself—were the best persons "to distinguish between true and false mysticism." Yes, he said, there had been medical exams of Pio done by trained medical doctors, but "it is clear that those exams were insufficient." After all, averred Gemelli, in Pio's case, here was a "poor sick man" of "very limited intelligence" suffering from "a notable degree of mental deficiency." In Gemelli's self-proclaimed expert estimation, there was just no way that such a stupid man of "such spiritual poverty" could receive a "gift so extraordinary as the stigmata."[280]

Perhaps Gemelli pondered in confusion how a man as gifted as himself had not received the stigmata. That would have surely made more sense to the psychologist-priest.

Applying what he considered the most sophisticated tenets of his own understanding of psychology and theology, Gemelli hypothesized that perhaps there was an "incubus succubus relationship" between Pio and his spiritual director, Padre Benedetto. To repeat: an "incubus succubus relationship." In Gemelli's estimation, perhaps Padre Benedetto, who he assumed to be another man of malice among this misbegotten coven of friars at San Giovanni Rotondo, was inserting these ideas of stigmata into Pio's deficient mind.[281]

As to how this novel "incubus-succubus" insertion by Benedetto was converted into the visible bleeding wounds of Christ in Pio's hands and feet and side, well, that was not explained by Gemelli.

The thirty-two-year-old Gemelli issued a long list of recommendations, including subjecting Padre Pio to a series of psychological exams and other interventions by "specialists," such as himself. Gemelli also recommended that authorities plaster one of Pio's arms and one of his legs.

Gemelli was just one clergyman who was vicious in his treatment of Pio. And the word *vicious* is a choice one, as *vicious* means to be full of vice. These men channeled the worst of their vices in service of slandering Padre Pio in the most heinous ways. They were not imbued with charity—nor with virtue—but consumed with vice, especially the vice of envy. They plotted against Pio while, in turn, contriving almost insanely imaginative notions that the quiet Pio (who spent endless hours in the confessional) was somehow plotting against them. It was nothing to hear comments from them like this from Frs. Michele De Nittis to Domenico Palladino regarding their despised Pio: "Well, Dumi, the hour of revenge has come!"[282]

They schemed ways to get the priest, who they convinced themselves was a nefarious deceiver. With terrible irony, these schemers convinced themselves that this holy priest was a schemer, just like them. They projected their own deceitful intentions and feelings on him.

Yet another minister, Fr. Giovanni Miscio, a jealous and unstable priest who had a parish in San Giovanni Rotondo, went to the level of extortion against Pio. This priest's crimes against Pio were so blatant that he was arrested by police. Cardinal Pietro Gasparri, a defender of Pio, was so outraged when he learned the details of Misco's conspiracy that he snapped, "Have him [Miscio] put in jail!" Precisely, that would have happened to Fr. Miscio if not for the relentless intervention of one clergyman who intervened again and again to save him: Padre Pio.[283]

Observers stood in amazement that Pio would intervene to spare the shameless Miscio. But Pio was nothing if not amazing. Miscio himself would be amazed at how Pio saved him and ultimately became a forever-grateful admirer of the friar.

And then there was Archbishop Pasquale Gagliardi's behavior toward Pio, which was so blatantly awful that everyone took notice. Bishop Alberto Valbonesi was so aghast at Gagliardi's foul actions that, in letters, he started customarily referring to Gagliardi as "the vile archbishop."[284] Gagliardi ultimately resigned, but not until after years of causing great anguish for Pio. He did his dirty deeds, besmirching the future saint's reputation. The damage was done.

Bishop Alessandro Macchi was likewise cruel. He dubbed the gentle Pio "a deluded man, lacking in humility." With a strange accusation intended to frame Pio as a country yokel, which was presumably a bad thing to be—or at least to the snooty Macchi—he said the priest used cheap "cologne." This bishop, this prince of the Church, threatened to nab Pio in the dark of the night, toss him in a vehicle, and usher him to Rome "just like he was a sack of straw."[285]

Yet another attacker, Fr. Paul-Pierre Philippe, pondered a similar solution for Pio. Actually, his plan was worse. He would not have let Pio anywhere near Rome or his home. Philippe insisted that Pio be removed from San Giovanni Rotondo and exiled to a convent far away. He denounced Pio as a "false mystic, who knows that his stigmata are

not from God." He accused him of living "a life of total immorality."
Pio was a "wretched priest, who profits from his reputation to deceive
his victims." Philippe concluded in a formal statement to the Vatican,
"The case of Padre Pio is the most colossal fraud that can be discovered
in the history of the Church."[286]

It was hard to find a more egregiously inaccurate case of character assassination of Pio than that of Fr. Paul-Pierre Philippe. Perhaps
equally alarming, this Dominican priest of severely flawed judgment,
who judged Pio with the worst of inaccurate aspersions, was nonetheless elevated to be a cardinal a decade after these statements by Pope
Paul VI. (Curiously, as we shall see, that is the same Paul VI who, on
March 9, 1952, when he was Archbishop Giovanni Battista Montini,
said, "Padre Pio is a saint."[287])

And worse still, Philippe had accomplices in his libelous smears
of Pio. And *libelous* is not too strong of a word. If Pio had not been
the selfless man of sacrifice and humility that he was—if he had been
like his critics—he could have sued Philippe. But such was not in the
character of this "wretched priest."

These malicious ministers were hellbent on destroying Padre Pio.
And here, too, *hellbent* is a choice word. In fact, Pio would often excuse
these destroyers by charitably proffering that their misbehavior was not
their fault but the fault of the devil. They were victims just as he was,
being assaulted and misled by the forces of darkness. Still, whatever
the culprit, they had helped the devil create a hell of the place. Pio
lamented that the blessed San Giovanni Rotondo was becoming like
"a dome over hell" in which he was imprisoned.[288]

This went on from the very first years when Pio received the stigmata
until the very end. The attackers never stopped coming, all the way into
the last decade of the Capuchin's life.

To that end, among the most forceful in pursuit of Pio was Msgr.
Carlo Maccari, who, on July 30, 1960, darkened the door of the friary
at San Giovanni Rotondo with his assistant, Fr. Giovanni Barberini
(who soon after left the priesthood and married). They came to conduct yet another intensive Vatican investigation of the priest, this one
at the behest of the new pope, John XXIII.

Maccari arrived much as Gemelli had four decades earlier, with preconceived suspicions. The friars at San Giovanni Rotondo said that Maccari, who dubbed Pio a "small and petty person," had entered the place "totally prejudiced against Padre Pio." Others said worse about Maccari and Barberini. Cleonice Morcaldi, a spiritual daughter of Pio, who Maccari believed was the feeble Pio's secret mistress, described Maccari and Barberini as "Puppets of Satan." Another spiritual daughter called Maccari a "devil from Hell."[289]

When Pio learned that Maccari wanted the bleeding seventy-two-year-old friar, who had trouble walking and could not even close his hands, to confess that he was having sex twice a week with Morcaldi, the stigmatist was as shocked as he was saddened. Pio tried to explain that even if he had desired to have sex with Morcaldi (he was a lifelong virgin), he could not physically do so.[290]

In November, the two priests nonetheless submitted a raunchy 208-page official report to the Vatican. Years later, after Pio died and his cause began moving toward canonization, Maccari wrote a letter to the Holy Office acknowledging in retrospect that perhaps he had been "too frank and harsh." But alas, he did not feel that way in 1960, as he contributed to making the holy friar's life a hell on earth. It really hurt Pio, not only emotionally but physically, taking a toll on his heart.[291]

Padre Pio's Defenders

The detractors of Padre Pio were countered, if not altogether halted, by good clergy, some of them at the highest levels, such as Cardinals Pietro Gasparri and Giuseppe Siri, and even popes like Benedict XV and Pius XII, the latter of whose death in 1958 was a major loss of a key Pio advocate at the height of the Holy See. In private comments during conversations on March 9, 1952, both Pope Pius XII and Archbishop Giovanni Battista Montini, later Pope Paul VI, referred to Pio as a "saint."[292]

Pope Pius XII (1939–58) was succeeded by Pope John XXIII (1958–63), the Vatican II pope, who unfortunately was conflicted over Pio, given the calumnious reports he was receiving from Pio's enemies. It took yeoman's work from men like Archbishop Andrea Cesarano of Manfredonia and Cardinal Siri to convince John XXIII not to denounce Pio.

"For months I defended Padre Pio to Pope John XXIII," said Siri later. "We spoke about him at every meeting we had. Each time we met we ended up talking about Padre Pio. The pope was a very good man, a true saint. But he was worried and confused about what was reported to him." As the likes of Frs. Paul-Pierre Philippe and Carlo Maccari tried to convince the Vatican otherwise, including a salacious charge that he was having an affair with a mentally unhinged woman named Elvira Serritelli, Cesarano pleaded directly to Pope John XXIII, "It's all slander. I've known Padre Pio since 1933."[293]

There was a particularly significant defense of Pio that carried considerable weight internally at the Vatican. Today, we know in retrospect that many high-ranking Vatican officials benefitted from a crucial investigative report filed by Bishop Raffaello Carlo Rossi, the official apostolic visitor sent by the Holy Office to secretly investigate Padre Pio in June 1921. A future cardinal, Rossi arrived at San Giovanni Rotondo on June 14, 1921, bringing with him an open attitude, a neutral mind, and a true charity. As the formal bishop inquisitor, Rossi stayed with the brothers for eight days, recording depositions and interrogating every friar, including Pio.

Whereas Gemelli had spent mere minutes with Pio, Rossi spent hours with the friar, interviewing Pio at length and carefully examining his wounds. He concluded in his report and depositions to Rome that Pio's wounds were of divine origin. Rossi's report was kept closed for the entirety of the long remainder of the century ahead. It was finally published in Italian in 2008 and in English in 2011 by Ignatius Press in a book by Professor Francesco Castelli of the Romano Guardini Institute of Religious Studies in Taranto, Italy. Titled *Padre Pio Under Investigation: The Secret Vatican Files*, it is highly recommended for students and scholars of Pio today.

Rossi's report includes fascinating depositions with Pio in which they candidly discussed supernatural occurrences ranging from the stigmata to bilocation to visions to the peculiar raging-high temperatures that the friar's body somehow occasionally reached.

As to the latter, Padre Pio inexplicably, at times, existed with temperatures that would have easily killed any mere mortal. He was notorious for literally breaking thermometers, with the mercury exploding. As Rossi reported, it was a matter of written record that, in one case, the friar reached a temperature of 118.4 Fahrenheit (yes, documented). Particularly fascinating, Pio reached this state under what Rossi and the others described as "special spiritual circumstances" (it was not a permanent state). It was a condition of "moral, rather than a physical illness." (Rossi did not say this, but perhaps it was like a physical, feverish reaction to the sins that the friar encountered in souls he met.) What raged in Pio at those moments was "like in a furnace," burning with heat, and yet he was not floored by the extreme situation. He operated normally. "And in fact," marveled Rossi, "a Brother attests that even under the strain of this fever, Padre Pio is not knocked down, but gets up, moves about, and can do everything. It can't be denied that this is most unusual and exceptional!"[294]

The interviews by Bishop Rossi were also intriguing for gaining a feel for Pio's personality and high intelligence. The latter emerges so clearly from Pio's recorded words in the transcripts; it is bizarre that Gemelli would have reported just the opposite, describing Pio as mentally deficient (further evidence that the assertion said more about Gemelli than Pio).[295]

As for the reported stigmata, Rossi affirmed, "The stigmata are there. We are before a real fact—it is impossible to deny." He repeatedly ruled out fakery or diabolical origins, doing so emphatically at both the start and end of his report. "Is it likely that they might be of diabolical origin?" Rossi opened. "I would like to begin by absolutely ruling out this . . . hypothesis." He reiterated in closing, "To summarize, what I believe can be certainly affirmed today is that the stigmata at issue are not the work of the devil, nor a gross deceit, a fraud, the trick of a devious and malicious person."[296]

The Rossi investigation was early on in Pio's experiences, in 1921. It would quietly have a major influence among high-ranking men at the

Vatican. Bishop Rossi was eventually elevated to cardinal by Pope Pius XI in 1930 and no doubt continued to defend Pio in his years ahead. He died in September 1948 at age seventy-one.

But perhaps the most vigilant defender of them all was a layman, Emanuele Brunatto (1892–1965), a close spiritual son of Pio and, in the mind of many, a hero. He took a more public, no-holds-barred, bull-in-a-china-shop approach to defending Pio, unconstrained as he was as a layman. Brunatto felt no need to abide by Church restrictions, especially as he was convinced that many of the churchmen trying to handcuff him were men of moral disrepute who deserved to be in jail.

Brunatto had a cunning, crafty side, partly an extension of a sinful lifestyle before Pio had saved him via a dramatic conversion experience. He still struggled with his wiles. He was intensely loyal to Pio, and he took no guff from morally tainted clergymen, no matter what their ranking in the Church. He was not one to reflexively bow to any priest, assuming all of them to be angels. He saw the evil intentions in those hounding the beloved Capuchin friar, and he did his best to stop them, which infuriated them even more. The vicious Padre Gemelli once growled at Brunatto, "I'll have you destroyed!" That was something at which Gemelli certainly excelled, especially at this moment when he wanted no one to stop him from destroying Padre Pio. Not intimidated, Brunatto snidely replied to Gemelli, "Thank you for your Franciscan advice."[297]

Like countless laity who had been genuinely rescued by Pio, and who daily witnessed the man's saintly holiness, Brunatto was appalled at the behavior of the clergy hellbent on ruining their beloved spiritual father. Brunatto, however, had the wit, the means, the courage, and, above all, the panache to do something about it. He was a working professional, a teacher. He could think, argue, present, and write. He would not sit back and watch this scandal in silence. Pio needed defenders, and Emanuele Brunatto rushed to the front lines.

Making Pio's mistreatment all the worse for Brunatto and everyone sickened by the slanders of Pio was the widespread knowledge that many of the friar's priestly persecutors were privately living lives of deplorable scandal and hypocrisy, falsely accusing Pio of indiscretions that they themselves engaged in daily. This infuriated everyone. But Brunatto did more than just stew in anger at the duplicity. He began collecting evidence and typing it up.

At one point, Brunatto threatened to blackmail the Vatican with a seething polemic he put together. Titled *The Anti-Christs in the Church of Christ*, it was scathing and, sadly, accurate. Even Pio was shocked to learn how much was true. He was told about the book by Bishop Luca Ermenegildo Pasetto and Msgr. Felice Bevilacqua, who were sent to San Giovanni Rotondo by then Cardinal Rossi, who read a draft and was shaken by its contents. Rossi, Pasetto, Bevilacqua, and other Vatican officials were fearful of how the book would traumatize the laity if published. When briefed by Pasetto and Bevilacqua, Pio calmly shrugged and advised that the Church simply "refute the episodes alleged in the book that could create a scandal." In the ensuing silence that followed, however, Bevilacqua's eyes filled with tears as he admitted to Pio that "unfortunately, those allegations are true."[298]

Brunatto was ready to publish his screed in French, letting the bombshell detonate. It was typical of Pio's tormentors to demand that the holy friar call upon his loyal son Brunatto to cease and desist, even as they knew Brunatto had them dead to rights in exposing their unholy private lifestyles. The obedient Pio did just that, passionately pleading with Brunatto not to publish so as to spare priests and their beloved Mother Church from public scandal. The unholy men exposed for their unholiness were hellbent on stopping Brunatto from exposing them, just as they were hellbent on stopping the holy priest Padre Pio from saying Mass, hearing confessions, and even continuing to stay at his friary.

Pio's persecutors should have been grateful for his extraordinary charity. But these men were not about charity. It was almost as if Pio's displays of heroic virtue inspired in them worse displays of vice.

"The Devil Won't Leave Me Alone"

By the spring of 1965, Padre Pio's spiritual and physical torments had really taken their toll. He was now approaching eighty years old. He had bled for much of his whole long life for the sin and sinners of the world. In some cases, those he offered penance for only spited him in return.

"Never in my life have I suffered so!" he declared to friends. Amid his many sleepless nights, his good friend Padre Alessio heard him often cry out, "My Jesus, my mother Mary, I offer up to you the groaning of my poor soul! Jesus, call me! I can't carry on anymore! Give me the obedience to die."[299]

No foe, of course, was ever as merciless to the friar as the devil and his legion of demons. Sure, fellow clergy made Pio's life miserable in a way they should never have done, but the forces of hell itself were relentless, with the dark power to penetrate the friar's cell day and night and torment him at all times. "The devils won't leave me alone for one minute!" he told Padre Alessio. Alessio said that Pio was very afraid of the demons and asked Alessio to stay with him in his room at night as often as he could. "Once I would be there," said Alessio, "he wouldn't be scared."[300]

It was not long after this that the Almighty heard Pio's pleas, at least partly. The Lord gradually granted His suffering servant some measure of relief in the final three years of his life. In 1966, the stigmatic wounds on Padre Pio's feet disappeared. The next year, 1967, the wound in his side stopped bleeding and healed. In the Easter season of 1968, which would be his final earthly Easter, the wounds on the back of his hands began to close; by mid-summer, they were gone. It was as if the Lord was giving Pio new signs—this time, signs that his end was drawing near, signs of life eternal. The wounds in his palms also began to heal, though the Lord continued to bless His suffering son with the palm wounds until his final minutes. The last crust on the Capuchin's palm wounds fell off at the moment of his death on September 23, 1968, at age eighty-one.[301]

There as witnesses to that final phenomenon were four fellow friars, including Padre Giacomo Piccirillo, who photographed the deceased Pio's hands, feet, and thorax that evening. Among those present the night that Pio died was the American Capuchin Fr. Joseph Martin, who later testified, "When they undressed the body—he died in the habit—they discovered that his wounds had completely healed, all five

of them, and there were no scars or signs that he had ever had them."[302]
Present for that was Dr. Giuseppe Sala, who had been Pio's physician
the final twelve years of the friar's life, regularly checking his stigmata,
his blood pressure, his blood work, and everything, and who now
marveled at the moment of his patient's death, "The hands, feet, and
trunk and every other part of the body showed no traces of wounds,
nor were there scars present on hand or foot, neither on the front or
back, nor on the heel, nor on the side, where in life there had been
visible and well-demarcated wounds. The skin in those places was the
same as that in every other part of the body."[303]

The skin color was suddenly normal in those spots. No hole marks,
no inflammation, no scars, no crusts, nothing. Not a trace. The wounds
that had bled constantly, daily, hourly, for fifty years, had now all vanished. The earthly divine plan for Pio was finished.

The suffering service of the now-legendary stigmatic friar was over.
It was the time for the Lord to grant Padre Pio his heavenly reward. He
would now intercede for sinners in a new realm.

Padre Pio's death was an international news story. The faithful flocked
in from all over the world. Italy's beloved son, surpassed in popularity
only by the Lord Jesus Himself and the Blessed Mother, had departed.

Millions of pilgrims from throughout Italy and the world poured
into tiny San Giovanni Rotondo to pay homage to their beloved son.
This was no simple loss. Like the loss of Jesus Christ, whom Pio certainly would never have equated himself with, the faithful lost a man
who they felt could literally cure them. His life had been an incredible
blessing to Italians especially during a traumatic period when their
country and its dictator had joined forces with Hitler and Hirohito.
They needed mercy. They were given by God a remarkable man of
mercy—one who shared Christ's sufferings and very wounds for a
half century.

Many of Pio's followers did not hesitate to shout "*Santo, subito!*" at
the time of his death—that is, "Saint, immediately!" But because of his
earthly tormentors among persecuting clergy, it would take the Vatican

a while to wade through bad reports and the volume of misinformation and disinformation. In all likelihood, the process was probably also delayed by the need for the men who maligned Pio and ached for his destruction to simply die. The processes of beatification and canonization took much longer than may have been expected for the most widely seen stigmatist in history.

Who could deny their very eyes? But alas, the devil had his minions to wreak havoc, sow discord, and smear the reputation of this good and holy Capuchin friar. The divine hand, however, also had a plan. And it so it came to pass that on June 16, 2002, during a very hot day in Rome, a crowd of over three hundred thousand came to hear the canonization ceremony where the pope declared Padre Pio a saint. That pope was John Paul II, whose papacy some believe Pio might have foreseen decades earlier. Fittingly, this future saint, too, was a suffering servant. Weakened and aching from the scourge of Parkinson's disease, the Polish pontiff on that June day recalled "the many trials that the humble Capuchin of San Giovanni Rotondo had to face." The Holy Father then asserted in the name of Holy Mother Church, "We declare and define Blessed Padre Pio of Pietrelcina a saint."[304]

Today, countless pilgrims continue to flock to San Giovanni Rotondo, laity, clergy, and popes alike, where they venerate the body of St. Padre Pio encased in glass. They do not see hands with holes, which the Lord cured before the faithful friar's death. But they do see a friar gifted with another supernatural phenomenon bestowed by the Lord: a body that is incorrupt. That seems an appropriate crowning touch for the wounded stigmatist from San Giovanni Rotondo.

CHAPTER 7

BLESSED ELENA AIELLO
(1895-1961)

Of all the stigmatists highlighted with chapters in this book, the least is known about a little nun from Calabria, Italy: Bl. Elena Aiello. In a way, that lack of awareness seems odd because, with the exception of Padre Pio and Therese Neumann, Aiello is the most contemporary of all the stigmatists in this book, living into the 1960s. Also, like Pio, she carries a high level of credibility given that the Church has declared her blessed. And given that this little nun had some big prophecies that speak to our times and nations, particularly Russia in this twenty-first century, one might expect her to be more well-known. But alas, she is not. Hopefully, the focus here in this book can help change that.

A Google search of Elena Aiello's name at the time of this writing yields only a brief Wikipedia entry; a profile at the website Mystics of the Church; a short bio at the website Countdown to the Kingdom, which drills down on her key prophecies, including the three days of darkness; and a few articles by Catholic news sites that briefly and almost perfunctorily reported on her beatification. (Wikipedia entries can be notoriously unreliable, but they must be dealt with by scholars, because they are usually the first source to pop up in a Google search and the most common source consulted; they cannot be ignored.) The Wikipedia entry does not shy from her stigmata, stating, "Aiello began experiencing the stigmata each Good Friday from 1923 to not long before her death. The first time that happened the Lord appeared in a white garment with the crown of thorns and placed it on her head prompting much blood to gush forth." The Wikipedia entry adds that a witness, a servant named Rosaria, was about to leave the house when she suddenly "heard wailing and was petrified to see Aiello covered in blood believing someone murdered her. Rosaria rushed to get Aiello's relations who saw the blood but saw she was still alive and so contacted the doctor and several priests. The doctor attempted to halt the bleeding but could not do so for three hours."[305]

Here, the Wikipedia entry linked to an entry on the Mystics of the Church website that was no longer posted.[306] It also linked to a biography of Sr. Elena posted on the website for the town of Montalto Uffugo, the place of her birth. The biography was done by a cousin of Elena.[307]

Wikipedia had little to rely on.

Fortunately, there is a reliable source on Aiello—a 1964 Italian biography titled *The Incredible Life Story of Sister Elena Aiello: The Calabrian Holy Nun (1895–1961)*, written by the respected Fr. Francesco Spadafora of the Pontifical Lateran University in Rome and translated into English by Fr. Angelo R. Cioffi. The authors were contemporaries of Aiello. It still remains the most authoritative source on her in English. It received the *nihil obstat* of Archbishop Antonius Trani (July 18, 1964) and the *imprimatur* of Bishop Aloysius Liverzani (July 22, 1964). That version was published in English in 1964 by Theo. Gaus' Sons, Inc., in Brooklyn.[308] A 2017 version was published by an India-based publisher.[309] This book is the source for most of the material on Sr. Elena posted on the websites Mystics of the Church and Countdown to the Kingdom.[310] Again, there is not much, but the material that we do have is valuable and most inspiring and intriguing.

Nostra Piccola "Santa" (Our Little "Saint")

Elena Aiello was born on April 10, 1895, in Montalto Uffugo, a town numbering about ten thousand inhabitants in the province of Cosenza in the Calabria region of southern Italy.[311] Her full name was

Elena Emilia Santa Aiello. The name Santa might have been given because the baby girl was born during Holy Week and shortly after the feast of San Francesco di Paola, the patron saint of Calabria. She was born on Holy Wednesday, the eve of the Triduum that commemorates Christ's passion.[312]

The family's *piccolo "Santa"* (little "Saint") was the eighth child of Teresina and Pasquale Aiello. Her mother, Teresina, unexpectedly died on December 1, 1905, leaving her many children behind. Another daughter, one-year-old Theresa, had died a month earlier. Pasquale, a respected tailor who was the son of a tailor, long outlived his late wife by fifty years, dying on November 16, 1955, at the age of ninety-four, and working to the very end of his days.[313]

Elena was baptized by Fr. Francesco Benincasa in the church of San Domenico.[314] The priest's name seems fitting, if not providential. The family had a special devotion to San Francesco (St. Francis), the great stigmatist, and so would Elena. She would experience apparitions of St. Francis, as well as the Virgin Mary and other saints. The visits from the Blessed Mother included visions of the future.[315] Moreover, the priest's last name, Benincasa, was also the family name of Italy's great female stigmatist, St. Catherine of Siena.

Like other stigmatists in this book, Elena was very devout from a young age, practicing daily penance and regularly praying for souls in purgatory. It was customary at the time for children in her village to receive their first Holy Communion no earlier than age twelve, but Elena had her first Eucharist at age nine, and she was confirmed at age eleven.[316]

Elena also had early sufferings related to her faith mission. Beginning on Christmas Eve in 1906, she suffered a fit of convulsive coughing that damaged her windpipe and voice for a year and a half. The medical treatments seemed to only cause her more pain. In 1908, at age thirteen, after saying the Rosary one evening, she made a promise to the Blessed Virgin of Pompei that she would become a nun if cured of her illness. That very night, the Blessed Virgin of Pompei appeared to her in a vision and assured her she would be healed. By morning, all of Elena's symptoms had vanished. She was healed.[317]

Elena badly wanted to become a nun. She was ready, but she was also too young at the time. In the interim, the horror that became known as World War I broke out in Europe in August 1914. Her righteous father supported her decision to enter the convent, but he asked her to postpone any action until after the tumult of the raging war.[318]

Finally, the catastrophic war stopped. With that, Elena joined the Sisters of the Most Precious Blood. On August 18, 1920, she left her village of Montalto with the mother general, Sr. Maria Co', for the convent in the town of Nocera dei Pagani.[319]

Sr. Elena eventually began an orphanage and a school for girls. In 1928, she started her own order: the Sisters Minims of the Passion of Our Lord Jesus Christ. It was inspired by an order of friars founded in the fifteenth century by San Francesco di Paola.[320] Pope Pius XII gave pontifical approval for the order in 1949.[321]

Suffering Soul

At first, Elena thrived. She was put in charge of sixteen postulants, a sign of the confidence that Mother General Maria had in her. But like so many stigmatists, she was immediately put to unexpected physical tests—well before the ultimate physical endurance of stigmata.

Very soon after joining the Sisters of the Most Precious Blood in August 1920, she was beset by an intestinal fever that afflicted her for a month. That was quickly followed the first Sunday in October with a severe pain in her left shoulder, apparently prompted by trying to help other sisters move a large case.

Elena tried to keep this pain private, but another nun, Sr. Emilia, urged her to bring it to the attention of the mother superior, and her confessor, Fr. Villanacci, ordered her to reveal the injury to Mother Maria. For whatever reason, little further attention was paid to Sr. Elena's condition until March, when the mother general happened to look through a small window and glimpse Elena fainting on the floor of the laundry room. To the shock of the nuns and the physician, it was discovered that the little nun's entire left shoulder up to her neck had become a solid black mass. A decision was made to operate immediately.[322]

A man described as "the Community Doctor" performed the "operation" on Holy Tuesday, March 25, 1921. Tied to her dormitory chair without any anesthetic, clutching a small wooden cross and staring at a painting of Our Lady of Sorrows, Elena remained still as the doctor cut into her. In the process, he severed some nerves, causing a stiffening of the shoulder and a locked jaw. For forty days after, she vomited. She was sent home to her father Pasquale and her siblings on May 2. Just before leaving the convent for home, Elena said that Jesus had twice appeared to her and asked if she was willing to embrace the cross He had prepared for her and to accept His plans for her with complete resignation.[323] (We will see this likewise with Jesus's invitation to Sr. Faustina Kowalska.)

When Pasquale saw his daughter, he was aghast. She had wasted away to such an extent that he hardly recognized her. She was too weak to bathe herself or even comb her hair. He was appalled to see that her left arm was paralyzed by a shoulder with an open, unhealing sore, purulent—oozing with pus—and swarming with worms. The frightened father took his daughter to a professor who was the director of the city hospital in nearby Cosenza, who told the patient, "Young lady, there is nothing that I can do for you, because they have butchered you. The doctor who performed your operation was not a surgeon: he cut the nerves. You may get your health back, but only by a miracle."[324] He noted that gangrene was setting in and advised Pasquale to sue. But Elena pleaded with her father not to seek compensation.

Over the next several months, her agony worsened. She was confined to bed at her home. She did manage to walk once a week to the convent to go to confession. She took a short cut to avoid people noticing her and her deformed figure. As summer neared an end in August, she developed a sharp pain in her stomach. She tried to take down liquid forms of food with a small spoon in the corner of her mouth, but her body rejected it. She went back to the City Hospital at Cosenza, where she was diagnosed with stomach cancer—atop the grave situation with her ugly shoulder.[325]

The doctor told Elena's sister Giovannina, "I am sorry for her but there is no cure for cancer." Elena, who had entered the room during the conversation, interrupted Dr. Cerrito, saying candidly, "My dear doctor . . . I will not die from this disease, because St. Rita is going to make me well."[326] It was here that a famous Italian stigmatist entered the scene: St. Rita of Cascia.

Healed through Saint Rita of Cascia

One of the most remarkable elements of the narrative of Sr. Elena's extraordinary life is the documentation and witnesses to the various phenomena that affected her. She left behind many letters, notes, and a notebook, and there were many observers who can attest to what happened with specific details and dates. St. Rita played a major part in allowing all of that to transpire.

After confidently informing Dr. Cerrito that St. Rita was going to make her well, Elena, albeit exhausted, stopped on her way home at nearby St. Gaetano parish church, where she fervently beseeched a statue of St. Rita that was venerated at that parish. As she prayed to the saint for a healing of her stomach, she saw what were described as "dazzling flames" around the statue. That same night, St. Rita appeared to Elena, requesting various devotional exercises to be held in her honor, including a triduum. Elena did just that, and Rita would appear to her again with more instructions, telling the young girl that she would be healed of her stomach ailment—though her sore shoulder would linger for a time because she needed to personally take on continued unique suffering in shared expiation for the sins of the world.[327]

The cure came at 5:00 a.m. on October 21, 1921. According to Elena's personal notebook, that morning, "St. Rita of Cascia appeared to me in a vision from her little niche, radiant with light. After walking around the room she approached the bed and, folding the coverlet, she placed her right hand on my stomach saying: 'Now you may eat anything you desire, because you are cured.'"[328]

Two sources who attested to St. Rita's miraculous intercession on this day were Elena's spiritual director and confessor, Msgr. Mauro, who later (after Elena's death) confirmed it to Elena's biographer, Fr. Francesco Spadafora, in Rome on October 20, 1963, and Elena's sister Evangelina, who from the adjoining room at the Aiello house saw a brilliant light seeping through the cracks of the door. Fearing that Elena's room was on fire, she summoned the family to come rapidly. When they entered, they found Elena speaking enthusiastically of Rita's vision and cure. She asked for food, which, theretofore, she had been unable to consume. They brought her a large cup of coffee and scrambled eggs, which she ate with no trouble. They also sent for Msgr. Mauro to inform him of what had just happened.[329]

A month later, on November 8, 1921, another remarkable visitor came to Elena. This time, it was Jesus Christ Himself, and He appeared in a way strikingly similar to how He would present Himself to Faustina Kowalska in Poland ten years later in 1931. That Friday evening, as Elena's biographer described it, "Jesus appeared to her in a white garment and from His wounded Heart, which was quite visible, a beam of light encircled her head." More than that, the beam of light was hot; it left a trace of burnt hair. Msgr. Mauro not only saw the burnt hair (as did Elena's sisters and others) but picked up some strips that lay on the floor, which he still kept in his possession four decades later, after Elena's death. As Elena's biographer put it, "Jesus gave her to understand that those rays represented his loving invitation to suffer in atonement for the sins of the world."[330]

This seems very much a precursor to St. Faustina's Divine Mercy image and message, which the Polish nun expressed thusly: "Eternal Father, I offer you the Body and Blood, soul and divinity, of Your dearly Beloved Son, our Lord Jesus Christ, in atonement for our sins and those of the whole world."

Meanwhile, Elena's shoulder affliction would continue for another three years. On May 10, 1924, she wrote a letter to Msgr. Mauro. It briefly informed the priest:

> Reverend Father,
>   Yesterday, about three o'clock in the afternoon, Jesus appeared to me saying: "My beloved daughter, do you wish to get well or to go on suffering?" "My Jesus," I replied, "one

feels so good when suffering with You. However, do whatever You wish." "Well," Jesus went on. "You shall recover, but I want you to know that every Friday I shall permit you to be in a state of depression, so that you may stay closer to me." So saying, He disappeared.

Begging a memberance in your holy prayers, and humbly kissing your hand, I am

Your most humble servant in Jesus Christ,
Elena Aiello[331]

We see here in Sr. Elena's case something we have seen with other stigmatists, namely, a gentlemanly offer by Jesus to lift the suffering, and yet a willingness by the stigmatist to accept the stigmatic suffering as a unique gift to share with Jesus. And thus, Jesus agreed with His little martyr that every Friday—identifying with His time on the Cross on Good Friday—Elena would share in that form of excruciating suffering. As for the purulent shoulder that infected her with pus and worms, that would be healed, as He said.

How and when would this happen? Who or what would be the instrument or intercessor for the healing? The answer came as May 22 approached—the feast day of St. Rita of Cascia, stigmatist and patron saint of hopeless causes, a condition that aptly described the hopeless state of Elena's bloated shoulder. The day could hardly come too soon. About a week and a half after her letter to Msgr. Mauro, Elena's family summoned Dr. Adolfo Turano, the family's physician, as the young woman's condition had worsened. A weak Elena told the doctor to fear not, relating again the story of her vision of St. Rita, who had promised to heal her the afternoon of May 22. The doctor gently responded by telling the family that the poor girl was so sick that she was obviously hallucinating.[332]

Elena expressed her confident reassurance to anyone who would listen. Her friend Gigia Mazza candidly snapped, "She is dying and she expects to establish a religious community!" To which Elena retorted, "Don't worry because St. Rita will cure me on the 22nd of this month."[333]

Elena was certain. Her confidence was buoyed again on the night of May 21, 1924. She recorded in her notebook that that night she had another vision of St. Rita, who told her, "Tomorrow after the Rosary, come close to my statue and I will cure you." Backing what Jesus had said, Rita told Elena that she would still endure the sufferings on Fridays, but the infected shoulder that was making her gravely ill would be healed.[334]

The moment at last approached. At 2:45 p.m. on May 22, Elena, after being dressed by her sister Emma and carried downstairs to the family parlor—"like a paralyzed person," said Emma—was laid on a sofa that faced a statue of St. Rita. What happened next was sworn to by Emma thirty-seven years later in an October 30, 1961, deposition made to Counselor Di Napoli four months after Elena's death.

Emma said that Elena, "showing unusual courage," pulled worms out of her shoulder with the aid of a mirror and some splinters. Emma helped push the worms out through the deep-seated wound, though to little avail: "But the more I pulled out, the more remained inside," recalled Emma. "Elena looked quite resigned while enduring that torture, but her faith in St. Rita was amazing. She felt perfectly sure she would be cured, but few people could believe it. After all she had been suffering for three long years."[335]

Also present with Emma and the family were some neighbors, including a man named Carlo Taormina, who was a notary public and frequent guest fond of Elena. The group waited: "We were trembling, restless, excited, unable to say a word," recalled Emma. They recited the Rosary together in front of the statue. Elena began praying in a quiet voice:

> From your sanctuary of mercy, o Saint of the impossible, and patron of desperate cases, do turn your eyes of mercy on me, and behold the anguish overwhelming me, the misfortune and misery gripping me: for there is no other one I may turn to. . . . O Saint Rita, powerful and glorious, come to my aid, and, in this direst need, grant me the grace I beg of you! You have promised it to me: You must grant it to me. You must not permit that I be called a liar![336]

Those who were present lifted up Elena, bringing her close to the statue of the incorrupt fifteenth-century stigmatist. Emma said that they "felt the impression" that the hand of St. Rita that had been turned toward the crucifix had reversed and turned toward Elena's left hand on the side of her wounded shoulder. They also felt both the statue and the niche that held it shaken by "some sort of vibration." It was 3:00, the start of the hour of mercy. Just then, suddenly, Elena cried out in joy, "I am cured, I am cured."[337]

Emma and all others were "perfectly astonished" by Elena's proclamation and yet "still skeptical." But then, with no assistance whatsoever, Elena strolled with ease to the balcony. She looked out a window toward a neighbor, a widow friend, lifted up her arms for the first time, and exclaimed, "Donna Valentina [Vescillo], look, I am cured." Emma asked to see the wound and found it suddenly, shockingly, healed. A scar was the only thing that could be seen.[338] As Elena herself marveled, "the wormy wound was no longer there."[339]

Sister Elena's Stigmata

Elena was healed of this infection that should have killed her, but there were more sufferings. Of course, there was the stigmata. This was a different kind of suffering, a higher suffering, a better suffering. This was not some bacterial infection from the fall of man. This was a shared form of Christ's redemptive suffering.

Sr. Elena's stigmata began on Good Friday 1923 and continued every Good Friday thereafter for thirty-eight years, up until her death. They included wounds on her hands, feet, side, and head. Her cousin writes:

> Sister Elena began suffering the stigmata every Good Friday from 1923 until her death. This stigmata was the wounds of Christ's passion and included wounds on her hands, feet, head and side. The bleeding from these wounds was profuse. Because it began in 1923 her stigmata was well documented by scientists, doctors, photographs and many witnesses. It also brought many faithful pilgrims to Montalto Uffugo on Good Friday in the hopes they would be able to see Sr. Elena and her stigmata.[340]

In one particularly striking episode related by her cousin and biographer, it was said that Elena's pierced hand hit the wall next to her bed, and the blood flowed down the wall and formed the face of Jesus Christ. It was reported that this image of the face of Jesus itself began to bleed "profusely on its own" from September 29, 1955, continuously until October 13, 1955. That was a turning point for Sr. Elena's own Christ-like bleeding. After that episode, after that date of October 13, 1955, her stigmata incidents returned only sporadically until her death in 1961.[341]

A key point of clarification: Most accounts of Sr. Elena's stigmata state that she bore the wounds of Christ consistently every "Good Friday" from 1923 on (though her cousin's statement asserts that the consistency changed in the autumn of 1955). Some of them seem to consider each Friday as "Good Friday." Several accounts record her receiving the stigmata on regular Fridays in addition to the once-per-year Good Friday of Holy Week. (As we have seen, this was common for many stigmatists, who experienced the marks not yearly but weekly on days like Thursday and Friday. Some observers consider each stigmatic Friday a version of "Good Friday" in effect, given that it reflects Christ's passion on that first Good Friday.) Overall, the Spadafora biography is not always clear. To give just one attestation as an example, Dr. Guido Palmardita, prefect of Cosenza from August 8, 1936, to March 24, 1939, which included the period when Sr. Elena's mother house was moved from the city of Cosenza to Rome, stated, "On two Fridays in March 1938, I personally attended the extraordinary phenomena together with the Major of the Carabineers and with Professor Santoro. I witnessed the painful wounds on the hands, on the feet, on the side, that bloody sweat, the visions, and in the end, the sudden transformation and disappearance of blood from that face now bright and radiant."[342] That would be two Fridays in March 1938—again, not merely one Good Friday each year.

Among the first to document the stigmata was Elena's physician, Dr. Adolfo Turano. As the family doctor, he was naturally summoned right away the first time that Elena experienced her painful bleeding. He recorded this on the first day of Elena's phenomenon:

On the First Friday of March 1923, about 3 P.M., I was called to the home of Elena Aiello. I found her lying down, her head leaning to one side, and the eyes half-open. Blood was oozing out of her forehead, streaming down on face and neck and utterly drenching her pillowcase. The very abandon of her arms, the lines on her face, so expressive of profound sadness, her head bowed down and turned to one side, her lips and eyes barely open, made her stand out as a picture of the true mystic.

Now and then she would take up a rigid posture, lift up her head, intently focus her wide-open eyes upon some invisible object and register various expressions on her face. By just looking at her, one could easily guess her emotions either of anguish and terror or of happiness and heavenly contemplation.[343]

And, in fact, precisely that was taking place. Elena was locked into some kind of heavenly communion, speaking to some figure who had transcended this earthly existence and had something to communicate to her via her suffering. Dr. Turano continued his observations of his most unusual patient:

When her face muscles contracted, blood would trickle down through the skin. Her bleeding was more abundant at the center of her forehead, but tiny drops of blood were also running down from her head. The moment the ecstasy was over, the patient, in a low but distinct tone of voice, would recount how she had seen Jesus bleeding on the Cross. In their excitement over that singular and amazing phenomenon, all the members of her family, her Confessor, relatives and friends, quickly assembled in her bedroom, where, to their surprise, Elena questioned them whether they had also witnessed the Divine Tragedy.[344]

According to Dr. Turano, this phenomenon lasted for three hours, during which the bleeding occurred "now and then," and the patient exhibited "some unusual features" on her face. And then, at a snap, after the three hours—the same period as Christ on the Cross—Elena "was her old self again." To be sure, she was "thoroughly worn out," but she "recovered very quickly," so much so that the next day, she got out of bed early and resumed her normal activities.[345]

The next year, for Good Friday 1924, which fell on April 18, 1924, Dr. Turano invited Dr. Fabrizio, "a Professor at the University of Naples and a man of considerable culture," to visit Elena and observe the phenomenon. Also present for that Good Friday was Counselor Di Napoli. These gentlemen were hardly the only witnesses. Word had spread so fast about the stigmatic nun that, in the words of Dr. Turano, "an enormous crowd had assembled." There were so many people from nearby villages and other localities—groups of pilgrims moving up and down the stairs of Pasquale's house, many of them in meditation—that it was difficult to manage them. The family actually feared that the floor of Elena's room would collapse from the weight of so many visitors packed around her bedside.[346]

And this time, observers received a special treat. This time, the second Good Friday that she bore the wounds of Christ, she not only bled from her forehead but was marked with stigmata on her feet and with some bruises on her knees. "I was a witness to that phenomenon from beginning to end," wrote Dr. Turano. Turano arrived with a photographer named Serra. They watched Elena's laments at being seemingly tortured turn to joy as the blood started trickling down her forehead and all over her face, as she cried out several times, "How light is this crown of thorns on my head! How small, O my God, is this torture compared to Yours!"[347]

The photographer, Serra, was puzzled and frustrated that no matter how hard he tried, he could not get his camera to click. Other authorities in the room included Dr. Matteo Caracciolo and Dr. Alfredo Scotti, the town's official physicians, as well as the mayor, two attorneys, and more. Professor Fabrizio chalked up the bleeding to "hysteria." Dr. Caracciolo, not known to be a pious man, objected, "As far as I am concerned, I see that in this case we are face to face with the supernatural."[348]

That was 1924. The same extraordinary activity would take place each Good Friday thereafter. All along, there were witnesses—not just parishioners and pilgrims but priests and physicians.

Here is a November 23, 1938, report from another physician, Dr. G. Battista Molezzi, who was then the physician for the Aiello family, to the Rev. Roberto Nogara, the archbishop of Cosenza, which needs to be quoted in full:

> What I am goin [sic] to write concerning Sister Elena Aiello, in whose body some amazing phenomena take place on Good Friday, is the result of my personal experience both at her home at Montalto Uffogo and in her Institute, "The Little Abandoned Girls" at Cosenza. I shall not deal with useless questions, neither shall I discuss religious matters. I shall simply report what I myself saw and felt on those Fridays. To be sure I was profoundly stirred on those days by the spectacle of the bleeding stigmata and by the awesome sight of that poor body convulsed with terrific pain.
>
> I shall not mention the few cases when Elena recovered instantly from serious illness without human remedies, but solely through direct supernatural intervention, as she herself admitted. Some day, if God grants me the grace and the strength to do so, I shall deal with them at length in a book that I hope to write on the life of this stigmatic Nun.[349]

Here we see a physician, a man of science, so struck by what he witnessed that he was prompted to write this report to the archbishop and even to desire to one day write a book on what he conceded was a stigmatic nun. He described the patient:

> Before going any further we should take into account the physical condition of Sister Elena. She consumes but a frugal meal consisting of some vegetables and water, yet she goes about filling her schedule of manifold duties that would break the fiber of even a robust constitution. And she does all this in spite of her continuous suffering.
>
> Indeed, it may be said of her that she lives by her daily fast which, though not as spectacular as is the case with stigmatic Theresa Neumann, it is quite remarkable just the same.

Worth remembering too is the fact that the bleeding on her stigmata occurs on Good Friday, at exactly the same hour as Jesus suffered on the Cross. Blood keeps oozing out of her forehead, apparently punctured by sharp thorns, from her side, her hands and her feet. On one occasion when Doctors pushed splinters through the wounds on her feet, we got the distinct impression that these had been pierced by actual nails.[350]

Dr. Molezzi had educated himself about the case of Therese Neumann, a German contemporary of Elena, who lived and died at nearly the exact same time (1898–1962) and who will be examined at some length in the pages ahead. Clearly, what he saw from Elena prompted him to dig further into other reported cases of stigmatists. Though indeed, as Dr. Molezzi noted, despite Elena's sparse food consumption, she exhibited remarkable physical endurance, more so than Neumann.

Note also Dr. Molezzi's observation that the oozing blood that started at exactly the time that Jesus was on the Cross came out of the little nun's head as if pierced by thorns. He and other doctors observed that the feet wounds seemed punctured by nails. Molezzi then wrote of the copious amount of blood from Elena at those Good Friday moments:

> The bleeding of the stigmata is so abundant as to utterly drench a lot of linen. Once the phenomenon is over, Elena reposes in a comatose stage, which is frequently interrupted by some painful visions. She stretches out her arms and keeps her eyes wide-open as if struck by a dreadful scene. On regaining consciousness she tells the story of having witnessed the Passion of Our Lord and of having partaken to that Divine Tragedy. After Good Friday all phenomena disappear at once. All that is left on her side, on her hands and feet, is some sort of a pink crust which stays on for good.
>
> It is also an extraordinary fact that Sister Elena, though so worn out, as if her very life were coming to an end, yet on Holy Saturday morning rises cheerful and strong as ever, just as if nothing unusual had happened to her on the previous day.[351]

Dr. Molezzi here affirmed and repeated what other physicians had been observing from Elena since the onset of the stigmata way back on Good Friday in 1923. She suffered intensely, akin to Christ on the Cross—even with arms opened wide—and then bounced back the next morning, chipper as always.

Dr. Molezzi then addressed the attempted strange quasi-clinical explanation of "hysteria," which somehow might have caused the bleeding, like clockwork, only on Good Fridays. The physician stated to the archbishop:

> Several attempts have been made to explain these phenomena on grounds of hysteria or of some impaired nervous system. But in all fairness I think that we should ask ourselves this simple question: "Is it because of our ignorance that we are unable to explain a biological and pathological case of phenomenology? Or is it rather because we are in presence of a mystery, which is elusive to human science?"[352]

No doubt, the doctor was speaking the clergyman's language here. Dr. Molezzi concluded to Archbishop Nogara:

> When all is said and done, this much is certain, i.e., that after viewing that poor body tortured by indescribable pain, as you leave that room, you cannot possibly forget that face smeared with blood flowing from forehead and both temples. It is not possible to forget the vision of that body agonizing with pain at the slightest touch on its wounds.
>
> Ordinary people and learned men stand by perplexed and perturbed, not knowing what to say or what to do. But fair-minded persons willingly admit that there must be some unknown and hidden power that shows the way how to solve the doubt by simply acknowledging that we are in presence of a mystery.
>
> Otherwise it would be humanly impossible that this soul, consumed with love, could supply strength to a body tortured by pain, unless it were supported by a Supreme Being.

That is what in my capacity, as the family physician, I can conscientiously attest concerning the life of Sister Elena Aiello.[353]

Again, that is a physician writing to the archbishop, not vice versa. Doubtless, the archbishop was likewise willing to ascribe this to the realm of supernatural mystery, to a higher power. And in his role as archbishop of Cosenza, the diocese of Elena Aiello, he was here doing his due diligence with the case of the reported stigmatist among his flock.

Throughout this long period of her stigmatic suffering on each Good Friday, beginning in 1923 and lasting until her death in 1961, there were reports like these from physicians and priests alike attesting to the supernatural phenomena they were witnessing from this little Calabrian nun.

Sr. Elena's spiritual director, Fr. Francis Sarago of the Minims, would write in a formal deposition shortly after her death, "Who could adequately measure the sufferings endured by this great departed soul? She suffered martyrdom in her body, where every single fiber was tortured. She was unable to take food, unable to move about, and was worn out by fever during her last years." In addition, "she suffered severe and painful hemorrhages that undermined her strength until the bell of departure tolled for her."[354]

But throughout these many years, there were more pains still—of a different sort. They were pains that spoke to that day and the days yet to come and that speak to us still.

Sister Elena's Visitations and Prophetic Visions

"But by far," continued Fr. Francis Sarago in his sworn deposition after Elena's death in June 1961, "more bitter were the tortures of her soul, because she intensely bewailed the evils afflicting the world."[355]

Sr. Elena Aiello was tormented by the welfare of souls. Akin to Jesus Christ in the Garden of Gethsemane, she was permitted a glimpse into the evils of the world, and it tormented her even more painfully than physical pains upon her person. "Hers was the agony of the victim freely consecrated to Jesus agonizing in the Garden," wrote Fr.

Sarago, "a truly perfect martyrdom and consequently a real redemptive work."[356] The little nun from Calabria was given visions not only in real time of the evils produced by her fellow children of God but of the evils to befall the world still years ahead.

Among the most remarkable of Elena's prophecies concerning her own day were those relating to Italian dictator Benito Mussolini in the spring of 1938, a year before World War II broke out, with *Il Duce* joining Hitler and the Japanese emperor as part of the Axis powers—a calamitous development and great embarrassment to so many Italians. Like Sr. Faustina Kowalska, who died in 1938 with similar catastrophic prophecies of the war ahead, Elena was racked by ominous visions of what was to befall Mussolini, Italy, Europe, and much of the world.

Hearing Elena's pronouncements of these visions as a live witness was the aforementioned Dr. Guido Palmardita, prefect of Cosenza from 1936 to 1939. He transcribed the nun's messages on several occasions throughout this period. Here are a few.

On March 24, 1938, Palmardita recorded a scene that Elena was witnessing at the foot of the Cross of Jesus Christ. She saw at the Cross the Blessed Virgin shedding tears along with Mary Magdalene, Martha, and angels who she said were gathering the drops of blood from the crucified Lord. Notably, Elena, in this particular vision, also described seeing fellow Italian stigmatist Gemma Galgani (who died in 1903) as well as a girl named Vera, a daughter of Prefect Palmardita, who had died eight months earlier, in July 1937, and who had been a close friend of Elena. She saw Gemma and Vera holding lilies at the scene, with the latter "sent by God to help me bear all the pain."[357]

This was not unusual for Elena. In addition to seeing deceased figures like Gemma Galgani, who had been beatified by Pope Pius XI in May 1933 and would be canonized by Pope Pius XII in May 1940, she also had visions and interactions with the likes of St. Theresa of the Infant Jesus (St. Thérèse of Lisieux) and (among others), of course, St. Rita of Cascia.[358]

On April 15, 1938, Palmardita recorded another message from Jesus to Elena: "Do you wish to come with Me to Gethsemane? You shall have to suffer for sinners. . . . The sin of impurity makes man loathsome. . . . Blessed are the clean of heart, because they shall see God. . . . Father, forgive them, for they know not what they do." Here, Elena had a vision of events in Italy. She stated, "A soldier's camp. Italy is going through a terrible time: but she will be safe because the Vicar of Christ resides there."[359]

Elena affirmed this a number of times in subsequent visions. Yes, Italy would suffer during a terrible time, especially because of the sins of Mussolini, who himself would have much to suffer for in the end. But as a whole, Italy would not be annihilated. It would be preserved by the mere fact that the Vicar of Christ resided there. It was blessed by the presence of the Vatican, St. Peter's Basilica, and its capital, Rome, is the Eternal City. The pope lives there as the living inheritor of the Chair of St. Peter. This would imbue Italy with a vital degree of supernatural protection.

Prophetic Warnings to Mussolini

But as for Benito Mussolini, alas, he would be in big trouble if he did not heed the warnings of the Lord, transmitted by this little Calabrian nun. And quite strikingly, just as an earlier Italian stigmatist, St. Catherine of Siena, managed to get the rapt attention of popes, this Italian stigmatist, Elena Aiello, had the ear of Mussolini. On April 23, 1940, the little nun boldly addressed this letter to *Il Duce*:

Cosenza, April 23, 1940

To the Head of the Government
Benito Mussolini
Duce:

I come to you in God's Name to tell you what God has revealed to me and what He wants from you. I was hesitating to write, but yesterday, April 22, the Lord appeared to me again, and bid me to tell you what follows:

"The world is going to ruin because of its many sins, particularly the sins of impurity, which have presently exceeded the very limits before the Justice of My Heavenly father. Therefore, you shall suffer and shall become an atoning victim for the world, especially for Italy where My Vicar on earth resides. My Kingdom is a Kingdom of peace: whereas the whole world is entangled in war. The Nations' Rulers are bent on acquiring new possessions: Poor fools! They don't know that, when there is no God, there is no victory either. Their hearts are filled with wickedness. All they do is to outrage, ridicule and despise Me. They are like devils sowing dissension, subverting people and seeking to drive into the sinful scourge of war even Italy, when [where] God is pleased with many souls, and where My Vicar on earth, the Pastor Angelicus, resides. France, so dear to My Heart, shall soon fall to ruin on account of her many sins, and shall be overthrown and ravaged like the ungrateful Jerusalem. I sent Benito Mussolini to preserve Italy from the precipice because of My Vicar on earth: otherwise, by now, she would be worse off than Russia."

"I have always shielded him [Mussolini] from many dangers. He must now keep Italy out of war, because Italy is a civilized country and it is the dwelling place of My Vicar on earth. If he is willing to do this, he shall receive many favors and I shall make all Nations respect him. But since he has made up his mind to go to war, tell him that, if he doesn't prevent it, he will be punished by My Divine Justice."

It is the Lord who has told me all this. Please, Duce, do not think for a moment that I am interested in politics. I am just an ordinary Nun looking after the welfare of abandoned little girls, and I am earnestly praying for your safety as well as the safety of our country.

Respectfully,
Sister Elena Aiello[360]

These were powerful words from a little nun standing afraid. As a sign of how immediately prophetic they were, note what she—via Jesus Christ—had warned about France: "France, so dear to My Heart, shall soon fall to ruin on account of her many sins, and shall be overthrown and ravaged like the ungrateful Jerusalem." This apolitical nun issued that warning from the words of Christ on April 23, 1940. Precisely that would happen to France just two and a half weeks later, when the Germans invaded on May 10, 1940. It took the Nazis mere weeks to ravage France like wolves. The country would spend the next four years under the jackboot of Hitler.

How could this little nun so uninterested in politics nail that ominous prediction so accurately? By her own cognizance, she could not. This, however, was the insight of the Lord Jesus that was given to her—to give to Mussolini.

And what about the warnings to Mussolini in this letter? Did he see this message from Sr. Elena? He sure did. Elena brought the letter with her on May 2, 1940, when she came to the Vatican for the canonization ceremony of fellow Italian stigmatist Gemma Galgani. The letter was delivered to Mussolini by his younger sister, Donna Edvige, who personally handed it to him four days later, on May 6. Donna Edvige (1888–1952) was a woman of faith who respected Elena, as did *Il Duce* himself. Mussolini had earlier heard about Elena from Dr. Guido Palmardita, prefect of Cosenza, and was said to have been "greatly interested" in her, to the point of having made a "considerable" personal financial contribution to the mother house. When he received this dispatch, Mussolini was said to have been "so perturbed," especially knowing how the winds of war were swirling.[361]

At this very moment, the Nazis were making plans to devour France. From there, Hitler would next attack England. By the end of May 1940, after relentless bombing, London was hanging by a thread, with Paris already bludgeoned by the Berlin beast.[362] Mussolini's German ally was wreaking havoc upon Europe. And yet, *Il Duce* marched forward nonetheless, blithely ignoring Elena's warnings, holding tight to an alliance with Hitler. It would be his downfall.

Sr. Elena and Mussolini's sister Edvige stayed in touch. Among their correspondence was a bracing May 15, 1943, letter sent by Elena from her hometown, where she and her fellow nuns and the girls under their protection had sought refuge from the Allies' bombardment:

Montalto Uffugo, May 15, 1943

My dear Donna Edvige:

You may have thought that, on account of my long silence, I may have forgotten you, whereas I remember you every day in my prayers. I am following the painful events now taking place in our beautiful Italy. We have left Cosenza on account of the bombardments. The enemy's barbarity has vented all its hatred by bombing the City of Cosenza thus bringing desolation and death to the population. I was bedridden because of my illness: three bombs fell close to our Institute, but the Lord, in His infinite goodness and mercy, has protected us. We have taken refuge at Montalto Uffugo, my native town, in order to protect the little girls from the danger of new raids.

Naturally, we are far from comfortable, but we are offering up all to God for the preservation of Italy. The purpose of this letter is that I wish to make another appeal to you, just as I did in the month of May 1940, when I was introduced to you in Rome by Baroness Ruggi for the purpose of giving you in writing whatever God had revealed to me concerning the Duce.

If you recall, on May 6, 1940, we were saying that the Duce had made up his mind to go to war, whereas, the Lord had warned him in my letter to keep Italy out of war, otherwise His Divine Justice would strike him. "I have always rescued him—said Jesus—from many a danger: now it is up to him to save Italy from the scourge of war because Italy is the dwelling place of My Vicar on earth. If he complies with My request, I will bestow great blessings on him and I shall cause all Nations to respect him, but, since he is determined to go to war, I want him to know that, if he persists, he will be severely punished by My Justice."

Ah! Had the Duce only listened to Jesus' words, Italy wouldn't be in such a terrible plight now. . . . I know that the Duce must feel quite dejected on seeing Italy, once a flourishing garden, now a barren field filled with diseases and deaths.

But, why persist in this terribly cruel war, when Jesus has stated that no one is going to achieve true victory?

Therefore, my dear Donna Edvige, please tell the Duce, in my name, that this is God's last warning to him. He is still in time to save himself by leaving all things in the hands of the Holy Father. Should he be unwilling to do so—said the Lord—Divine Justice shall quickly reach him. The other Rulers also, who play deaf to the counsel and directives of My Vicar, shall be overtaken and punished by My Justice.

Do you recall that, on July 7th of last year, you asked me what was in store for the Duce? Didn't I reply that, if he didn't listen to the Pope, he would wind up worse than Napoleon? Now I am going to repeat the very same words, "If the Duce is unwilling to rescue Italy and ignore the Holy Father, he will have a speedy downfall." Even Bruno is begging his father from the other world to save both Italy and himself. Quite often Our Lord says that Italy will be protected on account of the Pope, who is the atoning victim for this disaster. Therefore, the only way to achieve true peace in the world is the one that the Holy Father shall indicate.

My dear Donna Edvige, please remember that whatever Our Lord revealed to me has been perfectly fulfilled. Who has been the cause of all this ruin to Italy? Is it not the Duce's fault? Didn't he refuse to listen to the warnings of Our Lord Jesus Christ? Even now, he could somehow counteract the evil done provided he be willing to do what God wants of him. As for me I shall continue to pray for that intention.

Respectfully,
Sister Elena Aiello[363]

Again, like St. Catherine of Siena, this Italian stigmatist was speaking truth—that is, on behalf of Truth Himself—to power. If those powers chose to ignore these messages, it would be to their own peril. But these prophetic voices, the likes of Sr. Elena in the 1940s and Catherine of Siena six centuries earlier, had the nervous attention of these powerful men, just as John the Baptist had Herod's attention. Would they listen? They would not.

And for that, just as the little nun warned, Mussolini was severely punished. *Il Duce* had not heeded, in Elena's name, God's last warning to him. He still had time to save himself by leaving things in the hands of the Holy Father, Pope Pius XII. He did not. And now, he would indeed wind up worse than Napoleon. Napoleon had been permitted by his foes to live his final years in exile, ultimately dying in his bed on the island of St. Helena on May 5, 1821. Mussolini, by contrast, would be executed by Italian partisans (primarily Communists), strung up at a gas station in Milan next to one of his mistresses, and then ignominiously spat upon, and cut down, his bloody corpse dragged through the street by an angry mob.

Mussolini was killed on April 28, 1945, just two days before Hitler shot himself in the head, hence ending the war in Europe. His quick decline, however, had started in the autumn of 1943, not long after Sr. Elena's letter of final warning. Time ran out.

A somewhat touching end to this story of tragic woe was a letter sent to Sr. Elena five years later by Mussolini's surviving sister, Edvige. Dated "Holy Year 1950," Edvige addressed it to the "Very Reverend Mother" Elena, whom Mussolini's sister proceeded to refer to as a literal "Saint." It began:

> Seven years ago I had the honor and the pleasure to be received by you in the Convent of the Suore [Sisters] di Malta, Via Iberia, Rome. Since that day I never forgot that pleasant hour I passed in your company. I begged of you a special favor which I received. How could I have ever forgotten meeting a Saint? I find no words to tell you, my Very Reverend Mother, how often, in my distress as Mother and Sister, I have thought of you and of those prophetic words you wrote to me at the very beginning of the war. In April 1945, I lost my brother, my twenty-one year old son Joseph and the husband of my eldest daughter. All of them were murdered on the same day in Northern Italy.[364]

Here was a woman in pain, who likely never received much public empathy as the sibling of the catastrophic Italian dictator. Nonetheless, she was a sister, a wife, a mother, daughter, and a Catholic. In the letter, she proceeded to list for Elena her ongoing trials and tribulations, imploring the heavens for help—in fact, imploring Elena for help: "Very Reverend Mother," Edvige pleaded in conclusion, "under these trying circumstances affecting my poor children, so badly in need of help, I beg of you, with joined hands, to pray that God's blessing may descend upon them." She ended with the fullest confidence that Elena would grant her request, signing it "Affectionately Yours." The worldly sufferings of Edvige Mancini Mussolini would end on May 20, 1952, when she passed away at age sixty-three.

Additional Prophetic Messages

Sr. Elena Aiello's messages to Benito Mussolini certainly turned out to be prophetic. They were played out in World War II. But there would be more messages after the war. Some of them seem to speak to events that might have transpired during the Cold War, with violent revolutions and communism taking their toll in countries from the Soviet Union to China to the regions of Eastern Europe, Asia, Africa, and more. And yet, the language of some of these messages is so apocalyptic that they seem to deal with disasters that have not yet unfolded—or perhaps that God, in His providence, decided to hold back, forestall, and withdraw altogether.[365] Truly, only God knows. Nonetheless, here is what the little nun from Calabria foresaw.

Elena's biographer, Fr. Spadafora, ended his presentation of the many examples of Elena's prophecies with a very dramatic one that he, unfortunately, did not date for readers, though he carried with him the piece of paper that held the message, acknowledging that "its contents are very serious indeed. They resemble a page of the Apocalypse, containing, as they do, urgent warnings, appalling forebodings and a clear intuition that takes in all nations and also the fundamental reasons for all the human events." The message, given by the Blessed Virgin Mary, was offered by Elena (in my estimate) during the period of 1955–57. (The message is also printed, with a different translation that varies only slightly, at the long entry for Sr. Elena at the Mystics of the Church website, which dates the prophecy as December 8, 1956, the feast of the Immaculate Conception. That was also the date given by the publication *Divine Love*, which will be detailed below.) Here are what Fr. Spadafora dubbed "some of the more notable excerpts":

> People are offending God too much. Were I to show you all the sins committed on a single day, you would surely die of grief. These are grave times. The world is thoroughly upset because it is in a worse condition than at the time of the deluge. Materialism marches on ever fomenting bloody strifes and fratricidal struggles. Clear signs portend that peace is in danger. That scourge, like the shadow of a dark cloud, is now moving across mankind: only my power, as Mother of God, is preventing the outbreak of the storm. All is hanging on a slender thread. When that thread shall snap, Divine Justice shall pounce upon the world and execute its dreadful, purging designs. All the nations shall be punished because sins, like a muddy river, are now covering all the earth.
>
> The powers of evil are getting ready to strike furiously in every part of the globe. Tragic events are in store for the future. For quite a while, and in many a way, I have warned the world. The nation's rulers do indeed understand the gravity of these dangers, but they refuse to acknowledge that it is necessary for all people to practice a truly Christian life to counteract that scourge. Oh, what torture I feel in my heart, on beholding mankind so engrossed in all kinds of things and completely ignoring the most important duty of their reconciliation with God. The time is not far off now when the whole world shall be greatly disturbed. A great deal of blood of just and innocent people as well as saintly priests will be poured out. The Church shall suffer very much and hatred will be at its very peak.
>
> Italy shall be humiliated and purged in her blood. She shall suffer very much indeed on account of the multitude

of sins committed in this privileged nation, the abode of the Vicar of Christ.

You cannot possibly imagine what is going to happen. A great revolution shall break out and the streets shall be stained with blood. The Pope's sufferings on this occasion may well be compared to the agony that will shorten his pilgrimage on earth. His successor shall pilot the boat during the storm. But the punishment of the wicked shall not be slow. That will be an exceedingly dreadful day. The earth shall quake so violently as to scare all mankind. And so, the wicked shall perish according to the inexorably severity of Divine Justice. If possible, publish this message throughout the world, and admonish all the people to do penance and to return right away to God.[366]

The severity of this message speaks for itself. What else can be added? The only remaining questions are those of when and where.

All of the aforementioned messages, from the prophecies about Mussolini to this apocalyptic statement, are found in the 1964 biography of Elena Aiello, written by Fr. Francesco Spadafora and translated by Fr. Angelo R. Cioffi. As noted, the book received an official *nihil obstat* and *imprimatur* by, respectively, Archbishop Antonius Trani and Bishop Aloysius Liverzani. Thus, these prophecies carry a significant degree of weight, though the Church itself generally, as a rule, does not comment on the specific prophecies.

The *Divine Love* Revelations

In more recent years, long after the publication of the 1964 Spadafora biography, some quite significant additional prophecies attributed to Sr. Elena have been posted on the website Mystics of the Church, where they have been picked up by other Catholic websites.[367] The full entry for Elena at Mystics of the Church prints out to forty-four pages. The first twenty-eight pages come from the 1964 Spadafora book. On page twenty-nine come further passages with particularly stark prophecies. Glenn Dallaire, the editor of the Mystics of the Church website, lists the source of the previously unpublished prophecies as

Msgr. Cioffi, the translator of the Spadafora biography and a friend of Sr. Elena. According to Dallaire, these previously unpublished prophecies of Sr. Elena were provided by Cioffi to the late Stephen Oraze (1916–86), editor of the Catholic newspaper *Divine Love*, which was produced by the Apostolate of Christian Action, founded in Fresno, California, in 1958, and the prophecies were published there. Dallaire asserts that Msgr. Cioffi was nervous about publishing the messages because they were so severe. Dallaire says that Stephen Oraze got permission from his own bishop to publish them, with the bishop giving them his *imprimatur*.[368]

I contacted Glenn Dallaire to see if he was in possession of back issues of *Divine Love* so that I could confirm the quite dramatic quotations attributed to Sr. Elena, plus check for additional material of interest. Given that the long entry at Mystics of the Church had been written over a decade ago (first posted in 2011) by a colleague of Dallaire with whom he had lost contact, he was unable to retrieve them.[369] Fortunately, I did find one archive—only one—that had back issues. That archive is at the University of Dayton, a Catholic university that maintains a large amount of archival material on Catholic subjects. With the help of the staff at the university, I was able to find copies of *Divine Love* and, indeed, of Elena's prophecies published in the newspaper.[370]

What follows are several of these remarkable messages of Sr. Elena, many of which are similar to the aforementioned messages from the Spadafora biography, and some of which could well be the same messages (recall that Spadafora did not always give exact dates), differing in exact wording only because of varying translations.

In the very first issue of *Divine Love*, published July–September 1957, which no doubt was in part inspired by the editor receiving material like this, Stephen Oraze posted this prophecy from Sr. Elena,[371] which she had received three years earlier on Good Friday, April 16, 1954.[372] According to Elena, "Upon initiating the usual sufferings, about the hour of 1:00 p.m., Jesus appeared to me, covered with wounds and bleeding," and then He said to her:

Behold my child, see to what ends the sins of man have reduced me. The world has lowered itself in overflowing corruption. The governments of the people have risen like demons incarnated, and, while they speak of peace, they prepare for war with the most devastating implements to destroy peoples and nations. Men have become ungrateful to My Sacred Heart, and abusing My Mercy, have transformed the earth into a scene of crime. Numerous scandals are bringing souls to ruin. . . . particularly through the corruption of youth. Stirred up, and unrestrained in the enjoyment of the pleasures of the world, they have degraded their spirit in corruption and sin. The bad example of parents trains the family in scandal and infidelity, instead of virtue and prayer, which is almost dead on the lips of many. Stained and withered is the fountain of faith and sanctity—the home. The wills of men do not change. They live in their obstinacy of sin. More severe are the scourges and plagues to recall them to the way of God; but men still become furious, like wounded beasts (and harden their hearts against the Grace of God). The world is no longer worthy of pardon, but only of fire, destruction and death.

There must be more prayers and penances from the souls faithful to Me, in order to appease the just wrath of God, and to temperate the just sentence of punishment, SUSPENDED [uppercase original] on earth by the intercession of My Beloved Mother, who is also the Mother of all men.

Oh! . . . how sad is My Heart to see that men do not convert (or respond) to so many calls of love and grief, manifest by My Beloved Mother to errant men. Roaming in darkness, they continue to live in sin, and further away from God! But the scourge of fire is near, to purify the earth for the iniquities of the wicked. The justice of God requires reparation for the many offenses and misdeeds that cover the earth, and which can no longer be compromised. Men are obstinate in their guilt, and do not return to God.

The Lord Jesus urged the little nun to "make it known to all men that, repentant, they must return to God, and, in doing so, may hope for pardon, and be saved from the just vengeance of a scorned God." These were sins occurring at that time, and many clearly have gotten only worse since.

According to Elena, at that point, the Lord disappeared, and then His Blessed Mother appeared. She was dressed in black, with seven swords piercing her Immaculate Heart. With an expression of profound sorrow and tears running down her cheeks, she told Elena:

> Listen attentively, and reveal to all: My Heart is sad for so many sufferings in an impending world in ruin. The justice of Our Father is most offended. Men live in their obstinacy of sin. The wrath of God is near. Soon the world will be afflicted with great calamities, bloody revolutions, frightful hurricanes, and the overflowing of streams and the seas.
>
> Cry out until the priests of God lend their ears to my voice, to advise men that the time is near at hand. And if men do not return to God with prayers and penance, the world will be overturned in a new and more terrible war. Arms most deadly will destroy people and nations! The dictators of the earth, specimens infernal, will demolish the churches and desecrate the Holy Eucharist, and will destroy things most dear. In this impious war, much will be destroyed of that which has been built by the hands of man.

At this point, the Blessed Mother issued the gravest warning, foretelling a massive fire from the sky amid a period approaching three days of darkness. This cataclysmic event would destroy much of humanity. *Divine Love* printed this message in uppercase letters and bold for emphasis (I have included the original capitals for all of these messages as printed in *Divine Love*):

CLOUDS WITH LIGHTNING FLASHES OF FIRE IN THE SKY AND A TEMPEST OF FIRE SHALL FALL UPON THE WORLD. THIS TERRIBLE SCOURAGE, NEVER

BEFORE SEEN IN THE HISTORY OF HUMANITY, WILL LAST SEVENTY HOURS. GODLESS PERSONS WILL BE CRUSHED AND WIPED OUT. MANY WILL BE LOST BECAUSE THEY REMAIN IN THEIR OBSTINACY OF SIN. THEN SHALL BE SEEN THE POWER OF LIGHT OVER THE POWER OF DARKNESS.

Be not silent, my daughter, because the hours of darkness, of abandonment, are near.

According to the Blessed Mother, her intercession and pleading had held back the punishing hand of God thus far: "I am bending over the world, holding in suspension the justice of God. OTHERWISE THESE THINGS WOULD ALREADY HAVE NOW COME TO PASS. Prayers and penances are necessary because men MUST RETURN TO GOD and to MY Immaculate Heart—the Mediatrix of men to God, and thus THE WORLD WILL BE AT LEAST IN PART SAVED." She urged the nun, "Cry out these things to all, like the very echo of my voice. Let this be known to all, because it will help save many souls, and prevent much destruction in the Church and in the world."

In this same issue of *Divine Love*, editor Stephen Oraze published a second prophecy from Sr. Elena, this one given two years earlier on Good Friday, April 8, 1955. Again, a tearful Blessed Mother ominously forecast dark days and fire from the skies:

DARK AND FRIGHTFUL DAYS ARE APPROACHING! . . . LAUNCH FORTH INTO THE WORLD A MESSAGE TO MAKE KNOWN TO ALL THAT THE SCOURGE IS NEAR AT HAND. . . . If men do not amend their ways, a terrifying scourge of fire will come down from Heaven upon all the nations of the world, and men will be punished according to the debts contracted with Divine Justice. There will be frightful moments for all, because Heaven will be joined with the earth, and all the un-Godly people will be destroyed. SOME NATIONS WILL BE PURIFIED, WHILE OTHERS WILL DISAPPEAR ENTIRELY.

The Mother of Christ commissioned the nun, "You are to transmit these warnings to all, in order that the new generation will know that men had been warned in time to turn to God by doing penance, and thus could have avoided these punishments."

Sr. Elena asked the Lady, "But when will this come about?" The Blessed Mother replied, "My daughter, the time is not far off. When men least expect it, the course of Divine Justice will be accomplished. My Heart is so big for poor sinners, and I make use of every possible means that they may be saved. Look at this mantle, how big it is. If I were not bent over the earth to cover all with my maternal love, the tempest of fire would already have broken upon the nations of the world." Elena then exclaimed, "My Lovely Mother, never before have I seen thee with such a large mantle," prompting the Blessed Virgin to open her arms wide and explain, "This is the mantle of mercy for all those who, having repented, come back to my Immaculate Heart. See? The right hand holds the mantle to cover and to save poor sinners, while with the left hand I hold back the Divine Justice, so that the time of Mercy may still be prolonged."

A similar warning was published in the winter 1958–59 issue of *Divine Love*, this time relating Mary's message to Elena on December 8, 1956, the day of the Immaculate Conception, which (as noted earlier) had also been shared in the Spadafora book, though not dated and with a slightly varied translation.[373] The Blessed Mother forewarned:

> ALL NATIONS WILL BE PUNISHED because of the many sins that cover the world like a tide of mire. The forces of evil are prepared to unchain themselves in every part of the world with enraged fury. Tremendous will be the confusion that will come, because men are obstinate and will not heed my voice of Mother. The time is not far off when the world will be overturned. Much blood will be shed by the innocent; the just; the holy priests; and the Church will suffer much. Hate will reach its fullest measure. . . . A GREAT REVOLUTION WILL UNFOLD AND THE STREETS WILL BE RED WITH BLOOD.

Here, editor Stephen Oraze added a "special note," stating that Mary had given Elena "more specifics" in a July 2, 1958, message. Oraze described it this way: "God has no choice but to send the punishment because there is more sin now (in proportion) than at the time of the Deluge, and the evil surpasses the good. Italy will be washed in her own blood; France will be covered with rubble; much of the United States will be in the hands of the Communists, except one area which has turned to the Rosary. All people who have turned to the Rosary will have the special protection of the Blessed Virgin Mary."

It is hard to imagine how much worse those sins are today, in the twenty-first century, than in 1958. If those sins in 1958 were then worse than at any time since the Great Flood, today, the magnitude must be incalculably worse. And indeed, in the final chapter of this book, we will see messages from modern seers claiming just that. Such a vast ocean of sin means that humanity will be punished in a way never experienced since the Deluge. This time, however, it will come not from the waters but from the skies.

"Russia Will March Upon All the Nations of Europe," and Other Stark Visions

A few final prophecies from Sr. Elena are likewise staggering, dealing with Russia, the pope, priests, epidemics, weather calamities, and more. They can be found on various Catholic websites, with the Mystics of the Church website as their provenance. The Mystics of the Church site, in turn, cites the *Divine Love* newsletter as the original source.

Unfortunately, I could not confirm these prophecies via the archives of the University of Dayton, which regrettably are incomplete; the archives do not contain every edition of the *Divine Love* newsletter. Actually, the archives lack only one issue, and it happens to be the issue in which these prophecies were very likely published: issue number 86 (1982), the theme of which was titled "Prophetic Warnings."[374] This was a major edition of *Divine Love*, which nearly every issue thereafter referred to when re-invoking the dramatic prophecies. Rather than thereafter republishing the entire prophecies as they did in 1982, the editor and writers instead did a short recap throughout each major issue until the final issue of the newsletter was published in 1986, the year that editor Stephen Oraze died.[375] While it is hard to verify the exact language in the 1982 issue, the themes and subjects and much of the language in the Mystics of the Church entry on Sr. Elena are essentially identical to what *Divine Love* stated in these later editions.[376]

With those caveats, here are key excerpts of those prophecies, drawn from the full posts at Mystics of the Church.

On Good Friday, April 9, 1950, Sr. Elena Aiello asked the Blessed Mother amid her forecasts of world destruction, "What will become of Italy? Will Rome be saved?" The Virgin Mary answered Elena, "In part, by the Pope. The Church will be in travail, but the forces of Hell cannot prevail! You must suffer for the Pope and Christ, and thus Christ will be safe on earth; and the Pope, with his redemptive word, will, in part, save the world."

According to Sr. Elena, "The Madonna then came closer, and with a sad expression, showed me the flames of Hell." The Mother of Jesus told the nun, "Satan reigns and triumphs on earth! See how the souls are falling into Hell. See how high the flames are, and the souls who fall into them like flakes of snow, looking like transparent embers! How many sparks! How many cries of hate, and of despair! How much pain!"

This, of course, is language strikingly similar to what we have heard before from various visionaries describing souls falling into hell, including Sr. Lucia of Fatima, who used the exact same description of "transparent embers," and Anna Maria Taigi, who used the metaphor of snowflakes.[377] As for those souls falling into hell, they included some bad priests, which terribly saddened the Mother of Jesus. Elena quoted the Virgin Mary: "See how many priestly souls! . . . What torture, my daughter, in my maternal Heart! Great is my sorrow to see that men do not change! The justice of the Father requires reparation—otherwise many will be lost!"

And then this prophecy on Russia—namely, not on the Soviet Union per se, but on *Russia*: "See how Russia will burn!" asserted the Blessed Mother. Elena described what she saw of Russia: "Before my eyes there extended an immense field covered with flames and smoke, in which souls were submerged as if in a sea of fire." According to the Blessed Mother, this fire consuming Russia would come not from earthly warfare by soldiers or missiles but from angels in the heavens. "And all this fire," concluded the Madonna, "is not that which will fall from the hands of men, but will be hurled directly from the Angels." This would transpire, according to Elena, "at the time of the great chastisement or purification that will come upon the earth."

In another prophecy related to Russia and more, this one in 1959 (exact date not provided), Elena again asserted, quoting the direct words of Jesus, "The hours of darkness are near!" She again quoted the Blessed Mother, who warned through tears that "if men do not return to God, purifying fire will fall from the Heavens, like snowstorms, on all peoples, and a great part of humanity will be destroyed!" As for Russia, it would be a source of chastisement for a world that "must soon be purified." Elena said, in language from Mary printed in uppercase letters for emphasis, "RUSSIA WILL MARCH UPON ALL THE NATIONS OF EUROPE, PARTICULARLY ITALY, AND WILL RAISE HER FLAG OVER THE DOME OF ST. PETER'S. Italy will be severely tried by a great revolution, and Rome will be purified in blood for its many sins, especially those of impurity! The flock is about to be dispersed and the Pope must suffer greatly." Accordingly, said Mary, "The only valid means for placating Divine Justice is to pray and do penance, returning to God with sincere sorrow for the faults committed, and then the chastisement of Divine Justice will be mitigated by mercy. Humanity will never find peace, if it does not return to my Immaculate Heart as Mother of Mercy, and Mediatrix of men; and to the Heart of my Son Jesus!"

One wonders if the time for this has since passed, perhaps with Divine Justice placated, and maybe with the collapse of the Soviet Union in 1991. Then again, the word used consistently was not the *Soviet Union*, or *USSR*, but *Russia*. To be sure, the Soviet Union/USSR was often called simply "Bolshevik Russia" or plain "Russia." However, technically, in the time of Elena's prophecies, Russia was a part of the Soviet Union/USSR. Russia was one of fifteen Soviet republics. Today, post-1991 and into the twenty-first century, there is no Soviet Union/USSR, but merely Russia—that is, Vladimir Putin's aggressive Russia, the one that marched into Ukraine.

Speaking of which, Sr. Elena shared another warning on Russia in her Good Friday 1960 vision. She again quoted the Blessed Mother:

> Great calamities will come upon the world, which will bring confusion, tears, struggles and pain. Great earthquakes will swallow up entire cities and countries, and will bring epidemics, famine, and terrible destruction ESPECIALLY WHERE THE SONS OF DARKNESS ARE.
>
> In these tragic hours, the world has need of prayers and penance, because the Pope, the priests, and the Church are in danger. If we do not pray, Russia will march upon all of Europe, and particularly upon Italy, bringing much more ruin and havoc!
>
> I will manifest my partiality for Italy, which will be preserved from the fire, but the skies will be covered with dense darkness, and the earth will be shaken by fearful earthquakes which will open deep abysses. Provinces and cities will be destroyed, and all will cry out that the end of the world has come! Even Rome will be punished according to justice for its many and serious sins, because here sin has reached its peak. Pray, and lose no time, lest it be too late; since dense darkness surrounds the earth and the enemy is at the doors!

Again, more talk of Russia marching upon its neighbors, days of darkness, and the sins of priests and of Rome. In Rome, notably, sin had reached its peak, presumably including those of the clergy.

Continuing along these themes, here was another such message, this time offered on the feast of the Immaculate Heart of Mary, August 22, 1960, and this time pitting Russia directly against America. The Blessed Mother told Elena:

> The hour of the justice of God is close, and will be terrible!
>
> Tremendous scourges are impending over the world, and various nations are struck by epidemics, famines, great earthquakes, terrific hurricanes, with overflowing rivers and seas, which bring ruin and death.

> If the people do not recognize in these scourges (of nature) the warnings of Divine Mercy, and do not return to God with truly Christian living, ANOTHER TERRIBLE WAR WILL COME FROM THE EAST TO THE WEST. RUSSIA WITH HER SECRET ARMIES WILL BATTLE AMERICA; WILL OVERRUN EUROPE.
>
> The river Rhine will be overflowing with corpses and blood. Italy, also, will be harassed by a great revolution, and the Pope will suffer terribly.

The Blessed Mother here advised devotion to her Immaculate Heart and recitation of the Rosary as "Satan goes furiously through this disordered world." Satan would be inspiring Russia to this chaos.

To that end, here was one more such message, this time from Good Friday 1961. Calling her the "Sorrowful Madonna," Elena quoted the Blessed Mother: "People pay no attention to my motherly warnings, and thus the world is falling headlong evermore into an abyss of iniquity. Nations shall be convulsed by terrible disasters, causing destruction and death." And here again was Russia and the pope: "Russia, spurred on by Satan, will seek to dominate the whole world and, by bloody revolutions, will propagate her false teachings throughout all the nations, especially in Italy. The Church will be persecuted and the Pope and the priests shall suffer much."

At this point, Sr. Elena Aiello shared a grim vision that she foresaw: "Oh, what a horrible vision I see! A great revolution is going on in Rome! They are entering the Vatican. The Pope is all alone; he is praying. They are holding the Pope. They take him by force. They knock him down to the floor. They are tying him. Oh, God! Oh, God! They are kicking him. What a horrible scene! How dreadful! Our Blessed Mother is drawing near. Like corpses those evil men fall down to the floor. Our Lady helps the Pope to his feet and, taking him by the arm, she covers him with her mantle saying: 'Fear not!'"

What Elena described next certainly seems as though it would have applied to a communist Bolshevik Russia of the century past, or at least one would think. She described the red flag flying over St. Peter's dome and elsewhere, with these atheistic "evil brutes" shouting, "We don't want God to rule over us; we want Satan to be our master." In this instance, Elena said that the Blessed Mother told her that "Rome will not be saved, because the Italian rulers have forsaken the Divine Light and because only a few people really love the Church. But the day is not far off when all the wicked shall perish, under the tremendous blows of Divine Justice."

All of this begs the questions: Are these visions of the past that were mitigated or avoided or halted by our prayers? Did they come to the little nun from Calabria circa 1960 in the heart and height of the Cold War but were ultimately stopped thanks to the great efforts on behalf of peace and the dissolution of the Soviet "evil empire" by good men like Pope St. John Paul II and others who worked with him to peacefully end the Cold War in the 1980s, men like Ronald Reagan and Mikhail Gorbachev and Boris Yeltsin? Or do they apply yet to the future?

Only the Lord knows. This book can only share what Sr. Elena Aiello is reported to have shared. All we can do is watch and wait—and, as we have been exhorted to do, pray.

Sister Elena's Death and Posthumous Cause

Sr. Elena Aiello, this little Calabrian nun with mighty messages, died in Rome at 6:19 a.m. on June 19, 1961. Ten days later, on June 29, 1961, Fr. Bonaventura da Pavullo, superior council of the Capuchins and pontifical assistant to the Sisters Minims of the Passion, noted that Sr. Elena had so "remained faithful [to Christ] to the very end," including sharing His wounds, that she also shared in His final words from the Cross. She said in Latin, "*Fiat—Consummatum est!* (Be it done—It is consummated!)"[378]

As Fr. Bonaventura observed, she had "taken her flight to eternity" from this "Eternal City" of Rome that had become so dear to her "because it is the swelling place of the 'dolce Cristo in terra,' as she loved to say with St. Catherine [of Siena] when mentioning the Holy Father." Rome had thus acquired that special place in her heart. There, she had offered herself as victim to God not only for the people of the world but for the pope and for the Catholic Church—the chair of St. Peter and Christ's Church.[379] Her remains were interred in the motherhouse of her order.

Sr. Elena's special witness was summed up well by two authoritative witnesses to her life and suffering. One testimony comes from Fr. Bonaventura da Pavullo in a report on Elena that he signed from Rome on May 13, 1963, feast day of Our Lady of Fatima. He fondly recalled his visits with this bedridden and yet "ever charming" little nun in her final days when she was confined to a white bed on which she laid for about twenty hours each day. She would speak at length concerning "a hundred topics" and, with joy and sorrow, turn her attention to the events of the day "which she would interpret so accurately as to seem almost prophetic." As she did, she kept rosary beads wrapped around her wrists to call upon at any moment.[380]

Fr. Bonaventura called Elena "a truly valiant and strong woman, frail in body but of the Baptist and Catherine type," who did not hesitate to speak with the utmost frankness to rulers and heads of state, "albeit in a respectful way." She was humble as well as prayerful. And why? Because she had been uniquely called upon to suffer for the world's evils.

To that end, here is a final thought from her biographer, Fr. Spadafora, who said that Sr. Elena Aiello knew "that sin—not suffering—is the only real evil in this world." She thus happily agreed to endure severe personal suffering in order to help expiate the sins that spread evil throughout this world.[381] In so doing, Sr. Elena spread good throughout the world, especially in her home village, her native region of Calabria, and her beloved Italy.

Her reputation for holiness, already firmly solidified in Calabria and much of Italy, continued to spread quickly after her death. Only two decades later, on January 7, 1982, the process for her beatification was opened, with official approval from the Vatican's Congregation for the Causes of Saints.[382]

Nine years later, on January 22, 1991, Pope John Paul II declared her the Ven. Servant of God Elena Aiello. In April 2002, the process began of introducing and investigating an official miracle attributed to the intercession of Sr. Elena.[383] On April 2, 2011, Pope Benedict XVI formally recognized a miraculous healing attributable to the late

Sr. Elena's intercession, hence paving the road for her beatification on September 14, 2011. Serving the ceremony on the pope's behalf in Cosenza was Cardinal Angelo Amato, prefect for the Congregation of the Causes of Saints.[384]

The postulator for her cause of canonization is Enzo Gabrieli.[385] Sr. Elena Aiello is now Bl. Elena Aiello, and her move toward hopeful canonization continues. That process has not yet come to fruition, and, certainly, neither have all of the little nun's prophecies. For all of that, only time will tell. And as Elena Aiello would caution, it is in the hands of the Lord.

CHAPTER 8

SAINT FAUSTINA
(1905–1938)

The final stigmatist, profiled with a full chapter in this book, comes fittingly last. More than any other, she spoke to us about the Final Days. She was born Helena Faustina Kowalska, the third of ten children to Stanislaus and Marianna, on August 25, 1905, in the humble village of Glogowiec, in the heart of Poland.

But at that time, Poland was not technically Poland. This deeply devout Catholic country, so committed to Jesus Christ and His Blessed Mother, had been wiped off the world's maps. From 1795 to 1918, Poland did not exist in the eyes of the powers of the world. This blessed nation, which President Ronald Reagan would call "the martyred nation of Poland . . . a brave bastion of faith and freedom in the hearts of her courageous people," had been carved up by invaders.[386]

After World War I, however, God's Divine Mercy shined once again on the Polish people. Their nation was resurrected. But in truth, it never really disappeared, because the Polish people kept it alive through their culture—their music, their literature, their traditions, and their unifying faith. The nation was sustained by what a later Pole, the most famous of them all, Karol Wojtyla (1920–2005), the future Pope St. John Paul II, referred to as "memory and identity." Above all, it was sustained by its Catholic identity.

Few Poles in the twentieth century, other than Karol Wojtyla, felt and served that faith quite like Faustina Kowalska. Faustina and Karol both would witness more martyrdoms for Poland in its new century ahead, even after it was reconstituted as a nation by the WWI Allied powers after the Versailles conference. In the unique case of Faustina, however, it is more accurate to say that she *foresaw* those martyrdoms to come.

Faustina came from a pious family and was herself a committed Catholic. And yet, by her late teens, she was not committed to a clear plan for her life. She did feel the tug of a religious calling, but she kept putting it off, especially given that her parents had other plans for her. That would soon change in a dramatic way.

One evening in the summer of 1924, nineteen-year-old Faustina and her sister Josephine went to a dance in a park in the cheerful city of Lodz, which in just two decades would be ripped to shreds by ravenous wolves—totalitarian invaders. While at that dance, the teenage Faustina had a vision of Jesus. It would not be her last. It could not have left a greater impression. She was truly shaken.

Jesus Christ Himself, in the spirit and flesh, was suddenly standing next to the nineteen-year-old girl inside that dance hall. Amid the frivolity, He was suffering. Stripped of His clothing and covered with wounds, He had a message for her, formulated as a question: "How long shall I put up with you and how long will you keep putting me off?"[387]

One can scarcely imagine the young girl's shock. Her world must have froze. Imagine the scene. It was the Roaring Twenties, not just for America but for much of the world. The brutal First World War, then the deadliest in human history, was in the past, and it was time to have fun and live it up. It was party time for young people. But here was an arresting vision—unbeknownst to the girl, the first of many incredible visions and interactions with Jesus still to come—that would halt anyone near-dead in their tracks. Drew Mariani, in his book *Divine Mercy*, nicely captures the atmosphere at that dance:

> [W]hat's going on? One of the girls has just stopped in the middle of the floor. It's like she doesn't even see anyone around her anymore. Is she having a seizure? Should someone call a doctor?

But then she comes to herself again. She goes over to the edge of the room and sits down. Her sister is there taking care of her. Somebody tells us she has a headache. She'll be all right. We can go back to our dancing and laughing and eating. And we may never realize that what happened to that farm girl tonight will eventually change the world.[388]

No, we may never, perhaps even to this day. But for the girl, she was forever changed. "If you and I had been at that dance, we wouldn't have noticed anything very important going on," continued Drew Mariani. "We wouldn't even have seen anything interesting. If we'd been watching, we might have seen a farm girl with a headache or something. That would have been it. But what Helena saw changed her life completely."[389]

The girl dashed to a church—and not just to any church but to the Basilica of St. Stanislaus Kostka, named after one of the patron saints of Poland. There were a few people in the church, but like at the dance hall, Helena Faustina found herself alone with Jesus. She prostrated herself before the tabernacle and suddenly heard the words of Jesus. He instructed her, "Go at once to Warsaw; you will enter a convent there."[390]

Helena and her sister had been staying at the home of their uncle. She immediately went to her uncle's house and started packing her bags. "Helena! What are you doing?" her uncle asked. "I am going to Warsaw to enter a convent," she replied. The uncle knew of the tension between Helena and her parents on this matter of religious life. They were good, pious parents, though unwilling to give up their daughter.[391] The uncle protested, "You know that this will make your dear mother and father very sad and break their hearts!"[392]

Perhaps so. But Helena Faustina Kowalska had just experienced a call that could not be denied. "Jesus will take care of all my needs," she confidently told her uncle. Given the astonishing thing that had just happened, she had no doubts.

She tossed together a small bag that night and jumped on a train. She did not have her parents' permission, nor could she have sought it at the moment, given the lack of communication technology in 1924. Her parents had refused her request and intense desire to enter religious life, which she had felt since childhood. Nothing, however, could stop what she had just seen and been told.

Shortly thereafter, she would find herself in a convent, devoting her life completely to Jesus Christ—not that she was quickly welcomed. She knocked on many convent doors, and they refused her. At last, on August 1, 1925, she entered the convent of the Congregation of Sisters of Our Lady of Mercy on Zytnia Street in Warsaw. She took the name Maria.[393] "I felt immensely happy," she declared. "It seemed to me that I had stepped into the life of Paradise."[394]

Message of Divine Mercy

Sr. Maria Faustina Kowalska was about to take many steps into the life of Paradise. Actually, the lives of Paradise came to her. Faustina's religious life was not only a mix of joy, ecstasy, dedication, and obedience but also of suffering, torment, and illness. She was every bit the mystic, experiencing terrifying but profound visions and prophecies and often seeing and communicating directly with Christ Himself, with the Blessed Mother, with her guardian angel, and more.

Her most lasting vision that the world, too, came to see was given to her on February 22, 1931, while in her cell at the convent. Jesus appeared, clothed in white, with his right hand raised as if giving a blessing to the world, while the left hand touched a garment at His breast. From the opening in the garment, exuding from Jesus's Sacred Heart, were two large rays, one red and the other white, representing blood and water to heal the world of its sins. "In silence I gazed intently at the Lord," said Faustina. "My soul was overwhelmed with fear, but also with great joy."[395] The Christ figure instructed the nun, "Mankind will not enjoy peace until it turns with confidence to My Mercy."

Jesus asked Faustina to paint this image of Him displayed before her and to inscribe it with the words "Jesus, I trust in you." He told her, "I desire that this image be venerated, first in your chapel, and [then] throughout the world" (Faustina's *Diary*, section 47). He promised her that "the soul that will venerate this image will not perish. I also promise victory over [its] enemies already here on earth, especially at the hour of death" (*Diary*, 48). Since she was not a painter herself, artists were eventually commissioned.

Jesus also called for the entire universal Church to celebrate an annual feast of Divine Mercy. He said to her that same day, February 22, 1931, "I desire that there be a Feast of Mercy." He told her that He wanted the Divine Mercy image associated with the feast of mercy "to be solemnly blessed on the first Sunday after Easter; that Sunday is to be the Feast of Mercy" (*Diary*, 49).

That feast day would ultimately be established, but only after a long wait. When it was finally accomplished, nearly seventy years after her death, it would be done through the first and only Polish pope: John Paul II.

This was the major message and mission of Sr. Faustina Kowalska. She was assigned by the Lord as His special "secretary" and "administrator" of His mercy.[396] The world had fallen so far, so deep, that the Lord told Faustina that it required an "Ocean of Mercy" that Jesus alone could offer. He instructed the nun, "Mankind will not enjoy peace until it turns with confidence to My Mercy."

On the Eve of the Second World War

Faustina received this message on the eve of war—this time, a far worse global conflict, World War II—as a vast sea of horror approached Europe's shore. The message to the Polish nun could not have been more prophetic of what the world would need. Mercifully, she did not live to see it. With God's grace, she was spared the Holocaust to come, though so many who lived in Poland—a nation that lost more people as a percentage of its population in the war than any other country, including the largest number of Jews of any nation—did not. Sr. Faustina was called to her eternal home on October 5, 1938. Like Christ, she was only thirty-three years old. Like her Savior, she died a suffering, painful death, albeit even longer in duration, at the hands of a brutal case of tuberculosis. She was taken a year before Hitler and Stalin took turns devouring her beloved homeland and started World War II.

What had launched those mutual invasions of Poland from west and east in September 1939 was the agreement known as the Hitler–Stalin Pact, signed in Moscow on August 23–24, 1939. Christ had told Faustina that the world would need an ocean of mercy in the period ahead. What Hitler and Stalin consummated now ensured it.

That war launched the Holocaust. And yet, it is fascinating to see how Faustina, a year earlier, offered herself and her own suffering as a holocaust to God for the sins of the world. To that end, one of her most intriguing messages came on April 24, 1938. It would be the final April 24 message that Faustina would experience in this world, going on to be with her Lord six months later, on October 5, 1938. It was a Sunday, the Lord's Day. Moreover, it was the first Sunday after Easter Sunday—fittingly, the day that each year was to be declared the feast day of Divine Mercy.

What Faustina recorded in her diary that day seems especially appropriate given her message of mercy for the world. The revelations she received on April 24, 1938, beautifully encapsulate the fullness of what she was chosen to share. Here is what she wrote:

> On Sunday [April 24, 1938], the sister who had charge of the sick said to me, "Well, Sister, the priest will bring you the Lord Jesus today." I answered, "Good," and he brought Him. After some time, I received permission to leave my bed. So I went to Holy Mass and to spend time with the Lord, regularly.
>
> After the first examination, the doctor [Silberg] found that my condition was grave. "We suspect, Sister, that you do have the illness about which you spoke to me, but Almighty God can do all things."
>
> When I entered my room, I steeped myself in prayer of thanksgiving for everything the Lord had been sending me throughout my whole life, surrendering myself totally to His most holy will. A deep joy and peace flooded my soul. I felt a peace so great that, if death had come at that moment, I would not have said to it, "Wait, for I still have some matters to attend to." No, I would have welcomed it with joy, because I am ready for the meeting with the Lord, not only today, but ever since

the moment when I placed my complete trust in the Divine Mercy, resigning myself totally to His most holy will, full of mercy and compassion. I know what I am of myself. . .

Low Sunday. Today, I again offered myself to the Lord as a holocaust for sinners. My Jesus, if the end of my life is already approaching, I beg You most humbly, accept my death in union with You as a holocaust which I offer You today, while I still have full possession of my faculties and a fully conscious will, and this for a threefold purpose. (*Diary*, 1678–80)

The Polish nun offered herself as a holocaust, a living, suffering sacrifice for the sins of the world. Here was the threefold purpose that she offered to her Lord Jesus:

Firstly: that the work of Your mercy may spread throughout the whole world and that the Feast of The Divine Mercy may be solemnly promulgated and celebrated.

Secondly: that sinners, especially dying sinners, may have recourse to Your mercy and experience the unspeakable effects of this mercy.

Thirdly: that all the work of Your mercy may be realized according to Your wishes, and for a certain person who is in charge of this work. . .

Accept, most merciful Jesus, this, my inadequate sacrifice, which I offer to You today before heaven and earth. May Your Most Sacred Heart, so full of mercy, complete what is lacking in my offering, and offer it to Your Father for the conversion of sinners. I thirst after souls, O Christ.

According to Faustina's diary entry, at that very moment, "the light of God penetrated my being, and I felt that I was God's exclusive property." She experienced "the greatest spiritual freedom, of which I had had no previous idea." Simultaneously, she saw "the glory of The Divine Mercy and an infinite multitude of souls who were praising His goodness." She said that her soul was "completely drowned in God," and she heard these words of Jesus: "You are My well-beloved daughter."

There is much to take from this passage, which was the only entry made in her diary that week (she would not write again until May 1). Consider that Faustina began with the Eucharist that April 24. She had to get permission to leave her bed to attend Mass. Her condition had deteriorated that badly. Those familiar with her life know how much the Polish nun suffered. She was often in pain and agony and rarely felt well. Thus, for her to muster the strength to rise at this time, approaching her final months, was a sign of how much she endeavored to attend Mass.

Of course, Faustina was able to spend time with her Lord without going to Mass, by receiving the Blessed Sacrament in her bed or, in her case, by the totally unique visitations she so profoundly received. Nonetheless, going to Mass was special. It was a high point. She pulled herself there, even as her physician declared her condition "grave." It indeed was.

Did she lament this state? Did she cry aloud, bitterly asking God why He allowed bad things to happen to good people? Did she doubt God's existence? Quite the contrary, Faustina fully accepted her condition with joy and thanksgiving, surrendering herself totally to God's will. As she did, a "deep joy and peace" flooded her soul. The sense of peace was so overwhelming that she welcomed death at any moment. After all, ever since this secretary of mercy (as Jesus called her) had placed her complete trust in the Divine Mercy, she had been fully resigned to His most holy will.

The Polish nun welcomed death not merely for herself but as a sacrificial offering, a "holocaust" for others, a year before Hitler's Holocaust began killing so many beloved Jewish friends in Poland. She did so, while still in full possession of her faculties and conscious will, for a threefold purpose: first, to spread throughout the world the idea of a feast of Divine Mercy; second, so that sinners, especially those dying, could have recourse to that mercy; and third, so that the work of Christ's mercy could be realized. All of this, in turn, was offered to God the Father for the conversion of sinners. And at that point, she felt the literal rays of light of the Divine Mercy image—the rays that infused the ocean of mercy that the world would now need.

Faustina and Caterina—and Her Stigmata

It is fascinating to consider some of the very similar visions and revelations that St. Maria Faustina Kowalska seemed to share with another
suffering servant and stigmatist, St. Catherine of Siena, who lived six
centuries before the nun from Poland. We can start with Faustina receiving the stigmata. For Faustina, like Catherine, it was hidden stigmata.

That moment occurred after the Polish nun took her temporary
vows on April 30, 1928. She was twenty-two years old. She later, in
November 1936, detailed the moment in her diary:

> When I experienced these sufferings for the first time, it was
> like this: after the annual vows,[397] on a certain day, during
> prayer, I saw a great brilliance and, issuing from the brilliance,
> rays which completely enveloped me. Then suddenly, I felt a
> terrible pain in my hands, my feet and my side and the thorns
> of the crown of thorns. I experienced these sufferings during
> Holy Mass on Friday, but this was only for a brief moment.
> This was repeated for several Fridays, and later on I did not
> experience any sufferings up to the present time; that is, until
> the end of September of this year.[398]

That present time was September 1936. Thus, Faustina received
the stigmata—on her hands, feet, side, and head—first during a Holy
Friday Mass during the Easter season of 1928, for several Fridays. It
stopped after that, not returning again for another eight years, until
September 1936. When it did return, it was not a period of optimal
health for the Polish nun.

In the next line, Faustina notes in passing that she had tuberculosis during this time. She long suffered from the terribly debilitating
effects of the disease. One can scarcely imagine the pain she must have
endured when receiving the sting of stigmata atop the heaving bloody
coughs of tuberculosis. This was serious trauma. She continued:

> In the course of the present illness [tuberculosis], during Holy
> Mass one Friday, I felt myself pierced by the same sufferings,
> and this has been repeated on ever[y] Friday and sometimes
> when I meet a soul that is not in the state of grace. Although

this is infrequent, and the suffering lasts a very short time, still it is terrible, and I would not be able to bear it without a special grace from God. There is no outward indication of these sufferings. What will come later, I do not know. All this, for the sake of souls.[399]

Once again, when the stigmata returned, as when they first appeared in the spring of 1928, they came on a Friday during Mass and were repeated for several Fridays, though apparently not permanent, and again not visible. It is interesting, too, that Faustina would feel these pangs sometimes when encountering a soul not in a state of grace. She bore the pain of the sins of others.

She wrote about this moment again on another occasion. Writing on September 25, 1936, she stated, "I suffer great pain in my hands, feet and side, the places where Jesus' body was pierced. I experience these pains particularly when I meet with a soul who is not in a state of grace" (*Diary*, 705). Like Catherine of Siena, Faustina described the moment as coming to her during prayer, with "rays" of "great light" piercing her. And like Catherine, the wounds were concealed from others.

Other striking similarities between Faustina and Catherine include their similar states of ecstasy, their acute physical sufferings, their communications with Jesus and guardian angels,[400] their mutual ability to read human hearts and sense sin in others, their mutual spiritual betrothal (*Diary*, 912), and how both spoke of the Lord as (in the words of Faustina) "a kind of fire in my heart" (*Diary*, 432). It is also notable that both women wrote books in the final years of their lives, Catherine's *Dialogue* and Faustina's *Diary*, that remain absorbing accounts of their discussions with the God of the universe. In each of these written accounts, the Lord refers to the two young women as "My daughter."

Fittingly, among the most striking parallels between the two women is the ocean-like abundance of mercy they described. They spoke of how God desired His creatures to enter into that mercy. The Polish nun quoted the Lord, who ordered her, "Write: before I come as a just Judge, I first open wide the door of My mercy. *He who refuses to pass through the door of My mercy must pass through the door of My justice*"

(*Diary*, 1146). She quoted the Lord, "While there is yet time, let them have recourse to the fountain of my mercy" (*Diary*, 848).

Fr. Antonio Buoncristiani, the metropolitan archbishop of Siena, speaking about Pope Francis declaring a jubilee year of mercy (from December 8, 2015, through November 20, 2016), notes that St. Catherine of Siena in her letters and *Dialogue* continually spoke of mercy,[401] which Fr. Buoncristiani described in her case as "an immense ocean [of mercy] that dilutes everything."[402] Catherine said that God was above all just: He was mercy.

It is quite striking that Catherine in her *Dialogue* explicitly relates God speaking of His "abundance of mercy" and even His "doors of mercy."[403] Of course, six centuries later, these exact same expressions became signature phrases of Faustina. In our day, Pope Francis, by way of his bishops around the world, would institute literal "doors of mercy" in keeping with Christ's request to Faustina. Each diocese, everywhere across the globe during the Jubilee Year of Mercy, had a physical, designated Door of Mercy at a church somewhere in its diocese. In his official bull of indiction, *Misericordiae vultus*, Pope Francis declared that when these doors were opened at the beginning of the year, "the Holy Door will become a Door of Mercy through which anyone who enters will experience the love of God who consoles, pardons, and instils hope."[404]

Though both Faustina and Catherine spoke of this Door of Mercy, Faustina's words are particularly poignant because they were given as a precursor to God's warnings on the last days (more on that below).

Finally, in yet another similarity to St. Catherina of Siena, the Lord Jesus called Faustina to heaven, after a period likewise of great physical turmoil, at the same age: thirty-three. Like Catherine, and like Jesus Christ their Savior, Faustina died at age thirty-three.

St. Thomas Aquinas said that Christ's death age is the perfect age, and that with our own resurrections in heaven, if we are blessed to get there, we will all, like Christ at His death, be of that age. Aquinas cited Ephesians 4:13: "Until we all meet . . . unto a perfect man, unto the measure of the age of the fulness of Christ." Said Thomas, "Now Christ rose again of youthful age, which begins about the age of 30, as Augustine says

(*De Civ. Dei* xxii). Therefore others will rise again of a youthful age."[405]
For Faustina and Catherine, like Jesus, that was the age of thirty-three.

Visions of Hell

Such was the message of mercy, for then, for now. But then there were
other messages from St. Maria Faustina Kowalska, including some grim
ones, which Mercy Himself hopes to spare us of. There were warnings of hell.

Those visions seen by Faustina bore a striking resemblance to the
Fatima image of hell. The apparitions at Fatima took place in Faustina's
lifetime, namely, in 1917, when the Polish girl was twelve years old. At
that time, she was far from life in a convent or the life of a mystic. And
yet, her mystical vision of hell that later came in the convent carried
an eerie echo of what the three shepherd children—Lucia, Jacinta, and
Francisco—witnessed at Fatima.

The time was late October 1936. Faustina was doing an eight-day
retreat that began on October 20. It was one day during this retreat
that she was led by an angel to what she called the "chasms of Hell."
The Polish nun described it in her diary as a place of "great torture"
and "fire that will penetrate the soul without destroying it—a terrible
suffering." This hell was filled with darkness, and, despite that darkness,
"the devils and the souls of the damned see each other and all the evil,
both of others and their own."[406]

"I, Sister Faustina Kowalska, by the order of God, have visited the
Abysses of Hell so that I might tell souls about it and testify to its existence," she wrote in her diary. "The devils were full of hatred for me, but
they had to obey me at the command of God." She also saw, similarly
described by Dante, special sections reserved for specific agonies earned
in this fallen world. "There are caverns and pits of torture where one
form of agony differs from another," she recorded. "There are special tortures destined for particular souls. These are the torments of the senses.
Each soul undergoes terrible and indescribable sufferings related to the
manner in which it has sinned" (*Diary*, 741). Dante called this form of
punishment *contrapasso*, directly linked to the way that the sinner sinned.

According to Faustina, this was merely "a pale shadow of the things I saw. But I noticed one thing: That most of the souls there are those who disbelieved that there is a Hell." Akin to what the Fatima children experienced, she added, "I would have died at the very sight of these tortures if the omnipotence of God had not supported me."

Such had been the reaction of the shepherd children at Fatima when they were granted a vision of hell by the Blessed Mother on July 13, 1917. The vision was horrible, monstrous, terrifying—so much so that as the children were permitted this view, they were divinely infused with a protective grace that enabled them to observe the scene without being so mortified as to perish at the sight.[407]

Lucia later described it as a "sea of fire" filled with "demons and souls in human form, like transparent embers, all blackened or burnished bronze, floating about in the conflagration, now raised into the air by the flames that issued from within themselves together with great clouds of smoke . . . amid shrieks and groans of pain and despair, which horrified us." She said the demons could be distinguished by their "terrifying and repellent likeness to frightful and unknown animals, black and transparent like burning coals." (Recall that Sr. Elena Aiello also described "the souls. . . falling into Hell" as "looking like transparent embers.")

It was after this vision that the Lady taught a special prayer to the shepherd children, which we now know as the "Fatima Prayer" that ends each decade of the Rosary: "O my Jesus, forgive us our sins, save us from the fires of hell, lead all souls to heaven, especially those in most need of Thy mercy."

That redemptive mission of mercy was precisely the one charged to Sr. Maria Faustina Kowalska, who became Jesus's specially appointed apostle of mercy, herald of a veritable ocean of mercy, to save sinners from the fires of hell. Like the Fatima children nineteen years earlier, this vision was given to her less for her benefit than as a warning to larger humanity by order of God.

Frightening as this message might be, like Fatima, it provides a positive urgency to mercy. Through these visions and their messengers, the Divine is giving His children yet another chance. We are being warned to get ourselves in order, to stop sinning, and to seek conversion and redemption before it is too late.

"You Will Prepare the World for My Final Coming"

There were still more frightening visions and warnings from Sr. Maria Faustina Kowalska. They apply not to what the dead might receive in the afterlife but to what the living might experience here and now in our times—both in the twentieth-century past and perhaps the twenty-first century to come.

In her day, Faustina received dire communications regarding Poland, Europe, and Russia, all of which were approaching war. This was a war that would break out in her native Poland, of all places, in September 1939, eleven months after her death. It would come by way of a pact between two tyrants, Nazi Germany's Adolf Hitler and Bolshevik Russia's Joseph Stalin. They mutually invaded Poland in September 1939, hence launching World War II, the deadliest conflict in history. The words in Faustina's diary seem to forecast the impending trouble to come.

Regarding Russia, Jesus told her on December 16, 1936, "I cannot suffer that country any longer" (*Diary*, 818). This was the height of the crimes of Bolshevik Russia when Stalin was carrying out his purges and much worse. Ukraine, at that point, was enduring a forced famine imposed by Communists at the Kremlin in Moscow. That famine, known as Holodomor, saw five to ten million Ukrainians starve to death in the mid-1930s. The crimes against humanity carried out by the Bolsheviks were too vast to count. They included a war against the family, marriage, and the unborn. Bolshevik Russia was seeing levels of abortion theretofore unseen in human history.[408] And few crimes could equal the savage war on religion that the Marxist-Leninists orchestrated.[409] Indeed, it is hard to imagine the Lord suffering the country of Russia much longer.

Poland, unfortunately, had no choice but to suffer Russia much longer because it shared a border with the Soviet Union. The Nazis were defeated by May 1945, meaning they were henceforth expelled from Poland, but the Soviets remained in Poland through 1989. The martyred nation of Poland was occupied first by fascists and then much longer by Communists.

But Poland would be mightily blessed through this suffering. This period of trauma produced not only a saint like Faustina, who survived World War I but was spared living through World War II and the Cold War, but another saint, Karol Wojtyla (Pope St. John Paul II), who was born after World War I but experienced all the ordeals of World War II and the Cold War. He was born in May 1920 and would serve as pope from 1978 to 2005 in one of the most impactful papacies in history.

To that end, there is a prophecy from Faustina that relates to Poland but might also relate directly to the person of Pope St. John Paul II and the final coming of Christ. In one of her final messages from Jesus, she was told, "I bear a special love for Poland, and if she will be obedient to My will, I shall exalt her in might and holiness. From her will come forth the spark that will prepare the world for My final coming" (*Diary*, 1732).

Some interpret that spark to have been Karol Wojtyla himself, who, as Pope John Paul II, would prepare the world via his actions at the start of the new millennium with Faustina and Jesus's message of Divine Mercy. He would set in course—perhaps—the process of the full unfolding of the revelation. That unfolding is yet to come, very possibly today, in our times in the twenty-first century. Yes, that is a thought that gives serious pause.

Poland aside, here are further key messages from the Lord Jesus to Faustina relating to the end times. Jesus told the Polish nun flatly in May 1935 that she would be the vessel to prepare the world for His second coming. Here are His unmistakable exact words to Faustina: "You will prepare the world for My final coming" (*Diary*, 429). The messages in her diary relate to that mission of preparation.

Jesus went so far as to describe to Faustina a physical sign that the world could see in the form of a literal great darkness. He told her in August 1934, "Write this: before I come as the Just Judge, I am coming first as the King of Mercy. Before the day of justice arrives, there will be given to people a sign in the heavens of this sort: All light in the heavens will be extinguished, and there will be great darkness over the whole earth. Then the Sign of the Cross will be seen in the sky, and from the openings where the hands and the feet of the Savior were nailed will come forth great lights which will light up the earth for a period of time. This will take place shortly before the last day" (*Diary*, 83).

That is a powerful image. Read it again. Think about it. A period of darkness overwhelming the earth, interrupted only—and grandly—by a giant Sign of the Cross in the sky, providing the only light to a darkened world through the spots that bore the wounds of the Crucified One. We will give more attention to this in the concluding chapter of this book, underscoring related visions by other stigmatists.

As added attestation from the heavens, the Blessed Mother told Faustina this as well, on behalf of her beloved Son. She told the nun on March 25, 1936, "You have to speak to the world about His great mercy and prepare the world for the Second Coming of Him who will come, not as a merciful Savior, but as a Just Judge. Oh, how terrible is that day! Determined is the day of justice, the day of divine wrath. The angels tremble before it. Speak to souls about this great mercy. . . . Fear nothing" (*Diary*, 635—also see section 625 for another such message from Mary).

That end times message from the Blessed Mother in March 1936 was resumed by her Divine Son again at the end of the year. Faustina said that Jesus told her in December 1936, "Speak to the world about My mercy; let all mankind recognize My unfathomable mercy. It is a sign for the end times; after it will come the day of justice" (*Diary*, 848).

The message continued. Jesus said to Faustina on February 17, 1937, "Secretary of My mercy, write, tell souls about this great mercy of Mine, because the awful day, the day of My justice, is near" (*Diary*, 965).

And Jesus added in June 1937, "I am prolonging the time of mercy for the sake of sinners. But woe to them if they do not recognize this time of My visitation. My daughter, secretary of My mercy, your duty is not only to write about and proclaim My mercy, but also to beg for this grace for them, so that they too may glorify My mercy" (*Diary*, 1160). In another communication that same month of June 1937,

Jesus told her, "Write: before I come as a just Judge, I first open wide the door of My mercy" (*Diary*, 1146).

And then this dispatch to Faustina in February 1938: "In the Old Covenant I sent prophets wielding thunderbolts to My people. Today I am sending you with My mercy to the people of the whole world. I do not want to punish aching mankind, but I desire to heal it, pressing it to My Merciful Heart. . . . Before the Day of Justice I am sending the Day of Mercy" (*Diary*, 1588).

Are We Living Those Times?

Where does this bring us now? Well, truly, only God knows. But those of us who have studied not only Faustina but the twentieth century, the Cold War, communism, and Russia would be badly remiss not to offer a few observations.

The invasion of Ukraine by Putin's Russia, launched in February 2022, has been limited largely to Ukraine—but not totally. Western nations have poured in huge amounts of cash and military material to Ukraine to counter Russia. This has had the effect of halting Russia, killing countless tens of thousands of Russians boys and infuriating Vladmir Putin, who has not backed off and apparently will not be denied. If Poland gets directly drawn into the conflict with its own soldiers, as well as other NATO member nations, then so could NATO as a whole and the United States. Article 5 of the NATO charter declares that an attack against one NATO nation is deemed an attack against all. If NATO members like Poland, not to mention the Baltic states, are attacked by Russia, then the other NATO nations, by formal treaty, will go to war with Russia.

If that happens, a world war could be a very real possibility. Could this Polish nun's messages be timelier? Russia has invaded Ukraine, Poland's largest neighbor, with the possibility of igniting World War III. America and the entirety of the West is a vast cultural-moral disaster that grows more insidious day by day. Family and faith are under assault. The Western culture of Christendom is smoldering if not toast. The whole world is a wreck. The Church is a mess. If ever Faustina's warnings seemed to apply to the current world, they would seem to right now. And if ever the world seemed most in need of Divine Mercy, it is right now.

Canonization of Faustina

The extraordinary revelations given to Faustina a hundred years ago took time to make their way to the wider world beyond her cloistered cell. But precisely that would happen once she was canonized by Pope St. John Paul II in April 2000 as the first saint of the new millennium.

The Polish pope and Polish nun would be forever linked through this message of Divine Mercy. One particularly touching personal connection came with the pontiff's final minutes on earth. After suffering terribly during his final weeks in this world, as had Faustina, John Paul II died on April 2, 2005, which happened to be the vigil and eve of Divine Mercy Sunday, the special day he had instituted in 2000 at the canonization Mass of a little-known Polish nun named Sr. Maria Faustina Kowalska. The Mass for Divine Mercy was celebrated in the pope's room the evening he died.

In all, this Polish nun could not have been more prophetic in foreseeing what the world would need. And she did not live to see it. In God's mercy, she was spared the Holocaust to come. After offering herself as a holocaust, Sr. Faustina was called home by her Creator on October 5, 1938.

Jesus Christ had told Faustina that the world would need an ocean of mercy in the period ahead, and no other individual personally came to know and experience that quite like John Paul II, who in April 2000 sainted his native sister. The Polish pontiff there began, in homage to Faustina and her Lord's divine message, an international Divine Mercy Sunday.

Following the path and call of Faustina's revelation, the pope's teaching for this special day was that the blood and water that flowed from the pierced side of the crucified Christ was a holy fountain of mercy for the world, gushing open in atonement for humanity's sins, an eternal source of grace in the face of a rush of evil in the world. It was through the wounds of Christ, His pierced side and ruptured heart, that reparation was made continually for the whole world.

That message from a hidden Polish nun—so private that even the open wounds of her stigmata were hidden from us—is now gushing open for the world to heed. It is as open as the Lord's vast ocean of mercy available to us all.

CHAPTER 9

STIGMATISTS AMONG US

In the many centuries since the time of St. Francis of Assisi, there seems to have been a nearly unbroken, consistently running period of stigmatists living among us. And that is a long time. As noted at the start of this book, there have been an estimated four to five hundred stigmatists in total, with that number still growing to this day.

Let us take account of some of the stigmatists focused on in this book. Francis was born in the twelfth century and died in the thirteenth century and was followed by three well-known stigmatists born in the fourteenth century: Sts. Catherine of Siena, Rita of Cascia, and Frances of Rome. All three of those women became major figures in the Church. Then, to cite just a few examples, came the likes of Bl. Lucy of Narni, born in the fifteenth century, St. Catherine de Ricci, born in the sixteenth century, St. Veronica Giuliani, born in the seventeenth century, Bl. Anna Maria Taigi and Bl. Anne Catherine Emmerich, both born in the eighteenth century, followed by four prominent stigmatists born in the nineteenth century: St. Gemma Galgani, St. Padre Pio, Bl. Elena Aiello, and Therese Neumann (profiled in the next section). Several stigmatists profiled in this book—Galgani, Pio, Aiello, and Faustina—died in the twentieth century. And of course, these names are far from a complete sample of the various men and women reported to have borne the wounds of Christ.

This surely begs the question, namely, if there have been stigmatists in every century since at least Francis, born in Assisi way back in the 1180s, and with a number of high-profile cases over the last century or so—with accompanying photographs—then surely there are stigmatists among us today. Surely so. Well, then, who are they? Where are they?

There are indeed reported cases, and many are very controversial. Many are questioned, disputed, and rejected—as often happens in their own time. Oftentimes, unfortunately, the verdict of authenticity by the experts comes only years after the death of the subject. The Church has not taken a stand on most of the current purported cases. That will prompt many to question, dispute, and reject them, especially the cases raised by websites that seem sensational and on the fringe. I, too, tend toward healthy skepticism, at least as a starting point.

But again, recall that in their day, many of the heralded stigmatists in this book were questioned, disputed, and rejected. Padre Pio certainly was. He often faced doubters, including priests, bishops, and cardinals. And yet now, Pio is a saint, canonized in this century. St. Faustina's writings were debated for several decades after her death, prior to the intervention of Pope St. John Paul II. The likes of Anne Catherine Emmerich and Therese Neumann are still doubted and, in the latter's case, far from being canonized. Their cases ultimately could be rejected by the Catholic Church.

Of the alleged cases of stigmatists today, I cannot affirm what the Church has not affirmed. It is a risk to even share their names here in this book, anywhere. Nonetheless, it would also seem a great slight, highly shortsighted, not to consider the likelihood that surely our time should be no exception to some nine centuries of consistent stigmatists. Why would it be?

Thus, accepting the risk of naming a few names, I will list, in this chapter, just a few of those cases that have been reported, with the caveat to readers that we do not know if these claimed cases of stigmata are reliable. Importantly, many of them, like the approved stigmatic saints in this book, have laid claim to some mighty revelations, prophecies, and warnings. I will note those, too, again with the same caveat.

I shall keep these cases limited here to this chapter. In the final chapter that follows, which is focused on the warnings of stigmatists, I will focus primarily on figures examined in this book's individual chapters—that is, the Church-approved cases of individuals like Sts. Catherine of Siena, Elena Aiello, and Faustina.

Therese Neumann

Before looking at reported current cases in the twenty-first century, let's step back, not too far back, into the twentieth century, which witnessed an extraordinary case. One of the most famous examples of a recently reported stigmatist is Therese Neumann, who was born in 1898 and died in 1962. She is not covered with a full chapter in this book mainly because she has not reached the level of a Church-approved blessed or saint, though the process for her beatification, which has been long demanded by many, was formally opened in 2005.[410]

Therese was born on Good Friday, April 8, 1898, in the small village of Konnersreuth in northeastern Bavaria, Germany. She was the oldest of ten children. The primary biography of Therese Neumann was written by a German-born American named Adalbert Albert Vogl, who first met her as a friend of the family in 1927. He would spend more time with Therese and her family documenting her story and serving as her advocate than probably any other individual. He spent at least fifty years documenting her case and became "full[y] convinced" that her stigmata, visions, and more were a supernatural "gift from God." Like St. Thomas with Jesus—to whom Therese would humbly never dare compare herself—Vogl had the great benefit of seeing and touching the wounds himself.[411]

Vogl's book, *Therese Neumann: Mystic and Stigmatist, 1898–1962*, was published in 1987 by TAN Books. That book was an updated and expanded edition of his *The Life and Death of Therese Neumann, Mystic and Stigmatist*, published in 1978 by Vantage Press. The back cover of Vogl's 1987 book describes his subject as "perhaps the most visible stigmatist in the history of the Church," noting that countless people saw Therese briefly in her home or witnessed her ecstasies and suffering.

Vogl estimates that over the course of thirty-six years, Neumann "experienced Passion ecstasies some 725 times."[412]

So much of what this German mystic experienced flatly defied the laws of nature. She ate nothing and barely slept. Incredibly, for forty years, from 1922 until her death in 1962, Therese Neumann was nourished by nothing but the Eucharist. Vogl writes that after the spring of 1922, "it is an established fact that after that time she did not take any solid food in any way, shape or form for the rest of her life; thus her total abstinence lasted 40 years." And yet, she never ceased to steadily gain weight, with Vogl documenting that consistent gain across the decades, from 121 pounds in July 1927, for instance, ultimately up to 215 pounds in 1953. As for sleep, "she required little or no sleep," at best "known to relax for about thirty minutes on some days, but not every day."[413]

As for the Passion-like sufferings, Therese underwent those on Fridays, starting with her first episode on the first Friday of Lent, March 5, 1926. The bleeding ultimately would come from wounds in her hands, feet, head, side, shoulders, back, and even a "heart wound." The head wounds came from what Vogl described as a "Crowning of Thorns," specifically, nine wounds on her head.[414] Vogl's book includes a lengthy photo gallery with pictures both black-and-white and in color. Those photos include the marks on the back of Therese's hands and—most striking and even halting—bleeding that looks like it is coming from her eyes.[415]

One might assume that the blood around the eyes was emanating from her forehead and running down past and below her eyes.[416] However, according to Fr. Ulrich Veh, the vice postulator for the Neumann's cause for beatification, "She had cried tears of blood, just like Jesus at Gethsemane." Yes, that was blood coming from her eyes.[417] According to stigmatist expert Michael Freze, who studied Therese Neumann and interviewed Fr. Veh, she bled profusely from her eyes during her ecstatic vision of Christ shedding tears in the Garden of Gethsemane.[418]

In all, Vogl says that Therese's varied stigmatic wounds never disappeared, and "they were still imprinted on her body at the time of her death." He describes the wounds as "brownish-red in color, covered by a fresh scab, slightly raised from the rest of the skin." He personally attested, "I have touched the hand wounds on many occasions, and I can say honestly that the slightest scratch would have made them bleed." He said that when doctors first attempted to treat the wounds with the "best-known medicine and salves . . . the result was catastrophic. Blood and pus started to ooze through the bandages." Thus, "to prevent blood poisoning the doctors urged their removal."[419]

As an expert on Therese Neumann, Vogl noted that he had been repeatedly asked how many wounds she carried. He estimated, admittedly as a nonphysician and not an official examiner, "in the neighborhood of 45: wounds on the feet—two; wounds on the hands—two; heart wound—one; shoulder wounds and wounds from the Carrying of the Cross—about 30. Then, too, Therese had nine distinct head wounds from the Crowning of Thorns. All together one can easily come up with the number of 45 plus." And, of course, in all, the wounds put her in constant pain.[420]

Very interesting about Therese's mystical experiences and stigmata is what she had to say about the marks of Christ as related to St. Francis and St. Paul. Like Anne Catherine Emmerich, another German female stigmatist, Therese had visions of past events. These included the birth of Christ in Bethlehem, the murder of the Holy Innocents, the presentation of the Child Jesus in the Temple, Jesus multiplying the fishes, Jesus appearing to St. Thomas and the other apostles after the Resurrection, the death and assumption of the Blessed Virgin, the finding of the True Cross by St. Helena, Sts. Peter and Paul in prison, the death of St. Francis de Sales, the martyrdoms of Sts. Cecilia and Barbara, and much more.[421] As to Sts. Francis and Paul, in one of Therese's visions—again very much like Anne Catherine Emmerich—she claimed to have watched St. Francis receive the stigmata. This would have made Therese, along with Anne Catherine Emmerich, one of history's only witnesses to that extraordinary event, other than Francis's close companion Br. Leo. In fact, Therese watched the stigmatization from a heavenly provided vantage, closer than even Br. Leo could get. She had that particular vision during an ecstasy on the feast day of the stigmatization of St. Francis, which occurs every September 17.[422]

Therese's description of what happened that day in the thirteenth century matches the facts that we know from St. Francis's biographers. She named the mountain where the stigmatization occurred as Mt. Alverna, which she pronounced as "Alvernoo." She said that she had seen above Francis (in Vogl's words) "a cherub, a beautifully illuminated young man with very large wings," which seemed very similar to the figure that Francis and Br. Leo described, "above whom the Savior stood, in much greater illumination." While this was going on, Therese saw Francis kneeling reverently before the Lord.[423]

After Therese related this vision to Fr. Josef Naber, her spiritual director, the priest asked her who was the world's first stigmatic after Jesus Christ ascended into heaven. According to Vogl, "She did not hesitate one moment, and named 'St. Paul.'" That answer seemed to throw off Vogl and others who were present, until they consulted the Scriptures and learned of Paul's statement in Galatians about bearing the marks of Christ on his own flesh.[424]

Here we have in Therese Neumann a most unusual stigmatist with a unique connection to the first two stigmatists, Sts. Paul and Francis. Such was just one of so many spiritually remarkable things about this German woman.

Therese Neumann died on September 18, 1962. She was sixty-four years old. The woman lived an incredible life—one that many believe was a saintly life.

The Catholic Church had begun investigating Therese Neumann very early on, within months of the quickly circulating reports of her stigmata. Under the order of the archbishop of Regensburg, the first investigation began in July 1927. This was followed by decades of subsequent official investigations, which particularly picked up speed upon her death in 1962 and then continued through the 1970s and 1980s and on. Witnesses and friends clamored for her beatification. The start of that process would take some time, frustrating many of her contemporaries.[425]

Ultimately, the beatification process for Therese Neumann was officially opened on February 13, 2005, by Regensburg bishop Gerhard Mueller—the future cardinal and prefect for the Congregation for the Doctrine of the Faith. Thus, Therese Neumann is currently designated an official "servant of God" by the Catholic Church. Many consider her a modern saint, but her Church has not—at least not yet—reached that conclusion.

Stigmatists of the Twenty-First Century

Therese Neumann's death came in the same decade that saw the deaths of stigmatists Elena Aiello and Padre Pio, the latter of whom was far more widely known, a veritable giant of the faith, known around the globe as the priest with the stigmata. Therese, Elena, and Pio certainly count as recent stigmatists, attested to by eyewitnesses, examiners, and photographic evidence alike.

There were other stigmatists still later in the twentieth century, such as Marthe Robin, the French mystic and stigmatist born in March 1902 and who died in February 1981. At one point in her late twenties, Robin suffered a sudden permanent paralysis in her legs, atop years of previous significant suffering already, and remained bedridden for the remainder of her life—that is, for over fifty years. During her time in bed, Robin rarely slept or ate, being sustained only by the Eucharist—to repeat, for over fifty years. She also had visions, visitations, and apparitions and dealt with frequent attacks from the devil, including physical assaults. The devil was enraged by her sacrificial suffering for the sins of others.

A contemporary of Marthe Robin was Bl. Alexandrina da Costa (1904–55). Born in Balazar, Portugal, she likewise claimed visions and visitations, including from Jesus Christ. In September 1934, da Costa said that Christ asked her if she was prepared to join Him in His suffering on the Cross. She consented and purportedly received hidden stigmata. During her final thirteen years of life, she ate nothing but the Eucharist. She died on October 13, 1955, the anniversary of the day that the sun danced at Fatima in her native country of Portugal.

Likewise, born in this period was Marie Rose Ferron. She was born on May 24, 1902, in Quebec, Canada, the tenth child of a devout Catholic family. At age four, she and her family moved to Fall River, Massachusetts. She had her first vision of Jesus shortly thereafter. She soon became a suffering soul, stricken by a form of muscular paralysis at age thirteen. That and other health problems put Marie Rose in constant pain, and she became permanently bedridden. In 1925, her family relocated to Woonsocket, Rhode Island. The next year, she received the stigmata for the first time. Known as the "Little Rose," she was examined by many physicians, who were dumbfounded by her marks, particularly on her forehead, which were suggestive of some type of crown of thorns. Marie Rose died on May 11, 1936, at age thirty-three—the same age as Christ at His death.

Another remarkable modern stigmatist was Adrienne von Speyr (1902–67), the Swiss mystic known for particularly distinctive visions. Adding credibility to von Speyr's case was her family's academic and medical background and pedigree, and, more so, her own. She was a medical doctor and Catholic convert who became somewhat of a theologian in her own right, authoring over sixty books on spirituality and theology. Moreover, the prominent theologian and priest Hans Urs von Balthasar became a spiritual director and mentor to her and also a biographer of her. Von Balthasar was von Speyr's confessor for twenty-seven years.

Von Speyr left behind an extraordinary compendium of visions of various historical figures. She had an especially unusual charism, gifted with the ability to look back in time and see both saints and non-saints as they prayed. She claimed to be able to watch them and receive an understanding of their attitude toward God. Von Speyr dictated what she saw to von Balthasar. She observed individuals as diverse as St. Augustine and Wolfgang Amadeus Mozart, Sts. Thomas Aquinas and Joan of Arc, St. Teresa of Avila and Dante, St. Ignatius of Loyola and Joseph Haydn, Tertullian and Origen, St. Peter and Judas, and many more. "I see her [or his] prayer," von Speyr would typically begin her dictation. Or, in another case (St. Patrick): "His prayer is very close to God."[426] Her descriptions were fascinating and unlike those of any other visionary in the history of the Church.

But what about current-day stigmatists—that is, right now, in the twenty-first century, in our own day? Like with Therese Neumann, these modern cases have not received the Church's beatification or canonization. They are too recent. But that does not mean that they have not borne or are not bearing the wounds of Christ. In most of these cases, the Church has not yet come to a conclusion, and neither (necessarily) should we. Nonetheless, here are some notable reported cases from our own day.

As noted at the start of this book, Deacon Albert Graham, now in his nineties, continues to compile research on stigmatists. In May 2021, he had a list of eighty-nine stigmatists who had lived into and died in the twentieth century, some of which have been noted in this chapter. Here are just a few of Graham's names: Adrienne von Speyr (1902–67), Alexandrina Maria da Costa (1904–55), Antonio Ruffini (1907–99), Josefa Menéndez (1890–1923), Luisa Piccarreta (1865–1947), Marie-Julie Jahenny (1850–1941), Marthe Robin (1902–81), Marie Rose Ferron (1902–36), Sr. Rita Montella (1920–92), Maria Esperanza (1928–2004),[427] and Rhoda Wise (1888–1948), the American mystic from Canton, Ohio, who was a mentor to EWTN foundress Mother Angelica. As for stigmatists currently living or who had lived into the twenty-first century, Deacon Graham, in his 2021 list, had already come up with forty-five of them. Among those of today are Sr. Agnes Katsuko Sasagawa (the Our Lady of Akita seer), Luz de María de Bonilla, and Gisella Cardia, whom Graham (rightly) listed tentatively with a question mark.

I will discuss Sr. Agnes Katsuko Sasagawa at length in the next and final chapter. I shall close this chapter with a few words on Luz de María de Bonilla and Gisella Cardia.

Luz de María de Bonilla

Both Luz de María de Bonilla and Gisella Cardia have been featured prominently and are regularly highlighted with each passing prediction at the popular prophetic website Countdown to the Kingdom,[428] founded by Mark Mallett and run by Mallett, Christine Watkins, and

Daniel O'Connor.[429] Countdown lists a number of seers, including a few with reported stigmata. I will not here go into detail on each of them,[430] but two that stand out for their dramatic predictions, which I cannot, of course, confirm and which the Holy See has not commented on, are Luz de María de Bonilla and Gisella Cardia.

While Bonilla and Cardia do not bear the Church approval of the saints and blesseds profiled at length in this book (nor should we expect them to be, given that they are very current), I do want to at least acknowledge them as two alleged modern stigmatists/seers that have received quite a bit of attention. That attention has included plenty of attacks and controversy. I have also opted to include them because they are known for their claimed prophetic visions.

Luz de María de Bonilla is a reported stigmatist from Costa Rica, who later moved to and resides in Argentina. She is a wife, a mother of eight, and a Third Order Augustinian. Her many claimed mystical experiences began with what she said was a miraculous healing from an illness in 1990, which she said included a visitation from the Blessed Mother. Beginning on March 19, 1992, Bonilla says that the Virgin Mary began speaking to her regularly. Not long thereafter, she also claimed ongoing visits from Jesus and from Michael the Archangel.

Bonilla has typically conveyed one or two messages per week, which she says she is urged to share publicly. They are recorded in audio by two witnesses and transcribed by a nun and then posted on her website, revelacionesmarianas.com, from which they are regularly picked up and posted by Countdown to the Kingdom. She also published messages in a 2017 book, which, on March 19, 2017, had first received the *imprimatur* of Msgr. Juan Abelardo Mata Guevara, SDB, titular bishop of Estelí, Nicaragua. Bonilla is accompanied by her confessor, Fr. José María Fernández Rojas, as well as two other priests. These priests are involved in the process of reviewing the messages before they are posted at Bonilla's website.[431]

The messages by Bonilla are remarkable, if not outright staggering at times. They follow a consistent format regardless of whether they purportedly come from the Blessed Mother, Jesus, or Michael the Archangel. (This no doubt prompts suspicions that Bonilla's pattern is her own rather than of the Blessed Mother, Jesus, or Michael the Archangel.) The messages all tend to be lengthy, considerably longer than messages from other professed seers posted at Countdown to the Kingdom. Bonilla often makes very specific predictions about named countries, diseases, and impending natural disasters, especially about earthquakes ("the earth will shake"), that end up being questioned for lack of proof and are used against her credibility.[432] Many of the messages contain theological observations about the perverse state of humanity and often seem spot on, as if they very well could have supernatural origin.

The best source for examining the vast volume of Bonilla's predictions is Countdown to the Kingdom, which posts them all in an archive under her name.[433] Readers who are interested can go there. There are so many messages, including many that are severe and alarming, that I cannot give a sufficient sample here. Here are just a few examples, the first conveying a more theological observation and others relating to Bonilla's common warning about coming disasters and end times.

On April 2, 2021, which was Good Friday, Bonilla related this alleged message from the Blessed Mother:

> At this moment great confusion is being generated; human beings do not know what the Truth is, they do not know which way to go, because they do not know my Son. They have devoted themselves to living half-heartedly, without going deeper, without reasoning. . . . Sadly, a great majority are only Christians by tradition. This scourges my Son, crowning Him with thorns because of my children's lack of knowledge regarding Divine Work and Action. That is why my Son's People are being led like docile lambs facing any event whatsoever; they have no discernment, they do not go into events in depth. They believe that they love my Son, and yet in a moment everything vanishes like the waves of the sea, because they do not love my Son in spirit and in truth. . . . (Jn 4:23b) they do not look beyond what their eyes can see. . . they do not acquire knowledge. . . . In the end, they are people living in false religiosity. This wounds the Most Sacred Heart of my Son. They do not love Him in spirit and in truth. Being a

lukewarm people, they do not discern and are easily confused, even knowing how evil is proliferating, wanting to encompass all of humanity and to do harm to your bodies.[434]

That is a statement about the vast confusion, great sins, and false religiosity of our times that plainly seems hard to argue with. Many of Bonilla's messages contain observations like this about the wretched state of the modern world. They strike many of us as incontrovertible.

The messages from Luz de María de Bonilla that are perhaps more often viewed with suspicion, though no doubt also often accepted by many, are the forecasts of impending natural and spiritual disasters. To that end, here is another missive that Bonilla claimed to receive from the Blessed Mother, this time on June 10, 2023. Printed here in full, it is a good example of Bonilla's statements in terms of format, pattern, and content:

> Receive the blessing of this Mother who loves you.
>
> I bless you on this very special date; draw near to my Divine Son—live by Him and in Him, in a constant intimacy with souls who are faithful to my Divine Son. My Divine Son lives in each one of His children, guiding them, loving them, helping them, out of love and mercy, and in order to offer them eternal life. Beloved children, each of you is part of the Church that my Divine Son instituted; He dwells in you.
>
> Beloved children, as part of my Divine Son's mystical body, like my Son, you are and will be persecuted. My Divine Son suffers because of this, and as He asked Saul, He asks the persecutors of His children, "Why are you persecuting Me?" (cf. Acts 9,4)
>
> Beloved children, you know well that because of your love of my Divine Son, you are and will be persecuted severely by the enemies of the Church. Without doubting that you have received the Eucharistic Sacrament, truly present in the Holy Mass, nourish yourselves continually with the Eucharists you have received, together with times of Adoration before the Blessed Sacrament. Beloved children, you are my Divine Son's dwelling-place, and as such, be a worthy dwelling-place. Turn

away from worldly things and be creatures of good; love your brothers and sisters. My Divine Son is love, and His children must be love for themselves and for their brothers and sisters.

Very fierce trials are approaching for humanity in general. This is why I call you to be at peace with my Divine Son, so that before the great blackout that will occur, you would be illuminated by the Holy Spirit, not neglecting the duty to prepare yourselves prior to this great trial that will cause the downturn of the climate. Prepare yourselves!

It is painful for my Divine Son to see how war is ever nearer; it is painful for this Mother. . . . It is as if my children were preparing themselves for a party, and this is abominable.

Pray my children, pray for the countries whose rulers want to make the Church disappear and who want their people to disappear.

Pray, my children, pray and protect your health: sudden deaths caused by the wrongdoings of those who rule mankind are increasing.

Pray, my children, pray for my true instruments: they are being persecuted.

Pray, my children, pray for the United States: it will suffer. Pray for Chile, Ecuador, and Colombia.

Be worthy abodes of the presence of my Divine Son in each of you. I am here to intercede before my Divine Son for each of you. I do not separate myself from you: I love you with maternal love. Be faithful to my Divine Son and receive the Real Presence of my Divine Son, present in the Eucharist.

Serious anguish is approaching, and therefore I warn you to prepare yourselves with clothes for cold weather. The sun will be hidden; evil will seize on this fact in order to acquire dominion over a great part of humanity. My Divine Son is love, and being at peace with your brothers and sisters is a great good for the soul.[435]

It is common for Luz de María de Bonilla to issue warnings like this laid out in this pattern. Note the admonitions about enemies of the

Church, about trials for believers, about climate problems, and even of a "great blackout" with the sun being hidden. The latter would seem to be a portent of days of darkness, which will be examined in the final chapter of this book, given the severity of that singular warning from other stigmatists.

At the time of my finishing this book manuscript, Luz de María de Bonilla continues to offer such projections, including forecasts of World War III and statements that we are living in the final days. She relayed this alleged message from Mary, whom she has called "Mary Mother of the End Times,"[436] on August 13, 2023: "Dearly beloved of my Immaculate Heart, the Third World War will occur due to the rebellion, humanity's lack of conversion, and the rejection of my divine Son. Be assured that you are in the final stretch of the fulfillment of my prophecies."[437]

And this was the most recent posted warning from Luz de María de Bonilla, allegedly given by the Blessed Mother on September 25, 2023: "Children of my heart, these are the end times, not the end of the world, and although there are events yet to happen, the events are unfolding slowly, one after another, until the moment arrives when they will happen one on the heels of another, and this will mean great chaos for humanity." Perhaps akin to the warnings of St. Faustina about a great sign appearing in the sky, the message continued, "You are approaching moments when you will see a sign in the sky—not the one prior to the 'Great Warning' but prior to a serious event on earth. An event will occur that will leave human beings astonished." Bonilla, in the next line, delivered a striking prediction, one with unusual specificity: "A religious leader will die by unjust hands, unleashing worldwide astonishment."[438] Luz de María de Bonilla is a reported living stigmatist who often foresees such calamities. Whether her predictions are fulfilled remains to be seen, perhaps by us living today.

Gisella Cardia

Another such alleged seer and stigmatist living today is Gisella Cardia, an Italian woman in her early fifties.[439] Her case acutely demonstrates the highly problematic nature of dealing with purported stigmatists in our own day, as her stigmata and claimed apparitions have generated a firestorm of controversy, attacks, smears, and disinformation and have not been officially confirmed by her diocese, which is not surprising given how recent they are. Her diocese is now investigating.

In March 2016, following a life-changing visit to Medjugorje, Cardia began reporting mystical experiences from her home in the Italian lakeside village of Trevignano Romano, an idyllic community about thirty miles north of Rome.[440] She claimed that a recently purchased statue of the Blessed Mother in her home began shedding tears and blood. Particularly significant, Cardia soon started reporting regular messages from the Blessed Mother, which often came during public prayer gatherings at a hillside field overlooking Lake Bracciano. During several of these gatherings, which soon were thronged by pilgrims and accompanied by curious yet cautious clergy, witnesses claimed to see the sun doing unnatural things, akin to miraculous claims of the sun pulsating at Medjugorje. I have watched these videos, which were posted on online, including on YouTube; at Cardia's website, lareginadelrosario.org; and at the website of Countdown to the Kingdom, which chronicles Gisella's case closer than any other English website. The intriguing videos certainly lack polish. Readers can search these videos for themselves and make their own judgments.

Regarding stigmata or markings, Gisella first showed strange red scratchings of religious phrases on her arms, such as *Amore* ("Love"), *Abbiate fede* ("Have faith"), *Maria santissima* ("most holy Mary"), and *Popolo mio* ("my people"). Photos of these markings are posted on her website and at Countdown to the Kingdom and seem the most disturbing of her alleged phenomena. These marks would not be considered conventional stigmata; they have invited scorn and charges of fakery and even of having demonic origin, though the messages do contain holy phrases, even as they might not look holy to many observers (myself included). Cardia has more recently, however, claimed stigmata on her palms, and those subsequent images are much more traditional of stigmatists, not to mention seem much more impressive.[441]

Indeed, those recent visuals became a game changer, it seems, in the debate over Gisella Cardia. On March 24, 2023, after two years of incessant attacks on Cardia by the media, video was presented of her palms bleeding and allegedly exuding a fragrant oil (said to smell like myrrh) from circular stigmata marks. Filming and commenting on the phenomena were witnesses, including Dr. Rosanna Chifari Negri, a respected neurologist (MD and PhD) from Milan who for over a year monitored Cardia, and Peter Bannister, a British theologian who has closely studied Cardia. This video is on YouTube and should be watched by anyone offering an opinion for or against Cardia.[442] It is quite compelling and does not look phony. Cardia's hands appear to be showing stigmata, blood, and oil and are actively secreting. Dr. Chifari, in the video, narrates to the camera the details and places her professional reputation on the line. That video was accompanied by a second video recorded that same day from Cardia's home, in which Chifari and Bannister speak and read at length from a shared written testimony about what they had been witnessing.[443] (Bannister also speaks at length to the Cardia case in other videos posted online.[444])

It is surely no coincidence that shortly after these eye-opening videos were filmed and posted, Cardia's diocese, on April 14, 2023, announced that it was formally launching an investigation.

Up to that point, Cardia's case had generated a media circus in Italy. She came under fierce attack and a barrage of mockery (including allegations of financial fraud from a decade earlier in her previous line of work). Cardia did not shrink from the assault. She calmly faced the cameras and the salvos. The Italian media has given her situation very serious attention, with major television networks (including the dominant RAI and Mediaset Canale 5) doing news stories and interviews with her and her husband, Gianni. She subjected herself to TV talk-show debates with aggressive skeptics that became a near spectacle. I have watched these interviews and was highly impressed by her gentle demeanor throughout these hostile interrogations as she showed far greater grace than her hysterical, angry critics. In essence, the emergence of video of her claimed stigmata in March 2023 seems a fitting culmination to the sustained trials she underwent in the preceding two or three years.

Alas, in early April 2023, the woman from Trevignano Romano moved to another home in an undisclosed location. Immediately after that, her diocese, the Diocese of Civita Castellana, led by Bishop Marco Salvi, came forth with its April 14, 2023, announcement that it was beginning a formal examination into Cardia and her claims.[445] We should probably interpret her departure at that moment as likely resulting from advice that she avoid public appearances and allow the Church to do its work. No more media circuses. "The time required for a serious examination of the alleged phenomena requires thoughtfulness and various steps that are certainly not related to the speed of information in the media," reads the press release from the diocese. "It will be the concern of the bishop and the entire diocese to give further communications on the matter as soon as possible."[446] The investigation, of course, is crucial. Until Church authorities come to some degree of conclusion, we must be very cautious about the authenticity of Gisella's claimed heavenly messages. And what of those messages?

As with Luz de María de Bonilla, those messages from Gisella Cardia often have been quite dire. Given the lack of official approval by the Church, it would not be advisable here to lay out a long presentation of her numerous dramatic messages, but I will offer a sample for readers to have a feel for their content. American readers will be struck by how many of the messages from this Italian woman relate to their country. The following messages are the alleged words of the Virgin Mary, as related by Cardia (all are posted in English at Countdown to the Kingdom). Most of the below samples are excerpted from messages that typically run between one hundred and three hundred words in length, considerably shorter than the long dispatches from Luz de María de Bonilla:

May 19, 2020:

"Prepare safe refuges: prepare your houses as small churches, and I will be there with you. A revolt is ready, both inside and outside the Church."[447]

July 7, 2020 (amid the tumultuous American summer of 2020):

"Pray for America: because of its perversion it will drink the bitter cup."[448]

August 18, 2020 (amid the COVID-19 pandemic; this is the message in full):

"Dear children, thank you for having listened to my call in your hearts. I ask you to never abandon prayer: it will be the only weapon that will protect you. The Church is in conflict: Bishops against Bishops, Cardinals against Cardinals. Pray for America, because there will be great conflicts with China. My children, I ask you to make reserves of food for at least three months. I had already told you that the freedom granted to you would be an illusion—you will be forced once again to stay in your homes, but this time it will be worse because civil war is near. The new world order has already programmed everything and they want to manipulate your DNA and your minds; this is a project of Satan. I remind you to pay attention to vaccines. My children, do not accumulate money because a day will come when you will not be able to acquire anything. Famine will be severe and the economy is about to be destroyed. Pray and increase prayer cenacles, consecrate your homes and prepare altars within them. These are the warnings for these times; open your hearts and let the flame of the love of my Son Jesus enter them. Do not be far from God: everything now will depend on your choice. I bless you in the name of the Father, the Son and the Holy Spirit, Amen."[449]

September 3, 2020 (message in full):

"Beloved children, thanks for being here in prayer and thanks for having responded to my call in your hearts. My children, the Warning or Illumination will soon arrive, and I am here to ask you to make yourselves ready for this important event for humanity, when there will finally be the last opportunity to choose which side to take—that will be the moment. Preparing yourselves means making a good confession for cleansing your souls, nourishing yourselves often with the Eucharist—this will be the best way. Dear children, the Church is in the most total confusion, but I want to tell my Holy priests not to fear, because I and my Jesus, the only true Savior, will never abandon you. Children, my little ones, I am here to save you and to remind you to pray the Holy Rosary, a unique weapon against Satan. Children, you will be persecuted, there will be punching and spitting along your way, but do not fear, no one will ever be able to touch you, and whoever turns to God with great humility will be a witness to the Kingdom of Heaven and the Triumph of my Immaculate Heart. Children, always be lights burning in the world and be witnesses to my love; I am always waiting for you in this place blest by my Father. Now I bless you in the name of the Father, the Son and the Holy Spirit, Amen."[450]

September 8, 2020:

"Dear children, everything will fall, the sky will be tinged with red, the earth will shake as it has never done before. Children, it is useless thinking about a career and accumulating material goods because all this will no longer make any sense. [. . .] Do not give in to changes because they do not come from God. Children, my remnant will have nothing to fear because my angels and archangels will protect you. Pray for America, which will soon drink the bitter cup. Now I leave you with my Holy Blessing in the name of the Father, Son and Holy Spirit, Amen."[451]

April 3, 2021:

"Beloved children, thank you for being here in this blessed place and thank you for having listened to my call in your hearts. My children, my Son died out of love and to redeem you from sin; He rose again, overcoming death. My children, this is a special Easter because, from today, the signs that will come will be visible to many people, and above all you will see the greatest and long-awaited sign: nobody will be able to say that it was man-made."[452]

June 22, 2021 (full message):

"Dear children, thank you for having listened to my call in your hearts. Beloved children, pray, pray, pray: war is at the gates, pray for the powerful of the earth so that they might take decisions different from those already established. Pray for America, which will be punished for having accepted everything that is against God. Once again I tell you: if God and prayer are not in your lives, you will not have hope; raise up songs of praise and read the Bible during the day."[453]

August 24, 2021

"Pray much. . . for America that has turned its back on God by spreading and loving sin."[454]

Those are messages from Gisella Cardia that I have seen being posted in real time on her website and that of Countdown to the Kingdom. I saved, printed, and dated them. A quite remarkable prediction that she allegedly made, which predates my monitoring of her messages, allegedly came on September 28, 2019, when she reportedly related this message from Mary that would have predicted the COVID-19 pandemic: "Pray for China, because new diseases will come from there, all ready to infect the air by unknown bacteria." This striking prediction was noted by Catholic News Service in an August 2020 story (reposted by *Crux*) and by Countdown to the Kingdom, though CNS notes that it was unable to verify that the message was actually posted on that date, and Countdown likewise does not link to the original purported message.[455]

Note that the sample of messages provided here come from the years 2020 and 2021. More recently, Gisella Cardia slowed and nearly stopped the messages. They have been far less frequent in 2022 and 2023, paralleling the frequency of the public attacks against her. In all, what we have from Gisella Cardia are some striking messages. Are they authentic? Are her reported stigmata authentic? We must wait for the verdict of the Church and of history.

CHAPTER 10

THE PROPHETIC WARNINGS

This book has presented poignant visions and prophecies among the stigmatists. These include early messages and actions from the likes of St. Francis, a true reformer who genuinely repaired the Church, and St. Catherine of Siena, who also sought to restore the Church, urging popes to come back home to Rome. Catherine even conveyed condemnations from God on the scourge of sexual impurity and homosexuality among the clergy, exhorting them to holiness and repentance. Her words spoke not only to her day but to ours.

And then there are still other prophecies, some stark, dark forecasts, aimed directly at the last century and, perhaps, the current century, even the end times, or at least days of judgment that seem as though they could soon arrive if they have not already. If many readers today feel that we are on a precipice, well, so did the stigmatists.

Dragging us closer to the depths of recent times, Anne Catherine Emmerich, two centuries ago, spoke of the devil being unchained fifty or sixty years before the year of Christ 2000. She said that a certain number of other demons were to be let loose much earlier than Lucifer—perhaps in her own 1810s and 1820s, precisely the period when fellow Germans Karl Marx and Friedrich Engels were born, only to give birth to the communist ideology that would kill so many people in the period precisely fifty to sixty years before the year 2000.[456]

Emmerich, known mainly for her glimpses into the past, gave us something to think about in our era today. She was, in effect, speaking

227

to our times. And her fear of a bound Satan in the abyss of hell, being unchained and released for a period of time to wreak havoc, does not contradict the Scriptures. As noted earlier, Revelation 20:1–3 states, "Then I saw an angel coming down from heaven, holding in his hand the key of the bottomless pit and a great chain. And he seized the dragon, that ancient serpent, who is the Devil and Satan, and bound him for a thousand years, and threw him into the pit, and shut it and sealed it over him, that he should deceive the nations no more, till the thousand years were ended. After that he must be loosed for a little while." Again, Anne Catherine Emmerich's vision was not outside the bounds of the Holy Scriptures.

A number of the stigmatists in this book have spoken to our days and to a period of tribulation that might well occur in our era. Certainly, some of the reported stigmatists alive among us today, noted in the previous chapter, are speaking of just that.

But sticking mainly to the saints and blesseds profiled with chapters in this book, who died decades if not centuries ago, as well as other figures who have received formal recognition by the Catholic Church, this book will wrap up by highlighting three areas of prophetic visions of keen interest to everyone living today. The first comes from a figure who recently died and thus has not been honored as a saint or blessed, though her vision has received her bishop's official stamp of approval. These three visions are the 1973 messages of Sr. Agnes of Akita; statements by several stigmatists—including Bl. Elena Aiello, St. Faustina Kowalska, and Bl. Anna Maria Taigi (among others)—regarding their claims of a final-days phenomenon of "days of darkness"; and a recap in general of some of St. Faustina's remarkable prophecies that bear dramatically on our times. Such seems the most appropriate way to end this book. And ending with the Polish nun canonized as the first saint of the new millennium is particularly apt for our twenty-first century.

Sister Agnes of Akita

An extraordinary story of a visionary who lived in our day is Sr. Agnes Katsuko Sasagawa (1931–2024), known as the seer of Our Lady of Akita.

Sr. Agnes was not profiled with a full chapter of her own. She is neither a blessed nor a saint, and most people aware of her are unaware that she had stigmata—a fact confirmed by her bishop, Bishop John Shojiro Ito, in his official pastoral letter affirming the Akita visions.[457] Her personal life was kept so quiet that we know little to nothing about whether those stigmata continued. A number of the more reliable, careful articles on Agnes's interactions with the Blessed Mother at Akita do not mention her stigmata, instead focusing on her visions, which is not surprising in light of their dramatic nature. The entry for Our Lady of Akita at Wikipedia does mention Agnes's stigmata, providing more details than most sources. (Note: Wikipedia is not the most reliable source, but I offer it here because it is the first and most popular source that pops up when googling "Our Lady of Akita" and hence should be acknowledged or dealt with. Authors often are left no choice but to deal with Wikipedia, given its influence. For that reason, I sometimes in this book have cited Wikipedia.) Citing Japanese sources, the Wikipedia entry states that in June 1973, the nun developed bleeding wounds in her palms, which began as two red scratches in the form of a cross.[458] Other sources, however, note just one hand. Writing at EWTN, John Ata reports that Agnes's stigmata began with bleeding in her left hand on June 28, 1973.[459] Bishop Ito's pastoral letter mentions one hand, as did the Blessed Mother when she spoke to Agnes.[460]

Either way, the stigmatic experience came after Agnes's initial supernatural encounters, specifically with angels, and preceded her extraordinary messages from Mary. One might interpret her receiving the stigmata as preparation for the Marian visions to come. Indeed, particularly significant about Agnes are her incredible visions received at Akita. I have saved her story until now because of the nature of her warnings, applying to the end times.

Agnes's experiences occurred at her convent in Yuzawadai, a remote area on the outskirts of Akita, Japan. In her unique case, the Blessed Mother communicated not in the form of a mystical vision but through a wooden statue cut from a single block of wood from a katsura tree that became animated and spoke directly to the nun. The statue of Mary wept tears, perspired, and bled. Particularly striking, given our focus on the stigmata, the statue of Mary emanated blood from a cross-shaped wound in its right hand. That is to say, the statue of Mary on this occasion showed a mark of the Blessed Mother's crucified Son.

That action occurred on July 6, 1973, a little over a week after Agnes received bleeding stigmata on June 28, 1973—almost, perhaps, as a complement to the wound mark on Agnes's left hand.[461] In all, blood, sweat, and tears would emanate from the statue a reported 101 times from January 4, 1975, until September 15, 1981. These phenomena were carefully observed by many witnesses and tracked by scientists from the faculty at the University of Akita, who confirmed through laboratory testing that the bodily emanations were indeed of human origin. The blood, sweat, and tears were photographed and videotaped and even broadcast on Japanese television and can be viewed today in videos posted online—with proper caution.[462]

Church authorities were obviously struck by the reports from the convent. The presiding bishop, Bishop John Shojiro Ito of Niigata, visited immediately. Ultimately, after a long, detailed investigation, the diocese released a statement on April 22, 1984, declaring the incident of supernatural origin and worthy of veneration.[463] The statements bore a striking similarity to the messages from Our Lady of Fatima from May to October 1917. In fact, Bishop Ito underscored in his statement that "the message of Akita is the message of Fatima."[464] He called it "an update of Fatima and its promise."[465]

So, what is the message? It is quite powerful, if not alarming. Mary spoke to Sr. Agnes three times—the first apparition occurring on July 6, 1973, the second on August 3, 1973, and the last, surely not coincidentally, on October 13, 1973, which happened to be the anniversary of the final appearance of Mary at Fatima on October 13, 1917, the spectacular day of the Miracle of the Sun witnessed by some seventy thousand in Portugal.

In the first apparition on the morning of July 6, 1973, the first Friday of the month, the Blessed Mother lovingly greeted the nun with tender words of care about her ongoing condition of deafness and about the stigmata wound on her hand. As to the deafness, she told the nun she would be healed. In this and both of the following two incidents, the voice of Mary came from the wooden statue:

> My daughter, my novice, you have obeyed me well, abandoning all to follow me. Do you suffer much because of the handicap which deafness causes you? You will be assuredly healed. Be patient, it is the last trial. Does the wound in your hand give you pain? Pray in reparation for the sins of humanity. Each person in this community is my irreplaceable daughter.
>
> Do you say well the prayer of the Handmaids of the Eucharist? Then, let us pray it together.[466]

Both the Blessed Mother and Sr. Agnes then recited together the Eucharistic prayer of the nun's Institute of the Handmaids of the Sacred Heart of Jesus in the Holy Eucharist at Akita, which went like this:

> Most Sacred Heart of Jesus, truly present in the Holy Eucharist, I consecrate my body and soul to be entirely one with Your Heart being sacrificed at every instant on all the altars of the world and giving praise to the Father, pleading for the coming of His Kingdom. Please receive My humble offering of myself. Use me as You will for the glory of the Father and the salvation of souls.
>
> Most Holy Mother of God, never let me be separated from your Divine Son. Please defend and protect me as Your special child. Amen.

The Virgin Mary then asked the nun to "pray very much for the pope, bishops, and priests," before finishing by ordering her to "tell your superior all that passed today and obey him in everything that he will tell you. Your superior is wholeheartedly seeking prayers now."

That call to obedience to report the vision to her superior, that is, her bishop, was issued in each message from Our Lady of Akita to Agnes. As to her deafness, Agnes Sasagawa had previously lost her hearing while working as a catechist in the church of Myoko-kogen. The loss resulted in her being committed to a hospital for a time in the city of Joetsu. Bishop Ito later confirmed that her deafness was diagnosed by Dr. Sawada as an incurable total deafness. The condition was so severe that Agnes could no longer work as a catechist and was thus instead sent to the Institute of the Handmaids of the Sacred Heart of Jesus in the Holy Eucharist at Akita, where she committed herself full-time to a life of prayer. It was in that service that the Blessed Mother appeared to her. And with this appearance and promise of the Blessed Mother, Agnes's deafness, once medically determined as full and incurable, was now gone. She was healed.

The second apparition, on August 3, took an altogether different turn. It warned of a great chastisement to befall the entire world, as the wrath of God could no longer be held back:

> My daughter, my novice, do you love the Lord? If you love the Lord, listen to what I have to say to you. It is very important. Convey it to your superior.
>
> Many men in this world grieve the Lord. I seek souls to console Him. In order to appease the anger of the Heavenly Father, I wish, with my Son, for souls who will make reparation for sinners and the ungrateful by offering up their sufferings and poverty to God on their behalf:
>
> In order that the world might know the wrath of the Heavenly Father toward today's world, He is preparing to inflict a great chastisement on all mankind.
>
> With my son, many times I have tried to appease the wrath of the Heavenly Father. I have prevented the coming of the chastisement by offering Him the sufferings of His Son on the Cross, His Precious Blood, and the compassionate souls who console the Heavenly Father. . . a cohort of victim souls overflowing with love [ellipses original to Bishop Ito's letter].
>
> Prayer, penance, honest poverty, and courageous acts of sacrifices can soften the anger of the Heavenly Father.[467]

That message was preparation for a still more dire prophecy to follow on the anniversary of the Fatima Miracle of the Sun. On October 13, as Sr. Agnes knelt in prayer to say her Rosary in the convent chapel, Our Lady told her:

My dear daughter, listen well to what I have to say to you. And relay my messages to your superior.

As I told you, if men do not repent and better themselves, the Heavenly Father will inflict a great punishment on all humanity. It will definitely be a punishment greater than the Deluge, such as has never been seen before.

Fire will plunge from the sky and a large part of humanity will perish. . . [ellipsis original to Bishop Ito's letter] The good as well as the bad will perish, sparing neither priests nor the faithful. The survivors will find themselves plunged into such terrible hardships that they will envy the dead. The only arms which will remain for you will be the Rosary and the sign left by My Son (Eucharist).

Each day recite the prayers of the Rosary. With the Rosary pray for the bishops and priests. The work of the devil will infiltrate even into the Church. One will see cardinals opposing other cardinals. . . and bishops confronting other bishops [ellipsis original].

The priests who venerate me will be scorned and condemned by their confreres; churches and altars will be sacked; the Church will be full of those who accept compromises and the demon will tempt many priests and religious to leave the service of the Lord.

The demon is trying hard to influence souls consecrated to God. The thought of the perdition of so many souls is the cause of My sadness. If sins continue to be committed further, there will no longer be pardon for them.[468]

Once again, as we have heard from Sr. Elena Aiello and other stigmatists (repeated later in this chapter), this stigmatic Japanese nun conveyed from the Blessed Mother a forecast of a great fire from the sky that will scourge humanity with a chastisement worse than that of the Great Flood. The consistency among these twentieth-century warnings from stigmatists is remarkable. Also consistent is the statement from the Blessed Mother that God's righteous wrath can no longer be held back.

And yet, like at Fatima, there was a ray of hope to perhaps help mitigate the chastisement: people could stop sinning, repent, and make reparation. She also again urged prayer of the Rosary: "Pray very much the prayers of the Rosary. I alone am able still to save you from the calamities which approach. Those who place their confidence in me will be saved."[469]

Note, too, the undeniably prophetic statement from Sr. Agnes about cardinals and bishops opposing and confronting one another as the devil infiltrates the Church, a Church wracked by compromises and temptations. Such divisions are clearly thriving today in the Catholic Church, perhaps unlike at any time in centuries. But even well before, notably in the very time of this message to Agnes, the pope of her day, Paul VI, warned, during a June 1972 homily—the year prior to the Akita apparitions—that "the smoke of Satan has entered the Church."[470] Here in this third and final apparition on October 13, 1973, the Blessed Mother finished by faithfully telling the nun to relay this message directly to her superior, specifically naming "Bishop Ito, who directs your community." Agnes proceeded to faithfully do just that.

Bishop Ito went to the convent and witnessed the bleeding, sweating statue, as he would later attest in his Easter, April 22, 1984, letter affirming the events of Akita to be of "supernatural origin." "Since 1973, when the events began, eleven years have passed," he stated in his official pastoral letter. "As that was the first time I was a witness of the rather extraordinary events, I went to Rome to the Sacred Congregation for the Doctrine of the Faith in 1975 where I consulted Archbishop Hamer, deputy secretary of this Congregation." After what he described as an eight-year-long official investigation, which he said had included the testimony of more than 500 Christians and non-Christians, including the Buddhist mayor of the town, Ito concluded:

> After the investigation conducted up to the present day, I recognize the supernatural character of a series of mysterious events concerning the statue of the Holy Mother Mary which is found in the convent of the Institute of the Handmaids of the Sacred Heart of Jesus in the Holy Eucharist at Yuzawadai, Soegawa, Akita. I do not find in these events any elements

which are contrary to Catholic faith and morals. Consequently, I authorize, throughout the entire diocese, the veneration of the Holy Mother of Akita, while awaiting that the Holy See publishes definitive judgment on this matter.[471]

Beyond Bishop Ito, the Vatican has not issued a formal statement in support of or against the message at Akita. It is often claimed that Cardinal Joseph Ratzinger gave some type of personal approval in 1988 while serving in his crucial position as prefect for the Congregation of the Doctrine of the Faith under Pope John Paul II, but those reports are difficult to validate. That said, it has also been stated that, at the least, Ratzinger allowed for Bishop Ito's pastoral letter to be disseminated among the faithful, which indeed certainly appears to have been the case.[472] Obviously, the Holy See did not reject or stop the bishop's letter. As Bishop Ito confirmed in his official April 1984 pastoral letter, "after eight years of investigations, after consultation with the Holy See," the messages of Our Lady of Akita were approved by him.[473] And Ito clearly had Vatican support to do what he was doing.

Stigmatists on the Three Days of Darkness

One of the most significant prophecies given by stigmatists concerns a period of "days of darkness" (in most accounts, usually specified as three days) prior to the coming of Christ, the return of whom will literally pierce that darkness and illuminate the world and the consciences of all.

That darkness was noted earlier in the chapter on St. Faustina Kowalska, who, in her diary, related what Jesus told her in August 1934: "Write this: before I come as the Just Judge, I am coming first as the King of Mercy. Before the day of justice arrives, there will be given to people a sign in the heavens of this sort: All light in the heavens will be extinguished, and there will be great darkness over the whole earth." Only Christ Himself will penetrate the darkness: "Then the sign of the cross will be seen in the sky, and from the openings where the hands and the feet of the Savior were nailed will come forth great lights which will light up the earth for a period of time. This will take place shortly before the last day."[474]

Picture the scene because it foretells a grand sign to appear in the sky right before the last day: a vast darkness will envelop the entire Earth, followed by a massive Sign of the Cross seen in the air by all, from which will emanate "great lights" from the spots where the hands and feet of Christ Jesus bore the marks of the Crucifixion. Those wounds—known so acutely and personally by the stigmatists—would provide the only source of light to a world consumed by darkness. Christ alone will be our light.

These are the "days of darkness" foretold by certain stigmatists who themselves bore those marks of the Crucifixion. And among them, remember that St. Faustina is the messenger of Divine Mercy—its apostle, administrator, secretary, and saint. She and this message of hers must be taken seriously.

The days of darkness prophecy was also offered by Bl. Elena Aiello, coming to her in a Good Friday vision on April 16, 1954, while she was again in the throes of her stigmatic suffering. This is another of Elena's statements not reported in her original biography but later shared by Msgr. Angelo Cioffi and published by the *Divine Love* newspaper. Sr. Elena dramatically foretold the following in a message from the Blessed Mother. According to Elena, these were the words of the Virgin Mary:

> Clouds with lightning flashes of fire in the sky and a tempest of fire shall fall upon the world. This terrible scourge, never before seen in the history of humanity, will last seventy hours. Godless persons will be crushed and wiped out. Many will be lost because they remain in their obstinacy of sin. Then shall be seen the power of light over the power of darkness.[475]

Quite a scene: the world will be hit with a fire from the sky, a terrible scourge, theretofore never witnessed in the history of humanity.[476] A darkness will pervade the world for seventy hours (in essence, three days). And only then, after that period, the light shall emerge in glory to penetrate the darkness.

This cataclysmic moment was said to be not far off. In the words of the Blessed Mother to Elena on that Good Friday of April 16, 1954, "Be not silent, my daughter, because the hours of darkness, of abandonment, are near." In her Good Friday message the next year, April 8, 1955, Elena asked the Blessed Mother, "But when will this come about?" The Mother of Jesus replied, "My daughter, the time is not far off. When men least expect it, the course of Divine Justice will be accomplished."

In these messages, the chastisement would be a terrible "scourge of fire" coming from the skies, unlike anything ever before witnessed in the history of humanity. In fact, in so many of these messages, from Sr. Elena and Sr. Agnes of Akita and others, God's chastisement is not another massive flood—which He promised with the sign of a rainbow never to do again—but vast fire. And speaking of the language of the Flood, in so many of the prophecies by stigmatists, from Elena and Agnes and Faustina to certain alleged modern seers today, the voice of heaven insists that the sins of the world today are far worse than at any time in the history of the human race since the Great Flood.[477] And who could argue with that assessment? Surely, modern America and the West as a whole make Sodom and Gomorrah look downright puritanical by comparison.

Blessed Anna Maria Taigi on the Three Days of Darkness

As some readers probably know, there is still another powerful stigmatic messenger of the days of darkness vision. In fact, she is more directly connected to the days of darkness than any other figure. She is Bl. Anna Maria Taigi (1769–1837).

A native of Siena who moved to Rome, Taigi became an Italian mother of seven, a mystic, a visionary, a suffering soul, and a truly remarkable woman. This book did not devote a full chapter to Taigi, in part because very little has been written about or documented on her stigmata (akin to Sr. Agnes of Akita). She is noted as a stigmatist only occasionally, if not rarely. She is so acknowledged by Deacon Albert E. Graham in his *Compendium of the Miraculous*, though Graham offers only a single-word opening acknowledgment of her being "stigmatic."[478] Quite conspicuous is the absence of any mention of her stigmata at the website of the Mystics of the Church as well as the write-ups on Taigi at Wikipedia, the *Catholic Encyclopedia*, Catholic Exchange, EWTN, in Joan Carroll Cruz's *The Incorruptibles* (Taigi's corpse was incorrupt for a time), and other sources.[479] Thus, the vast majority of modern sources do not mention Tiagi's stigmata, which is unfortunate. As this book argues, the marks of the stigmata ought to be considered a deeper mark of authenticity to any alleged seer's visions and prophecies.

That said, the principal biography of Taigi, written by the Jesuit Fr. Albert Bessières, which remains the go-to authoritative source on Bl. Anna Maria Taigi, and which received the *nihil obstat* and *imprimatur* of the Church, does note that she had hidden stigmata.[480] That acknowledgment is stated only briefly, almost in passing, and with no details. This might partly explain why most modern sources have not focused on her stigmata—though perhaps the primary reason is that most sources focused on Taigi look mainly at her prophecy on the three days of darkness, which seems to almost wholly define her.

But again, the book by Fr. Bessières notes the stigmata. In a section delineating Taigi's many sufferings, Fr. Bessières states, "Racked by pains in her bowels and in her joints, by chronic rheumatic troubles, by asthmatic shortness of breath, by a hernia that impeded all her movements, by the miraculous hand which was torn by invisible stigmata, everything about her was dislocated, so to speak, including the soles of her feet and the joints of her bones."[481]

This is not an expansive acknowledgment, but it is there. More significant to those interested in the life of Taigi—and to us today—were her many remarkable visions and prophecies, both predictive of her own times and, possibly, those yet to come. She often came to these visions by staring into the sun, a process that did not hurt her eyes; the sun, from her purview, turned into a disc-like substance that served almost like a screen upon which she could see images, including alarming images. Fr. Bessières describes this process as Taigi's "terrifying visions in the mysterious sun."[482]

Those terrifying visions most saliently included her prophecy on the three days of darkness. Taigi is so prominently linked to that vision that the brief Wikipedia entry on the three days of darkness (yes, there is one on Wikipedia) highlights her as the foremost name associated with the prophecy. It states:

> The Three Days of Darkness is an eschatological prophecy of future events, held by some Catholics to be true. The prophecy foretells three days and nights of "an intense darkness" over the whole earth, against which the only light will come from blessed beeswax candles, and during which "all the enemies of the Church. . . will perish." [. . .]
>
> Blessed Anna Maria Taigi (1769–1837) is the most known seer of the Three Days of Darkness and describes the event in this way:
>
> "There shall come over the whole earth an intense darkness lasting three days and three nights. Nothing can be seen, and the air will be laden with pestilence which will claim mainly, but not only, the enemies of religion. It will be impossible to use any man-made lighting during this darkness, except blessed candles. He, who out of curiosity, opens his window to look out, or leaves his home, will fall dead on the spot. During these three days, people should remain in their homes, pray the Rosary and beg God for mercy. All the enemies of the Church, whether known or unknown, will perish over the whole earth during that universal darkness, with the exception of a few whom God will soon convert. The air shall be infected by demons who will appear under all sorts of hideous forms."[483]

Wikipedia's source for that quote from Taigi is an 1863 book that is not fully sourced, though the passage is very similar to other books of the era that quote similar Taigi statements almost verbatim (most likely differing merely according to varying translations from the original Italian).[484] The quotation does accurately reflect her thinking.[485]

Oftentimes, those quoting Bl. Anna Maria Taigi do not provide a citation or, at best, offer only a partial citation. Significantly, however, this prophecy appears to be legitimately connected to Taigi. She indeed seems to have said it. Let us return to the most authoritative book on her, written by Fr. Bessières.

Fr. Bessières first relates the words of Anna Maria Taigi to Msgr. Raffaele Natali, who was her spiritual confessor, confidante, and what Bessières describes as "her priest-secretary." Natali is considered for Taigi what Fr. Raimondo di Capua was to Catherine of Siena, with his collection of her writings considered by many the first draft of effectively her memoirs. In the words of Natali, "She told me that Our Lord was intending to cleanse the world and His Church for which He was preparing a miraculous rebirth that would be a Triumph of His Mercy."[486]

This language calls to mind that of St. Faustina, who talked about days of darkness as a precursor to the triumph of Christ's mercy. Fr. Bessières follows Natali's description by adding from Bl. Taigi, "The same vision was presented to the eyes of the Beata on many occasions. She saw the earth enveloped in flame; darkness covering it; immense edifices flung down; the earth and the heavens as it were in agony; the ordeal followed by a universal renewal. And all that would come to pass when the Church seemed to have lost all human means of withstanding persecution. The ordeal would make manifest 'the secret thoughts of the hearts.'"[487]

Here, we see a reference to what many observers today have come to construe as a sort of "illumination of conscience" that will purportedly come to everyone at the great moment of Divine Mercy that will arrive with those days of darkness. Fr. Bessières gave more detail on Taigi's vision:

> The disc of the sun was surrounded by a crown of thorns. The tableaux were never seen in the center of the disc, but only in the surrounding rays. Yet one day she saw the sun opening, and from it issued torrents of blood, while the Blessed Virgin interceded to mitigate the scourges God had prepared. This was a symbol of the great and critical tribulations through which God was going to purify the Church. A terrifying cyclone seemed to be loosed: the heavens took fire, there were earthquakes, plagues, revolutions, riots, massacres, battles, black airships traversing the skies and covering the earth with

fire and darkness. When she looked at the sun to discern any particular object, all the rest vanished.

She saw the peoples of most distant lands in detail as clear "as the facade of a neighboring house"; she saw the scourges threatening each nation, the causes of them, their remedies; the disorders of each class of society whether clerical, aristocratic, or lowly.[488]

This was, of course, a quite astonishing vision for a woman who lived centuries before what anyone might imagine as "black airships." Fr. Bessières quoted both Msgr. Natali and Fr. Callistus, who likewise was a spiritual confidante of Taigi and later wrote a biography of her. Callistus related an incident in which Taigi, akin to later visionaries such as the Fatima children,[489] one day remarked on the number of dead who went to heaven, hell, or purgatory. According to Callistus, Taigi said that very few of the souls that she saw passing went straight to heaven; rather, "many remained in Purgatory, and those cast into Hell were as numerous as flakes of snow in mid-winter."[490]

Here, Fr. Callistus likewise spoke of Taigi's vision of days of darkness. The priest said in an official deposition that "during many successive days she saw impenetrable black darkness cover the earth." This was a literal "physical darkness." Fr. Natali also spoke with specificity. According to Fr. Bessières, Fr. Natali was asked about this period of darkness by a "great number of people" and "was quite definite in telling them all that the darkness would last three days, and during that time only blessed candles would give any light."[491]

So, here we have several sources, including priests who knew Anna Maria Taigi, attesting to her vision of three days of darkness, which they affirmed contemporaneously to a "great number of people" at the time. Anna Maria Taigi, a Church blessed, foresaw three days of darkness.

Marie-Julie Jahenny on the Three Days of Darkness

And there are still more modern stigmatists who have prophesied this ominous vision. Another is the French stigmatist Marie-Julie Jahenny. Known as the "Brittany Stigmatist" (or "Breton Stigmatist"),

Marie-Julie Jahenny was born on February 12, 1850, in the village of Blain in Brittany, France. She died on March 4, 1941. She received the stigmata on March 21, 1873, when she was twenty-three years old, and purportedly carried the marks for the remainder of her long life until her death at age ninety-one. That may have been the longest duration for any stigmatist. In her case, they constituted five wounds, including the crown of thorns and a shoulder wound representing Christ's wound from carrying the cross.

Unlike Anna Maria Taigi, Elena Aiello, or Faustina Kowalska, Jahenny has not been recognized as a blessed or saint (a key factor in this book not devoting a chapter to her), but there have been a number of accounts of her mystical life of apparitions, visions, prophecies, and stigmata. Unfortunately, many of these writings—whether articles or books—are very poorly done and not well sourced. They are sloppy, undermining their reliability, and no doubt further contributing to the lack of attention given by scholars to Jahenny. The French mystic has not benefited from a capable biographer carefully laying out her messages in a clear and organized account that others would feel comfortable relying upon. Nonetheless, to those who pay close attention to prophecies of the three days of darkness, Marie-Julie Jahenny cannot be ignored, given that she actually made more statements on this subject than even Anna Maria Taigi. There are many such statements.

An early biography of her was done by Marquis de La Franquerie, a contemporary of Marie-Julie, a historian (including of religion), and an author of many books, including several on Marie-Julie.[492] That biography is titled *Marie-Julie Jahenny: The Breton Stigmatist*.[493] This is a primary go-to source for those quoting Jahenny.[494] Regrettably, English translations of the book posted online are poorly formatted and difficult to discern; at times, it is hard to decipher what Jahenny said versus what she was quoting others as saying (including the Blessed Mother and Lord Jesus). A better organized effort is a December 2011 work, 591 pages in length, by E. A. Bucchianeri, titled *We Are Warned: The Prophecies of Marie-Julie Jahenny*, which can be accessed for free online.[495] Unfortunately, that book likewise does not benefit from a major publisher.

With those caveats in mind, here is what this fairly modern French stigmatist is reported to have prophesied. The Marquis de La Franquerie book quotes Jahenny forecasting three days of darkness that "Will be on a Thursday, Friday, and a Saturday. Days of the Most Holy Sacrament, of the Cross and Our Lady." It quotes a September 20, 1882, message to Jahenny from the Blessed Mother, who allegedly told her, "The Earth will be covered in darkness, and Hell will be loosed on Earth. The thunder and lightning will cause those who have no faith or trust in my Power, to die of fear."[496]

Jahenny herself (this quote seems to be from her and not the Blessed Mother) went on to say that "during these three days of terrifying darkness, no windows must be opened, because no one will be able to see the earth and the terrible color it will have in those days of punishment without dying at once. . . . The sky will be on fire, the earth will split. . . . During these three days of darkness, let the blessed candle be lighted everywhere, no other light will shine."[497]

In another Jahenny message, this one from the Blessed Mother on December 8, 1882, Jahenny related (quoting Mary), "No one outside a shelter . . . will survive. The earth will shake as at the judgement and fear will be great." She said that "the candles of blessed wax alone will give light during this horrible darkness." Jahenny conveyed these words of the Blessed Mother: "Everything will shake except the piece of furniture on which the blessed candle is burning. This will not shake. You will all gather around the crucifix and my blessed picture. This is what will keep away this terror." Moreover, "During this darkness the devils and the wicked will take on the most hideous shapes . . . red clouds like blood will move across the sky. The crash of thunder will shake the earth and sinister lightning will streak the heavens out of season. The earth will be shaken to its foundations. The sea will rise, its roaring waves will spread over the continent."[498]

Jahenny was also purportedly given such images by Jesus Christ Himself. Here is a January 4, 1884, message that she claimed to have received from Christ:

> There will be three days of physical darkness. For three days less one night, there will be a continual night. The blessed wax

candles will be the only ones that give light in this terrible darkness: only one will suffice for three days, but in the homes of the wicked, they will not give any light. During these three days and two nights, the demons will appear under the most hideous forms. You will hear in the air the most horrible blasphemies. The lightning will enter your homes, but will not extinguish the candles; neither wind, nor the storm can put them out. Red clouds like blood will ride across the sky. The crash of thunder will shake the earth. Sinister lightning will cut across the dense clouds, in a season when they never occur. The earth will be shaken down to the foundations. The sea will rise thundering waves that will spread across the continent (tidal wave). Blood will flow in such abundance that the earth will become a vast cemetery. The corpses of the wicked and the righteous ones will litter the ground. The famine will be great. Everything will be in turmoil and three-quarters of men will perish. The crisis will break out suddenly.[499]

Those are just a few of many stunning statements like this from Marie-Julie Jahenny regarding the days of darkness. From Jahenny, we might well have more such remarks on the three days than we have even from Bl. Taigi and Bl. Aiello and St. Faustina. Among the visionaries, the consistency is impressive: with Jahenny and Taigi, a period of three days is specified, and with Aiello, effectively the same (she stated seventy hours).[500]

Finally, some thoughts on this related to Padre Pio. It should be acknowledged here that the days of darkness prophecy has also been attributed to stigmatist Padre Pio in numerous online sources claiming certain letters and statements from the holy friar. An alleged letter from Padre Pio is cited by proponents, whereas doubters point to a purported letter from his Capuchin Order, contending that the claimed Pio letter is not legitimate.[501] This is a debate and controversy that I cannot resolve here, but as this book has shown, there are plenty of quotes from other stigmatists on the days of darkness, regardless of what the great Padre Pio might have stated.

That said, we might consider a relevant Pio-related observation by the famed Capuchin's close friend Fr. Joseph Martin. Martin was asked by author Michael Freze about the incessant attacks on Pio by the devil and about the general presence of evil in the world today. Martin answered with an assessment not only on demonic forces but on the end times: "Satan and his cohorts . . . are creatures of hate; they cannot love. They are incapable of love—just solid hate, you see? We are living at the end of the Apocalyptic age, and the diabolical forces are very strong now."[502]

That was clearly a message and lesson that Fr. Martin had gotten from Padre Pio. Other stigmatists, including Anne Catherine Emmerich, had warned of the same in regard to our age. Padre Pio lived precisely amid that specific time in the later twentieth century when Emmerich said that Satan was to be unchained and unleashed. As the world moves toward the end of that age, edging closer to the apocalyptic time, the forces of hell will be more active than ever.

What Does the Bible Say?

Quite significantly, we must pause to consider what the New Testament may or may not state about a period of darkness. It is crucial to note in conclusion that Holy Scripture likewise talks about days of darkness, as well as destruction by fire, scourges of fire, the last judgment coming unexpectedly, Christ's triumphant return in the sky, and other great signs, whether in the book of Revelation or elsewhere in Sacred Scripture.[503] That, of course, is vital to remember in this discussion.

Among the four Gospels, Matthew 24:29–31 states, "Immediately after the tribulation of those days the sun will be darkened, and the moon will not give its light, and the stars will fall from heaven, and the powers of the heavens will be shaken; then will appear the sign of the Son of man in heaven, and then all the tribes of the earth will mourn, and they will see the Son of man coming on the clouds of heaven with power and great glory; and he will send out his angels with a loud trumpet call, and they will gather his elect from the four winds, from one end of heaven to the other." It must be noted here that some have interpreted "the sign of the Son of Man" (Matthew 24:30) as possibly a literal sign of the cross in the sky. Mark 13:24–27 likewise states, "But in those days, after that tribulation, the sun will be darkened, and the moon will not give its light, and the stars will be falling from heaven, and the powers in the heavens will be shaken. And then they will see the Son of man coming in clouds with great power and glory. And then he will send out the angels, and gather his elect from the four winds, from the ends of the earth to the ends of heaven."

Is this darkness an altogether different thing from what some of the aforementioned stigmatic seers were forecasting? Maybe, maybe not. Only the Lord knows. As a poignant precursor, perhaps, also note that the book of Exodus (10:22–23) speaks of "thick darkness in all the land of Egypt three days," during which "they did not see one another, nor did any rise from his place for three days." That was a literal type of three days of darkness in the Old Testament, at least as applied specifically to the Egyptians (albeit not the whole world). Thus, there most certainly would seem to be a precedent for God ordaining such action.

God the Father seems to be willing to show His mighty disapproval of sinners by meting out such a form of punishment—that is, by removing the light and enveloping people in darkness. That is especially so when the people reject the Light Himself. Consider one more revealing example from the New Testament:

The Gospels further note this phenomenon at the moment that Jesus Christ died on the Cross: "And there was darkness over the whole land until the ninth hour, while the sun's light failed" (Lk 23:44–45). That came at three in the afternoon. And for three days, the earth accepted the spiritual darkness of the earthly death of Christ until He rose again. Was that a precursor to what is to come, perhaps very soon? We shall see. And we shall see if our stigmatists have this right.

Remembering the Warnings of Saint Faustina

As noted, St. Faustina likewise foresaw days of darkness. It was among her visions of the last days. In this closing section, we need not repeat all of her vivid prophecies here, provided as they were in the chapter devoted to her, but it would seem a fitting end to this book to finish with Faustina's prophetic messages. Of all the figures in this book, she carries a special weight for our day. Her writings, namely, her *Diary*, arguably carry a credibility that other writings from other alleged seers often do not possess. She bears a special stamp of approval as not only a canonized nun but the first recognized saint of our new millennium.

Let us end with the words of this canonized Polish nun, from her warnings of end days to her rays of hope, from her calls for justice to her message of mercy. In May 1935, the Savior of the world, Jesus Christ, told Faustina Kowalska, "You will prepare the world for My final coming" (*Diary*, 429). Those words to ultimately the first saint of the new millennium demand to be taken seriously by all of us today. Surely, they cannot be too far off.

And yet, they were not mere words of warning intended to scare us. They were accompanied by exhortations to prepare us. And as so often with these heavenly signals given to our stigmatists, they were accompanied by motherly words from the Divine Son's Blessed Mother. On March 25, 1936, the Virgin Mary pleaded to Faustina, "You have to speak to the world about His great mercy and prepare the world for the Second Coming of Him who will come, not as a merciful Savior, but as a Just Judge. Oh, how terrible is that day! Determined is the day of justice, the day of divine wrath. The angels tremble before it. Speak to souls about this great mercy. . . . Fear nothing" (*Diary*, 635).

Yes, it will be terrible. But be not afraid. The Just Judge of wrath also offers great mercy to those who seek it. That mercy might not mean survival in this world as calamities strike, indeed perhaps as a mass fire from the sky, but it will mean survival forever in the far more important, better, and lasting life in the next world, the world of heaven, to which every soul should desire to go. That is our ultimate destination. We live not for this world but for the next.

The Catholic Church teaches married couples that one of their primary tasks ought to be to help their spouses get to heaven. We might add that the task should include helping to get our families, friends, and loved ones to heaven also. That ought to be especially our task right now, at this moment, especially if the warnings of the stigmatists apply to us right now in our days. And even if they do not apply to our days at this moment, in this decade, they are vital words of warnings for every soul in every day, as every person made in God's image is destined for earthly death and then eternity in either heaven or hell.

In December 1936, Jesus Christ told St. Faustina, "Speak to the world about My mercy; let all mankind recognize My unfathomable mercy. It is a sign for the end times" (*Diary*, 848). Two months later, in February 1937, He told her, "Secretary of My mercy, write, tell souls about this great mercy of Mine, because the awful day, the day of My justice, is near" (*Diary*, 965). She wrote it in her diary, as commanded. Several months later, in June 1937, she also wrote this: "But woe to them if they do not recognize this time of My visitation" (*Diary*, 1160). And, hence, Faustina was further told in February 1938, "In the Old Covenant I sent prophets wielding thunderbolts to My people. Today I am sending you with My mercy to the people of the whole world" (*Diary*, 1588).

The hour is near. The hour is always near for all of God's children, for each of us, at any time and on any day, regardless of whether our times are the ultimate end times. We each have our own end time. We had best have our souls ready for that moment. Seek God's mercy now and at all times. Try to live a holy life and help your family and friends likewise to live right and to get to heaven. That is the message and goal for all times.

Among their visions and messages and truly incredible lives, our stigmatists urged nothing less. They had much to tell us and to show us, especially with their divine markings. But above all, they wanted to show us a divine glimpse of heaven and how to get there.

ACKNOWLEDGMENTS

I write these acknowledgments and submit this book manuscript to the publisher on October 4, 2023, the feast day of St. Francis, while sitting before the Blessed Sacrament. Likewise appropriate, a key date toward finishing this manuscript was September 17, 2023, the day the Church formally marks the moment that St. Francis received the stigmata. To my knowledge, September 17 is the only liturgical feast day that honors the receiving of the stigmata by a Church figure.

Providentially, on that September 17 morning, I was writing what turned out to be the last section of this manuscript before going through my closing chapter-by-chapter editing: it was the section on Padre Pio receiving the wounds of Christ. In fact, I was writing the paragraph comparing Sts. Padre Pio and Francis receiving the stigmata when my daughter Abigail informed me that it was the feast day of St. Francis receiving the stigmata. I smiled, and I even let out a cheer and fist pump. How profoundly fitting, I thought. The whole process of writing this book was inspiring. It was so refreshing to write a book on something as edifying as this one on these holy men and women, as opposed to, say, another work on a wretched subject like communism and Karl Marx.

Along the way, there were other providential moments when key individuals stepped in to help with some significant research finds.

Among them, I am grateful to Hunter Oswald, my Grove City College student researcher, to Connie Shaw of our college library staff, and to University of Dayton staffers Chris Tangeman and Stephanie Shreffler for their assistance in finding back issues of the *Divine Love* publication that contained the prophecies of Sr. Elena Aiello. Those back issues were not easy to find. I am indebted to Hunter for his several days carefully combing through all of them, taking pictures, and transcribing text. This was the only archive we could find anywhere that contained old issues of that long-defunct publication.

I am especially grateful to Jaclyn Nichols, my Grove City College student assistant for two years. I particularly appreciated her work mining names and data from the University of Antwerp's Ruusbroec Institute's compilation of stigmatists. Also, Jaclyn did the index for this book.

I would like to thank my daughters Abigail and Gianna, as well as our dear family friend Jenny, for helping with the difficult task of picking the cover for this book. The TAN designers provided superlative options. We agreed on the beautiful portrait of St. Catherine of Siena, but there were so many good choices that it was not an easy decision. I also thank Abigail for her research on Bl. Lucy of Narni.

At TAN Books, I am so appreciative of Conor and Kevin Gallagher, Jason Gale, Patrick O'Hearn, and everyone who had a hand in this book or who simply do what they do daily for this wonderful Catholic publishing house that so excellently and devoutly does the Lord's work.

Finally, and most importantly, I thank my family, my kids, and especially my wife, Susan, for their support, love, and help in giving me the time to write, and the Lord Jesus, the Blessed Mother, my guardian angel, and all the angels and saints for their inspiration, protection, and intercession. I am particularly mindful of the inspirational images placed prominently in our home, namely, those of Padre Pio, Catherine of Siena, Faustina's Divine Mercy, and the large San Damiano cross that hangs in our living room, constantly evoking the inspiration of St. Francis of Assisi.

These images will always remind me of the stigmatists. May they pray for us and for me.

Paul Kengor
October 4, 2023, feast day of St. Francis of Assisi

ENDNOTES

1 Cardinal Stanisław Dziwisz, *A Life with Karol: My Forty Year Friendship with the Man Who Became Pope* (New York: Image, 2008), 136.

2 See Deacon Albert E. Graham, *Compendium of the Miraculous* (Charlotte, NC: TAN Books, 2013), 37, 39, 240–42, 263, 347.

3 I will discuss this quotation later in the Francis chapter. There are varying translations of the statement.

4 Graham, *Compendium of the Miraculous*, 195.

5 C. Bernard Ruffin, *Padre Pio: The True Story* (Huntington, IN: Our Sunday Visitor, 2018), 386–87.

6 Adalbert Albert Vogl, *Therese Neumann: Mystic and Stigmatist, 1898-1962* (Rockford, IL: TAN Books, 1987), 36-7.

7 Notably, some commentators who accept the Shroud of Turin as legitimately an image of the crucified Christ contend that the image shows a Jesus with nail marks through His wrists. I cannot confirm if that is an accurate interpretation that therefore should convince the world that Jesus was crucified through the wrists or that stigmata through the palms are not truly representative of Christ's nail marks. We might further note here that countless artwork shows a crucified Jesus through the palms, not the wrists.

 Fr. Robert Spitzer, SJ, PhD, was recently asked about this possible contradiction. Spitzer answered that there is no contradiction because the Romans would have pounded the nails through Jesus's palms downward through the back of the wrists, thus leaving blood marks on the shroud at the spots of the wrists. Spitzer said that this was the Romans' procedure. (Source: Spitzer speaking on *Father Spitzer's Universe*, EWTN, January 28, 2024.) Of course, this would not explain the case of stigmatists like St. Francis and Padre Pio having holes all the way through their hands, from the palms to the back of the hand, rather than exit wounds at their wrists.

8 I consulted colleagues with expertise in Hebrew and Greek, one of whom raised this "wrists" vs. "hands" objection. One of them told me the following: Only John's Gospel contains the narrative about Thomas (John 20:24–28), and that narrative is the only one in the New Testament that specifies "hands"

and "side/rib." The Liddell-Scott lexicon lists "hand" as the common use of the word, but says, "also the hand and arm, the arm, χεῖρα μέσην ἀγκῶνος ἔνερθεν Il.; χεῖρες ἀπ' ὤμων ἀΐσσοντο Hes.; so, ἐν χερσὶ πεσεῖν into the arms. . . ," so L-S finds that "hand" can extend its meaning to "arm." Similarly, the Lexicon by Bauer-Arndt-Gingrich-Danker has "hand" as the most common use, but also "The arm may be meant as in my arms (Hes., Theog. 150; Hdt. 2, 121, 5 εν τω ωμω την χειρα; Herodas 5, 83 εν τησι χερσι τησ εμησι; Paus. 6, 14, 7; Galen, De Usu Part. 2, 2 vol. I p. 67, 1 Helmreich; Longus 1, 4, . . .)." Interestingly, by metonymy, the term can be used for less than a hand, for a finger, as at Luke 15:22: ". . . and put a ring on his hand. . ." So the lexical information itself is probably not determinative. I suspect the historians consult Roman records and later practices to determine whether pierced "hands" could sustain the weight of a body. From what I've read, some suggest that the Greek word *cheir* (χείρ) for "hand" includes the wrist and that the Romans were generally trained to place nails through Destot's space (between the capitate and lunate bones) without fracturing any bones. Another suggests that the Greek word for "hand" also includes the forearm and that the nails were placed near the radius and ulna of the forearm.

9   See Michael Freze's criteria on false vs. authentic stigmata: Michael Freze, *They Bore the Wounds of Christ* (Huntington, IN: Our Sunday Visitor, 1989), 217.

10 On this, see Rev. Charles M. Carty, *The Stigmata and Modern Science* (Charlotte, NC: TAN Books, 1974), 26–27.

11 Frank M. Rega, *Padre Pio and America* (Charlotte, NC: TAN Books, 2015), 60.

12 See also Graham, *Compendium of the Miraculous*, 204.

13 Freze, *They Bore the Wounds of Christ*, 8.

14 Freze, 11.

15 I will later note the current case of Gisella Cardia, from Trevignano Romano, Italy, an alleged stigmatist who has been wildly ridiculed by media.

16 For sources on Dr. Antoine Imbert-Gourbeyre's data cited in this section, see Freze, *They Bore the Wounds of Christ*, 200; and Graham, *Compendium of the Miraculous*, 205.

17 Freze, *They Bore the Wounds of Christ*, 292–93.

18 Freze, 301.

19 Freze, 200.

20 I am not aware of any survey or polling data among Protestants regarding their acceptance or nonacceptance of the notion of stigmata.

21 The database is posted online at https://mediahaven-stigmatics.uantwerpen .be/index.php. I am indebted to my research assistant, Jaclyn Nichols, for her careful combing through the database and breakdown of various categories of stigmatists. Jaclyn provided me with a very detailed Excel spreadsheet that was enormously helpful.

22 Unfortunately, we cannot say that all of these alleged stigmatists have been Church-approved or are clearly authentic. But the stigmatists on these particular lists seem to be largely accepted. Those who compiled the lists have done

so with a notable degree of care and reliability.

23 For examples, see Freze, *They Bore the Wounds of Christ*, 185–87.

24 Freze, 188.

25 Michael Freze lists Menendez as a stigmatist. See Freze, 273–74.

26 See Freze, 197.

27 On incorruptibility and Sts. Frances of Rome, Catherine de Ricci, and Veronica Giuliani, see Joan Carroll Cruz, *The Incorruptibles* (Charlotte, NC: TAN Books, 2012), 96–7, 172–73, 233–34.

28 Even the secular world has taken notice. See the striking photo of Padre Pio's incorrupt body encased in glass published in the *New York Times* on March 17, 2018: "Pope Francis Makes Pilgrimage to Honor a Rock-Star Saint," *New York Times*, March 17, 2018, posted at https://www.nytimes.com/2018/03/17/world/europe/pope-francis-padre-pio.html.

29 My thanks to my daughter Abigail for sharing her research and insights into Bl. Lucy for this section.

30 "Walter Hooper at Narni city," Narnia.it, http://www.narnia.it/hooperdisc.htm, accessed May 17, 2023.

31 Lady Georgiana Fullerton, "Blessed Lucy of Narni," Narnia.it, http://www.narnia.it/lucia1_eu.htm, accessed May 17, 2023.

32 Fullerton, "Blessed Lucy of Narni"; and Graham, *Compendium of the Miraculous*, 373–74.

33 Graham, *Compendium of the Miraculous*, 374; and Fullerton, "Blessed Lucy of Narni."

34 Graham, *Compendium of the Miraculous*, 374.

35 Cruz, *The Incorruptibles*, 139; and Graham, *Compendium of the Miraculous*, 374.

36 Cruz, *The Incorruptibles*, 140; and Graham, *Compendium of the Miraculous*, 374.

37 Cruz, *The Incorruptibles*, 140.

38 Cruz, 140.

39 "Walter Hooper at Narni city."

40 See Fr. Michael Di Gregorio, *The Precious Pearl: The Story of Saint Rita of Cascia* (Staten Island, NY: Society of St. Paul, 2020), 35.

41 Di Gregorio, *The Precious Pearl*, 3.

42 Biographer Fr. Michael Di Gregorio, OSA, takes issue with that widely accepted view of Paolo. See Di Gregorio, 12–16.

43 Di Gregorio, 24–30. On St. Nicholas of Tolentino, see Bob and Penny Lord, *Visions of Heaven, Hell, and Purgatory* (1996), 65–76.

44 Di Gregorio, *The Precious Pearl*, 38.

45 Di Gregorio, 39.

46 Di Gregorio, 39–40.

47 More than one person who visited St. Rita's chapel has told me that they could smell the perfume very clearly and abundantly.

48 Cruz, *The Incorruptibles*, 103–04.

49 Cruz, 103.

50 I speak from personal experience, upon a visit to Assisi in June 2014.

51 See Cruz, 103–05; Graham, *Compendium of the Miraculous*, 332; and Freze, *They Bore the Wounds of Christ*, 261.

52 Di Gregorio, *The Precious Pearl*, 40.

53 Andre Vauchez, *Francis of Assisi: The Life and Afterlife of a Medieval Saint* (New Haven and London: Yale University Press, 2012), 28.

54 Some accounts list the year as 1206. Vauchez, who has carefully studied all the earliest accounts of Francis's life, said that the incident took place at the end of 1205. See Vauchez, *Francis of Assisi*, 25.

55 Some have reported that the Christ figured said *casa*, meaning "house," rather than *chiesa*, meaning "church." Either way, house or church would have referred to the same thing, meaning that house/church where Francis was there praying, and perhaps by extension the larger House/Church that was the Catholic Church. Vauchez uses "house." See Vauchez, *Francis of Assisi*, 25. The Italian version that I have cited is a common translation. This version is found in the literature provided at the tomb of St. Francis in Assisi, which I collected during my visit in June 2014.

56 Michael Goonan, SSP, *The Crucifix That Spoke to St. Francis* (Staten Island, NY: St Pauls USA, Alba House, 2000), 7.

57 See, among others, Goonan, *The Crucifix that Spoke*, 8. I have personally visited the church and seen the cross.

58 Vauchez, *Francis of Assisi*, 220.

59 Vauchez, 129.

60 See Vauchez, 129, 217.

61 Thomas composed the book in 1228–29. It was published in 1229. Among others, see Vauchez, *Francis of Assisi*, 19.

62 Vauchez, 218.

63 See the translation posted as "Medieval Sourcebook: Thomas of Celano, *First and Second Lives of Saint Francis*," https://sourcebooks.fordham.edu/source/stfran-lives.asp.

64 See Bret Thoman, "St. Francis might have been the first to receive the stigmata," Aleteia.org, September 20, 2021, https://aleteia.org/2021/09/20/st-francis-might-have-been-the-first-to-receive-the-stigmata/.

65 The mess has become so chaotic that many of these "churches" are not really churches.

66 Bl. Raymond of Capua, *The Life of St. Catherine of Siena: The Classic on Her Life and Accomplishments as Recorded by Her Spiritual Director* (Charlotte, NC: TAN Books, 2011), 8, 11.

67 Thomas McDermott, OP, "St. Catherine of Siena and leaving the Church," *Catholic World Report*, April 28, 2023.

68 Sigrid Undset died in June 1949. Her *Catherine of Siena* was originally published in Norway in 1951 and then first published in English in 1954 by Sheed and Ward. It was recently republished in 2009 by Ignatius Press.

[69] A very recent biography is Shelley Emling's *Setting the World on Fire: The Brief, Astonishing Life of St. Catherine of Siena* (New York: St. Martin's Press, 2016).

[70] Bl. Raymond of Capua, *The Life of St. Catherine of Siena*, 157.

[71] Bl. Raymond of Capua, *The Life of St. Catherine of Siena*.

[72] Bl. Raymond of Capua, *The Life of St. Catherine of Siena*, 8.

[73] According to Fr. Raimondo, Catherine "frequently [had] intimate conversations" with Mary Magdalene, and often conversed with St. Paul the Apostle, "whom she never mentioned without delight," John the Evangelist, St. Dominic, St. Thomas Aquinas, and "most frequently of all, the virgin of Montepulciano, Agnes." See Bl. Raymond of Capua, *The Life of St. Catherine of Siena*, 157.

[74] Bl. Raymond of Capua, 9–10.

[75] Bl. Raymond of Capua, 144–45.

[76] Bl. Raymond of Capua, 146.

[77] Bl. Raymond of Capua, 147, 152, 173.

[78] Bl. Raymond of Capua, 154.

[79] Bl. Raymond of Capua, 154.

[80] Bl. Raymond of Capua, 154–55.

[81] Bl. Raymond of Capua, 154–55.

[82] Bl. Raymond of Capua, 155–56.

[83] Bl. Raymond of Capua, 156–57.

[84] St. Catherine of Siena, *The Dialogue of St. Catherine of Siena* (Charlotte, NC: TAN Books, 2010), 185.

[85] Here I will quote from the original classic edition that was not purged by modern cleansers of political correctness. My source is Algar Thorold's authoritative translation (which received the official Church *imprimatur* and *nihil obstat*) from the original Italian, *The Dialogue of the Seraphic Virgin Catherine of Siena* (London: Kegan Paul, Trench, Trubner & Co., 1896). The full book can be found online as a PDF at https://ia801209.us.archive.org/17/items/seraphicvirginca00cathuoft/seraphicvirginca00cathuoft.pdf. Cited hereafter as simply *The Dialogue*. Several versions in the public domain do not include the material originally in St. Catherine of Siena's *Dialogue* that pertain to the sins of homosexual acts.

[86] See McDermott, "St. Catherine of Siena and leaving the Church."

[87] St. Catherine of Siena, *The Dialogue*, 270–71. The names of the five cities are not specified in *The Dialogue*. One assumes that Sodom and Gomorrah are among the five. Sodom and Gomorrah were actually part of the so-called Pentapolis of five cities identified in Wisdom 10. Also see Genesis, particularly Genesis 19.

[88] *The Dialogue*, 271.

[89] *The Dialogue*, 272.

[90] *The Dialogue*, 272–73.

[91] *The Dialogue*, 273–74.

[92] *The Dialogue*, 275.

93   This section refers to buying and selling in the temple, those "who lend money with usury," those who "clothe and fatten" themselves with the property of the Church, and other sins of greed and abuse. *The Dialogue*, 282–3.

94   *The Dialogue*, 283.

95   S. A. McCarthy, "The Homosexual Infestation of the Catholic Church," *Crisis Magazine*, June 22, 2023.

96   See Salvatore Cernuzio, "The Pope: 'If there is doubt of homosexuality, it is better not to let the seminarian enter,'" *La Stampa*, May 25, 2018.

97   See "Pope Francis 'worried' about homosexuality in the priesthood," BBC News, December 2, 2018; see also Fr. Roger J. Landy, "Pope Francis on the 'Gay Mentality' That Has 'Influenced the Church,'" *National Catholic Register*, December 12, 2018.

98   McCarthy, "The Homosexual Infestation of the Catholic Church."

99   McCarthy.

100   See Owen J. Blum, OFM, trans., *The Letters of Peter Damian, 31–60*, vol. 2 of *The Fathers of the Church: Mediaeval Continuation* (Washington, DC: The Catholic University of America Press, 1990), 15–38.

101   McDermott, "St. Catherine of Siena and leaving the Church."

102   Quoted by McDermott, "St. Catherine of Siena."

103   McDermott, "St. Catherine of Siena."

104   Ven. Anne Catherine Emmerich, *The Life of the Blessed Virgin Mary: From the Visions of Anne Catherine Emmerich* (Charlotte, NC: TAN Books, 2013), v.

105   Carl E. Schmöger, *The Life and Revelations of Anne Catherine Emmerich* (Charlotte, NC: TAN Books, 2012), 1:23.

106   Schmöger, *The Life and Revelations*, 27–31.

107   Emmerich, *The Life of the Blessed Virgin Mary*, v; and Schmöger, *The Life and Revelations*, 1:126.

108   Schmöger, *The Life and Revelations*, 1:182–83.

109   Schmöger, 1:182–83.

110   Schmöger, 1:183.

111   Schmöger, 1:183–84.

112   Schmöger, 1:184.

113   On the doubters whom Emmerich dealt with, very similar to those who disparaged Padre Pio, see Schmöger, *The Life and Revelations*, 1:267–69, among others.

114   Schmöger, 1:103, 184–85.

115   Schmöger, 1:185–86.

116   Schmöger, 1:186.

117   Schmöger, 1:187–89.

118   Schmöger, 1:187–89.

119   Schmöger, 1:187–89.

120   Schmöger, 1:201.

121   Schmöger, 1:201–07, 213–19, 222–23.

122   Schmöger, 1:207–08.

123 Schmöger, 1:272.
124 See Schmöger, 1:227–28, 236, 273, 354.
125 Schmöger, 1:238, 104.
126 Schmöger, 1:250, 255.
127 Schmöger, 1:251.
128 Schmöger, 1:250.
129 Schmöger, 1:250–52.
130 Schmöger, 1:255.
131 Schmöger, 1:256.
132 Schmöger, 1:292–93.
133 See also Schmöger, 1:468–69.
134 Schmöger, 1:325, 346.
135 Emmerich, *The Life of the Blessed Virgin Mary*, v.
136 On Brentano, see Schmöger, *The Life and Revelations*, 1:xxiii–xxiv, 346–68.
137 Anne Catherine Emmerich, *The Dolorous Passion of Our Lord Jesus Christ* (Charlotte, NC: TAN Books, 2012), 243–44.
138 Emmerich, *The Dolorous Passion*, 149–51.
139 Schmöger, *The Life and Revelations*, 1:316.
140 Emmerich, *The Dolorous Passion*, 348.
141 Emmerich, *The Dolorous Passion*, 349.
142 See Paul Kengor, *The Devil and Karl Marx* (Gastonia, NC: TAN Books, 2020), 4.
143 See Pope Pius XI, *Divini Redemptoris*, March 1937, https://www.vatican.va/content/pius-xi/en/encyclicals/documents/hf_p-xi_enc_19370319_divini-redemptoris.html.
144 See my lengthy discussion in Kengor, *The Devil and Karl Marx*.
145 See Paul Thigpen, *Saints Who Saw Hell* (Charlotte, NC: TAN Books, 2019), 42–43, 48–49.
146 Thigpen, *Saints Who Saw Hell*, 42–3.
147 Schmöger, *The Life and Revelations*, 1:391.
148 Schmöger, 1:511.
149 Schmöger, 1:511.
150 Schmöger, 1:511–12.
151 Schmöger, 1:512.
152 Schmöger, 1:512–13.
153 Schmöger, 1:513–14.
154 Schmöger, 1:515.
155 Schmöger, 1:516.
156 Carl E. Schmöger, *The Life and Revelations of Anne Catherine Emmerich* (Charlotte, NC: TAN Books, 2014), 2:296.
157 Schmöger, *The Life and Revelations*, 2:248.
158 Schmöger, 2:248–9.
159 Schmöger, 2:250.

160   For instance, in a message on August 10, 1822, she stated, "I see the Holy
      Father in great distress. . . . I fear the Holy Father will suffer many tribulations
      before his death, for I see the black counterfeit church gaining ground, I see its
      fatal influence on the public. . . . He is very feeble, quite worn out by distress,
      anxiety." This pope in that vision is old and ailing, as Pius VII was at that time.
      He would die the next year. Schmöger, 2:261–62.

161   Some Catholics, especially those who experienced the unusual time of two
      simultaneously living popes, namely, Pope Emeritus Benedict XVI and Pope
      Francis, have speculated that Emmerich's prophecies of the two popes might
      have been aimed at Benedict and Francis, but to the contrary, she made clear
      that the two popes were one ancient and one modern, and she designated
      the former as Boniface IV. (Also, it is unprecedented to have a current pope
      along with a "pope emeritus" as well.) For a good analysis of this, see Steve
      Skojec, "Anne Catherine Emmerich and the Two Popes," OnePeterFive.com,
      May 5, 2016.

162   Schmöger, The Life and Revelations, 2:251.

163   Schmöger, 2:251–52.

164   Pope John Paul II, "Beatification of Five Servants of God: Homily of John
      Paul II," Vatican, October 3, 2004.

165   Ven. Fr. Germanus, CP, The Life of St. Gemma Galgani, trans. Fr. A. M. O'Sul-
      livan, OSB (Charlotte, NC: TAN Books, 2012), 3.

166   Bob and Penny Lord, Visionaries, Mystics, and Stigmatists (self-published
      through Journeys of Faith publishing, 1995), 320.

167   Germanus, The Life of St. Gemma Galgani.

168   In all, Sophia sums up its presentation of both the diary and autobiography (I
      assume that the latter are mere portions) under St. Gemma Galgani, The Diary
      of Saint Gemma (Manchester, NH: Sophia Institute Press, 2022).

169   St. Gemma Galgani, The Diary of Saint Gemma, 7–8.

170   Galgani, 7–8.

171   Germanus, The Life of St. Gemma Galgani, xxi.

172   Galgani, The Diary of Saint Gemma, 119–20. See also Galgani, 122–23.

173   Galgani, 41.

174   Germanus, The Life of St. Gemma Galgani, xxiii.

175   Germanus, xxiii.

176   Galgani, The Diary of Saint Gemma, 49–50, 57–58.

177   Note: Gemma does not give the date of this moment, but according to the
      timeline in her autobiography, it was during the month of April 1899. See
      Galgani, 73–79.

178   Galgani, 77.

179   Galgani, 85.

180   Galgani, 85–6.

181   Galgani, 87.

182   Galgani, 101.

183   Galgani, 129. See also Galgani, 134, 142–43.

184 Germanus, *The Life of St. Gemma Galgani*, xxiii.
185 Germanus, xxiii–xxiv.
186 Germanus, xxiii–xxiv.
187 Germanus, xxiii–xxiv.
188 Germanus, xxiv.
189 Germanus, 76.
190 Germanus, 77–78.
191 Germanus, 77–78.
192 Germanus, 77.
193 Germanus, 79.
194 Germanus, 86–87.
195 Germanus, 88.
196 Germanus, 88.
197 The foreknowledge of earthly events detailed in this section relate to Gemma's death and her mother's death. I am not familiar with any major prophecies or predictions by Gemma akin to those of Sr. Elena Aiello relating to politics and global affairs. I asked Glenn Dallaire of the website Mystics of the Church, who has much material on Gemma, if he was aware of any information on prophecies and predictions. Glenn answered in an email from June 13, 2023, "As for St Gemma Galgani and prophecies, Venerable Father Germano CP never published any that I'm aware of, except for the one where she said that while the Passionist[s] wouldn't have her in life, but that they would have her in death, and as you know that's exactly what happened. Aside from that they never published any prophecies that she may have made. I'm not surprised in a way because they're [there] already was a good deal of skepticism surrounding all of the extraordinary mystical Graces that she was given. So Father Germano in his wisdom may have set any prophecies aside. That's just my own speculation."
198 See Bob and Penny Lord, *Visionaries, Mystics, and Stigmatists*, 330–31.
199 Galgani, *The Diary of Saint Gemma*, 13.
200 Galgani, 13.
201 Galgani, 13.
202 Galgani, 14.
203 Ven. Fr. Germanus, *The Life of St. Gemma Galgani*, 298–99.
204 Germanus, 304–05.
205 Germanus, 304–05.
206 Fr. Germano here wrote, "The greatest suffering of Our Lord in His Agony on the Cross was, according to the Saints, His apparent abandonment by His Eternal Father. Add that abandonment, too truly real, by men. Of all this He Himself complained from the Cross, and Gemma in this also had to be like Him." Germanus, 321.
207 Germanus, 312.
208 Germanus, 312.
209 Germanus, 317–19.

[210] Germanus, 317–19.

[211] Germanus, 320–21.

[212] Germanus, 320–21.

[213] Germanus, 320–21.

[214] Germanus, 322.

[215] Germanus, 323. In St. Gemma's day, the Easter Vigil was kept in the morning, which would explain why it could be said that she died on "the Solemnity of Our Lord's Resurrection," even though it was Saturday.

[216] See Pope Pius XII's Letter of Decree, "Sanctitudinis Culmen," on the occasion of Gemma's canonization, May 2, 1940, https://www.stgemmagalgani.com/2013/05/pope-pius-xii-letter-of-decree-for.html.

[217] Germanus, 188.

[218] Germanus, 188.

[219] Germanus, 188.

[220] Germanus, 188–89.

[221] Germanus, 189.

[222] Germanus, 189–90.

[223] Germanus, 189–90.

[224] Germanus, 190.

[225] Galgani, *The Diary of Saint Gemma*, 115–16.

[226] Galgani, 132.

[227] Galgani, 137–38.

[228] This was recorded by Gemma on Saturday, August 4, 1900. See Galgani, 117.

[229] Galgani, 107.

[230] See Matt Baglio, *The Rite: The Making of a Modern Exorcist* (NY: Doubleday, 2009), 2.

[231] Francesco Vaiasuso, *La Mia Possessione* (Milan, Italy: Edizione Piemme, 2012), 228–29.

[232] Glenn Dallaire, "St. Gemma Galgani in today's battle against evil," Mystics of the Church, last updated in July 2012, posted at https://www.stgemmagalgani.com/2009/05/exorcisms-intercession-of-st-gemma.html and https://www.stgemmagalgani.com/2009/05/exorcist-st-gemma-padre-pallotti-cp.html, retrieved July 13, 2023.

[233] Bree Dail, "Wife and Mother of Four Describes Experience of Possession, Exorcism," *National Catholic Register*, December 11, 2019.

[234] Msgr. Stephen Rossetti, "Demons Hate Gemma," March 5, 2022, posted in his Exorcist's Diary at his website, https://spiritualdirection.com/2022/03/05/demons-hate-gemma, retrieved July 13, 2023.

[235] See also, among others, Philip Kosloski, "Why St. Gemma Galgani laughed in the face of the devil," Aleteia.org, April 11, 2018; and Paul Thigpen, *Saints Who Battled Satan* (TAN Books, 2015).

[236] See polling data in Thomas C. Reeves, *America's Bishop: The Life and Times of Fulton Sheen* (San Francisco: Encounter Books, 2001), 1.

[237] Ruffin, *Padre Pio: The True Story*, 24.

238 According to Ruffin, Grazio (whose nickname was Orazio) lived in the Ma-honingtown neighborhood of the city of New Castle. I personally know New Castle, which is a short drive (less than thirty minutes) from the town where I currently live and also from the town (Butler, Pennsylvania) where I grew up. Ruffin says that Orazio shared a frame house on Montgomery Avenue with some fellow immigrants from their hometown of Pietrelcina and "worked as a foreman of the hands on a farm." Ruffin's source is a June 20, 1985, in-terview with Riparta Masone De Prospero of New Castle. See Ruffin, *Padre Pio*, 34, 476n.

239 Ruffin, 28.

240 Ruffin, 32, 57.

241 Among others, see Fr. Pascal Cataneo, *Padre Pio: Glimpse into the Miraculous* (Boston: Pauline Books & Media, 2013), 137–38.

242 See, among others, "St. Padre Pio on Listening to Your Guardian Angel," Aleteia.org, May 17, 2015.

243 See Ruffin, 360–61 (on seeing into the future), 365–70 (bilocation), and 353–64, 371–90, 453–62 (on miracles and miraculous healings). Also recom-mended among modern works translated into English is Fr. Pascal Cataneo's *Padre Pio: Glimpse into the Miraculous*. For examples of bilocation in Cataneo's book, see pages 72–74 and 90–91. Also striking is Cataneo's account (94–95) of the dead baby in the suitcase, a well-known incident in which Pio is report-ed to have possibly saved a baby that had died en route to his friary. When the distraught mother arrived, her child appeared to be dead. Pio took the baby in his arms and assured the mother that the baby was only sleeping. The child suddenly awoke and seemed perfectly fine, healed of the prior ailment. This was attested to by Dr. Sanguinetti, who was a direct witness.

244 Renzo Allegri, *Padre Pio: Man of Hope* (Cincinnati, OH: Servant/Franciscan Media, 2000), 130–31.

245 Ruffin, *Padre Pio: The True Story*, 285–86.

246 George Weigel, *Witness to Hope* (New York: HarperCollins, 1999), 83. Note: Weigel's source on this was Pope John Paul II himself, whom Weigel interviewed.

247 That statement is the typical rendering of the quotation, most often cited. The Padre Pio Foundation posts a slightly different quotation reportedly from Pio: "Angelo, I cannot say no to this request." See "The friendship be-tween Saint John Paul II, and Saint Pio of Pietrelcina," posted at https://sain tpiofoundation.org/news/facts. Most sources use the "this man" version.

248 Weigel, *Witness to Hope*, 435.

249 Weigel, 435.

250 Weigel, 153. Wojtyla said just that in an interview with George Weigel thirty-five years later.

251 Ruffin, *Padre Pio: The True Story*, 435.

252 Weigel, *Witness to Hope*, 894n.

253   Ruffin, *Padre Pio: The True Story*, 434. Ruffin writes that once Wojtyla be-
       came pope, "rumors spread that on that visit [in 1947], Padre Pio prophesied
       that he would become pope. Actually, he did not." But Ruffin oddly pro-
       ceeds to give no evidence whatsoever regarding how he knows that Pio did not
       prophesize that.

254   Weigel shrugged off such reports as a "legend." Weigel, a friend and scholar
       who I greatly respect, has a very cynical temperament. Strangely, Weigel in
       his mere endnote (894n) says of his personal interview with Pope John Paul
       II on December 13, 1997, "During this conversation the Holy Father did not
       mention the legend that Padre Pio had predicted Wojtyla's election as pope
       during his confession. The Holy Father's emphasis on the brevity, clarity, and
       simplicity of Padre Pio as a confessor tells against the legend which, if true,
       John Paul would quite properly have regarded as a private matter." But that
       is hardly evidence that the claim is a mere "legend." Weigel states candidly
       that he did not ask John Paul II about the story during his interview with the
       pontiff. It was not mentioned at all during their conversation. Why should he
       assume this as concrete evidence for or against the story?

255   Oddly, the next line in that quotation from Stickler reads, "Wojtyla believed
       when he was created a cardinal, the prophecy was realized." But obviously, the
       position of cardinal—there are usually at least a hundred cardinals at any giv-
       en moment (241 at the time of this writing)—is plainly not the highest post
       in the Church. The position of pope is the highest post in the Church. See
       Jonathan Kwitny, *Man of the Century: The Life and Times of Pope John Paul II*
       (Henry Holt and Co., 1997), 101.

256   Kwitny's material on Wojtyla and Pio appears on pages 100–01 and 179. His
       views on Pio are outrageous. He offers a brief, snide treatment loaded with
       one-sided material that suggests Pio was a fanatic and fraud. His portrayal is
       woefully superficial and inaccurate. He writes of longtime Lutheran pastor C.
       Bernard Ruffin, whom he quotes very selectively *against* Pio, "Ruffin, obvious-
       ly a devout Catholic, is convinced that Pio was everything he claimed to be."
       See Kwitny, *Man of the Century*, notes on page 687.

257   My sources for this section include Cataneo, *Padre Pio: Glimpse into the Mi-
       raculous*, 6–7; Frank M. Rega, *Padre Pio and America* (Charlotte, NC: TAN
       Books, 2015), 54–55; Ruffin, *Padre Pio: The True Story*, 138–41; and Allegri,
       Padre Pio: Man of Hope, 71–75.

258   Francesco Castelli, *Padre Pio under Investigation: The Secret Vatican Files* (San
       Francisco: Ignatius Press, 2011), 199–203.

259   Castelli, *Padre Pio under Investigation*, 202; and Allegri, *Padre Pio: Man
       of Hope*, 73.

260   Allegri, *Padre Pio: Man of Hope*, 73.

261   Quoted by David Gress, "The Second Fall," *National Review*, July 12, 1999.

262   Michael D. Hull, review of John Keegan's *The First World War*, published in
       Military History, February 2000, 66.

[263] See my detailed discussion in Paul Kengor, *A Pope and a President* (Wilmington, Delaware: ISI Books, 2017), 13–28.

[264] See, among others, Ruffin, *Padre Pio: The True Story*, 138.

[265] Fr. Charles Mortimer Carty, *Padre Pio: The Stigmatist* (TAN Books: Charlotte, NC, 1989), xi–xiii.

[266] Carty, *Padre Pio: The Stigmatist*, 286.

[267] Carty, 286.

[268] Carty, 286–7.

[269] See Ruffin, *Padre Pio: The True Story*, 15, 157.

[270] Carty, *Padre Pio: The Stigmatist*, 287.

[271] Carty, 287–88.

[272] Carty, 288.

[273] Carty, 289.

[274] Carty, 289.

[275] Carty, 289–90.

[276] Carty, 290.

[277] Carty, 291.

[278] Carty, 291–92.

[279] Carty, 182–84.

[280] Carty, 184.

[281] Carty, 184.

[282] Carty, 412.

[283] Carty, 245–49.

[284] Carty, 250.

[285] Carty, 257.

[286] Carty, 421.

[287] Carty, 12.

[288] Carty, 249.

[289] Carty, 15, 411–15.

[290] Carty, 414–15.

[291] Carty, 419, 427.

[292] Carty, 12.

[293] Carty, 421–22.

[294] Castelli, *Padre Pio under Investigation*, 107, 126–27, 206.

[295] See, for instance, Castelli, 199–201, 228–30, among others.

[296] Castelli, 107–10.

[297] Ruffin, *Padre Pio: The True Story*, 218.

[298] Ruffin, 262–65.

[299] Ruffin, 443.

[300] Ruffin, 444.

[301] Ruffin, 451.

[302] Freze, *They Bore the Wounds of Christ*, 293.

[303] Ruffin, *Padre Pio: The True Story*, 158–59, 451.

[304] Pope John Paul II, "Statement at Canonization Mass for Padre Pio of Pietrelcina," St. Peter's Square, June 16, 2002.

[305] "Elena Aiello," Wikipedia entry, posted at https://en.wikipedia.org/wiki/Elena_Aiello#cite_note-MC-1, retrieved June 5, 2023.

[306] See "Blessed Elena Aiello—Mystic, Stigmatic & Foundress," entry at Mystics of the Church website, posted at https://www.mysticsofthechurch.com/2011/09/blessed-elena-aiello-mystic-stigmatic.html, retrieved June 8, 2023.

[307] "Blessed Elena Aiello: A Saintly Cousin," website of Montalto Uffugo, posted at http://www.montaltouffugo.net/elenaaiello.html, retrieved June 6, 2023.

[308] Fr. Francesco Spadafora, *The Incredible Life Story of Sister Elena Aiello: The Calabrian Holy Nun (1895–1961)*, trans. Fr. Angelo R. Cioffi (Brooklyn, NY: Theo. Gaus' Sons, Inc., 1964). Fortunately, a PDF of the document is available online, posted at https://ia801608.us.archive.org/33/items/TheIncredibleLifeStoryOfSisterElenaAielloTheCalabrianHolyNun/The-Incredible-Life-Story-Of-Sister-Elena-Aiello.pdf, retrieved June 8, 2023.

[309] See Spadafora, *The Incredible Life Story of Sister Elena Aiello*, first published in 1964 and reprinted and translated in 2017 by Kalpaz Publications (Delhi, India).

[310] Several of the more stirring (and apocalyptic) quotations attributed to Elena at those two websites are not found in the 1964 Spadafora book but attributed to other sources, which I will detail later in this chapter. See, respectively, Mark Mallett, "Three Days of Darkness," Now Word Reflections on Our Times, August 17, 2007, and https://www.mysticsofthechurch.com/2011/09/blessed-elena-aiello-mystic-stigmatic.html, both retrieved June 8, 2023.

[311] Spadafora, *The Incredible Life Story of Sister Elena Aiello*, 11.

[312] See "Blessed Elena Aiello: A Saintly Cousin."

[313] Spadafora, *The Incredible Life Story of Sister Elena Aiello*, 11–12; and "Blessed Elena Aiello: A Saintly Cousin."

[314] "Blessed Elena Aiello: A Saintly Cousin."

[315] "Blessed Elena Aiello: A Saintly Cousin."

[316] Larry Peterson, "This saint bore the stigmata every Good Friday for 38 years," Aleteia.org, July 6, 2018.

[317] Spadafora, *The Incredible Life Story of Sister Elena Aiello*, 14.

[318] Spadafora, 14.

[319] Spadafora, 18–19.

[320] Francesco di Paola (also known as Francis of Paola), 1416–1507, was the founder of the Order of Minims. He was born in the town of Paola, located in the southern Italian Province of Cosenza, Calabria.

[321] Peterson, "This saint bore the stigmata every Good Friday for 38 years."

[322] Spadafora, *The Incredible Life Story of Sister Elena Aiello*, 18–19.

[323] Spadafora, 18–19.

[324] Spadafora, 22.

[325] Spadafora, 22–23.

[326] Spadafora, 23.

327 Spadafora, 23–24.
328 Spadafora, 24.
329 Spadafora, 24.
330 Spadafora, 24–25.
331 Spadafora, 33.
332 Spadafora, 33.
333 Spadafora, 38.
334 Spadafora, 35.
335 Spadafora, 34.
336 Spadafora, 34–35.
337 Spadafora, 34–35.
338 Spadafora, 35.
339 Spadafora, 35.
340 "Blessed Elena Aiello: A Saintly Cousin."
341 "Blessed Elena Aiello: A Saintly Cousin."
342 Spadafora, 99–100.
343 Spadafora, 131.
344 Spadafora, 131.
345 Spadafora, 131–32.
346 Spadafora, 132–33.
347 Spadafora, 133.
348 Spadafora, 133–34.
349 Spadafora, 134–35.
350 Spadafora, 134–35.
351 Spadafora, 135–36.
352 Spadafora, 135–36.
353 Spadafora, 135–36.
354 Fr. Sarago deposition printed in Spadafora, *The Incredible Life Story of Sister Elena Aiello*, 4.
355 Spadafora, 4.
356 Spadafora, 4.
357 Spadafora, 99–100.
358 On St. Thérèse and Elena, see Spadafora, *The Incredible Life Story of Sister Elena Aiello*, 40, 53.
359 Spadafora, 100–01.
360 Spadafora, 102–03.
361 Spadafora, 102–03.
362 Among others, see the excellent work by John Lukacs, *Five Days in London: May 1940* (New Haven, CT: Yale University Press, 2001).
363 Spadafora, *The Incredible Life Story of Sister Elena Aiello*, 103–05.
364 Spadafora, 105–06.
365 There have been many statements among saints and various seers about God perhaps withdrawing a planned punishment because of prayers or certain requested actions among the faithful. Consider Fatima, for instance. There are

assurances that if certain prayers and actions are taken—such as people changing and mending their ways, repenting, or the pope consecrating Russia—
then certain calamities will not befall us.

366 Spadafora, 117–19.

367 See "Blessed Elena Aiello—Mystic, Stigmatic & Foundress," entry at Mystics of the Church website, posted at https://www.mysticsofthechurch.com
/2011/09/blessed-elena-aiello-mystic-stigmatic.html, retrieved and printed
June 9, 2023.

368 "Blessed Elena Aiello—Mystic, Stigmatic & Foundress." The exact citation
at the Mystics of the Church website states, "Monsignor Cioffi, the translator of her biography and friend of Sister Elena, sent these previously unpublished prophecies of Sister Elena to the late Steven Oraze, Editor of
the edifying Catholic newspaper, 'Divine Love' which was produced by the
Apostolate of Christian Action in Fresno, California. At first Monsignor Cioffi
was nervous about publishing the messages because they were so strong and
thought that people wouldn't accept them. Mr. Oraze took them to his Bishop
who gave them the Imprimatur and he published them. At that time, 'Divine Love' contained the only public printing of these messages. The 'Divine
Love' staff received direct confirmations from Heaven that they were to publish
the messages more than once for all the world to see. It is now clear that they
are more relevant now than ever before. Here they are taken directly from this
newspaper." Retrieved June 9, 2023.

369 Email correspondence with Glenn Dallaire, June 9–11, 2023.

370 My excellent research assistant, Hunter Oswald, who lives near Dayton, went
to the archives in July–August 2023 and did terrific work finding all of the
articles. I am indebted to his fine work and also the assistance of University of Dayton staffers Chris Tangeman and Stephanie Shreffler. The *Divine
Love* back issues are housed in the university's US Catholic Special Collection
archives.

371 Initially in *Divine Love*'s pages, Sr. Elena was referred to only generally as a
stigmatized nun in Italy. But by the late 1970s and into the 1980s, she was
noted explicitly by name.

372 The prophecy appears in this article: Rt. Rev. Msgr. William C. McGrath, PA,
"America! . . . Sodom or Nineveh," *Divine Love*, vol. 1, no. 1, July–September 1957, 5.

373 Stephen Oraze, "The Plot to Destroy America," *Divine Love*, vol. 2, no. 2,
Winter, 1958–1959, 3.

374 We do not know why the archive lacks that one issue. Perhaps it was never in
the archive to begin with, or perhaps someone took it from the archive. We
have no explanation. As a historian, I have dealt with archives for decades. This
is not the first time that I have encountered a situation in which a crucial set
of papers happens to be missing.

375 For example, issue no. 96, published in 1984, stated this of the Elena prophecies we shall see momentarily: "She also foretold the problems in the Church; the corruption of youth; wars, revolutions and religious persecutions; THE RUSSIAN INVASION OF EUROPE, AND WORLD WAR III; some nations would be purified, while others would disappear entirely; Communist uprisings in Italy and France; the capture of the Holy Father by the Red; and eventually a Divine intervention, in which the forces of good would be delivered from the forces of evils—perhaps in the promised triumph of the Immaculate Heart of Mary."

376 For instance, see these editions of *Divine Love*: vol. 25, nos. 2–3–4, issue no. 89, Second-Fourth Quarters, 1982, "Updated Coming World Housecleaning" issue; vol. 26, no. 2, issue no. 91, Second Quarter, 1983, "Updated Defending the Faith" issue; vol. 26, nos. 3–4, issue no. 92, Third-Fourth Quarters, 1983, "Mary, Help of Christians" issue; vol. 27, no. 1, issue no. 93, First Quarter, 1984, "All That Matters Is Souls" issue; vol. 28, no. 1, issue no. 95, First Quarter, 1985, "Crosses—Weapons for Peace" issue; and vol. 27, no. 2, issue no. 94, Second Quarter, 1984, "Rosaries for Peace" issue.

377 I will discuss these later in this book, but for the record, as of now: Lucia described the hell witnessed by her and Jacinta and Francisco as a "sea of fire" filled with "demons and souls in human form, like transparent embers, all blackened or burnished bronze, floating about in the conflagration." Anna Maria Taigi stated that "those cast into Hell were as numerous as flakes of snow in mid-winter." Fr. Albert Bessieres, SJ, *Wife, Mother & Mystic: Blessed Anna-Maria Taigi* (Charlotte, NC: TAN Books, 2012), 158n.

378 Fr. Bonaventura da Pavullo deposition printed in Spadafora, *The Incredible Life Story of Sister Elena Aiello*, 5.

379 Spadafora, 5–6. See also Spadafora, 8.

380 Spadafora, 125–27.

381 Spadafora, 117–19.

382 See "Le Tappe Verso La Beatificazione" (The Stages towards Beatification), posted at the website of the Suore Minime della Passione di N.S.G.C. (the Minim Sisters of the Passion of Our Lord Jesus Christ), http://www.suorem inime-cosenza.it/, retrieved June 12, 2023.

383 See "Le Tappe Verso La Beatificazione."

384 Communicato Stampa (Press Release), "Il Papa Benedetto XVI ha firmato il decreto della Venerabile Serva di Dio Elena Aiello" (Pope Benedict XVI has signed the decree of the Venerable Servant of God Elena Aiello), Archdiocese of Cosenza-Bisignano, April 2, 2011.

385 Peterson, "This saint bore the stigmata every Good Friday for 38 years."

386 President Ronald Reagan, "Address at Commencement Exercises at Eureka College," Eureka, Illinois, May 9, 1982.

387 *Diary of Saint Maria Faustina Kowalska* (Stockbridge, MA: Marian Press, 2015), xv; and Sr. Sophia Michalenko, *The Life of Faustina Kowalska: The Authorized Biography* (Cincinnati, OH: Servant Books/Franciscan Media, 1999), 22–24.

388 Drew Mariani, *Divine Mercy* (Green Bay, Wisconsin: Relevant Radio, 2021), 12.

389 Mariani, *Divine Mercy*, 14.

390 Michalenko, *The Life of Faustina Kowalska*, 23.

391 On this, see the insightful, inspiring book by Patrick O'Hearn, *Parents of the Saints* (Gastonia, NC: TAN Books, 2022). The book includes several sections on Faustina's parents, as well as sections on the parents of stigmatists Gemma Galgani and Padre Pio.

392 Michalenko, *The Life of Faustina Kowalska*, 23.

393 *Diary of Saint Maria Faustina Kowalska*, xv.

394 *Diary of Saint Maria Faustina Kowalska*, xv.

395 "The Apostle of Divine Mercy: Saint Maria Faustina of the Congregation of Sisters of Our Lady of Mercy (1905–1938)," published by the Congregation of Marians of the Immaculate Conception (Stockbridge, Massachusetts, 1993).

396 See *Diary of Saint Maria Faustina Kowalska*, sec. 570, among others.

397 These were temporary vows, which Faustina referred to as "annual vows," because they were repeated for five years. She took them at this time on April 30, 1928. See *Diary of Saint Maria Faustina Kowalska*, sec. 303, 673n.

398 She wrote about this in November 1936. According to Sr. Michalenko, she wrote about it on November 20, 1936. See *Diary of Saint Maria Faustina Kowalska*, sec. 303, 673n; see also Michalenko, *The Life of Faustina Kowalska*, 139.

399 *Diary of Saint Maria Faustina Kowalska*, sec. 303; and Michalenko, *The Life of Faustina Kowalska*, 139.

400 For a particularly moving passage on guardian angels, see *Diary of Saint Maria Faustina Kowalska*, sec. 630.

401 The PDF version of Algar Thorold's authoritative translation of *The Dialogue of the Seraphic Virgin Catherine of Siena* (see earlier full citation) shows the word *mercy* appearing 163 times.

402 Fr. Buoncristiani interviewed for documentary, *St. Catherine of Siena*, done by EWTN Television and *Salvaimonasteri* (Save the Monasteries), produced by Elisabetta Valgiusti, 2016.

403 See *The Dialogue of the Seraphic Virgin Catherine of Siena* (Algar Thorold original translation), 124 (chapter LVIII) and 59 (chapter XXI) for, respectively, "abundance of mercy" and "doors of mercy."

404 See "Frequently Asked Questions about the Jubilee of Mercy," United States Conference of Catholic Bishops, https://www.usccb.org/beliefs-and-teac hings/how-we-teach/new-evangelization/jubilee-of-mercy/frequently-asked -questions-about-the-jubilee-of-mercy.

405 See *Summa Theologiae Supplementum*, Question 81, Article 1. For an easily accessible online reference, see https://www.newadvent.org/summa/5081.htm.

406 *Diary of Saint Maria Faustina Kowalska*, secs. 725–741.

407 I wrote about these comparable visions in a May 5, 2017, piece for *National Catholic Register*, titled "Fatima and Faustina Offer Striking, Frightening Visions of Hell." Also, at the *Register*, Joe Pronechen wrote an April 23, 2017, piece, "Fatima and Divine Mercy Are Eternally Linked," listing some parallels between Divine Mercy and Fatima, especially the crucial common message of repentance and mercy.

408 See, among others, my article "November 1920–2020: A Century of Abortion in Russia," *Catholic World Report*, November 17, 2020.

409 See Paul Kengor, *The Devil and Karl Marx*.

410 I also chose to exempt Therese because she did not have prophetic visions relating to our times today.

411 Adalbert Albert Vogl, *Therese Neumann: Mystic and Stigmatist, 1898–1962* (Rockford, IL: TAN Books, 1987), xv.

412 Vogl, *Therese Neumann,* 11.

413 Vogl, 23–26.

414 Vogl, 7–9.

415 See photo gallery in Vogl, *Therese Neumann,* 88–84 to 88–44 (black and white) and 3–6 (color). Also see the photos in Michael Freze, *They Bore the Wounds of Christ*, 228, 233–34.

416 Again, see photo gallery in Vogl, *Therese Neumann,* 88–4 to 88–44 (black and white) and 3–6 (color).

417 Quoted in Freze, *They Bore the Wounds of Christ*, 300.

418 Freze, 281.

419 Vogl, *Therese Neumann,* 9–10.

420 Vogl, 10.

421 Vogl, 29–31.

422 Vogl, 31.

423 Vogl, 31.

424 Vogl, 36–37.

425 See Vogl, 80–88, 139–40, 147–60.

426 See Adrienne von Speyr, *Book of All Saints* (San Francisco: Ignatius Press, 2008), 229.

427 On Maria Esperanza, see Jim Graves, "'She had a heart for souls': The life and cause of Servant of God Maria Esperanza de Bianchini," *Catholic World Report*, July 21, 2019.

428 See https://www.countdowntothekingdom.com/our-contributors/.

429 For a gentlemanly, charitable critique of Countdown to the Kingdom, made in the spirit of being constructive, see Jimmy Akin, "What is Countdown to the Kingdom?" *Catholic Answers*, December 14, 2021, posted at https://www.catholic.com/magazine/online-edition/what-is-countdown-to-the-kingdom.

430 Two other alleged stigmatists featured at the website are Eduardo Ferreira (Brazilian) and Marco Ferrari (an Italian priest). See https://www.countdowntothe kingdom.com/why-eduardo-ferreira/#messages and https://www.countdownt othekingdom.com/why-marco-ferrari/#messages.

431 See Bonilla's biography at Countdown to the Kingdom: https:// www.countdowntothekingdom.com/why-luz-de-maria-de-bonilla/.

432 See, for instance, Susan Brinkman, "Beware of So-Called 'Church Approved' Coronavirus Prevention," *National Catholic Register*, May 20, 2020.

433 The archive is posted at https://www.countdowntothekingdom.com/why-luz -de-maria-de-bonilla/.

434 See message, "Luz—When the Seal of the Beast Comes," April 2, 2021. https://www.countdowntothekingdom.com/luz-when-the-seal-of-the-beast -comes/.

435 See message, "Luz—You Are and Will Be Persecuted Severely," June 10, 2023, posted at https://www.countdowntothekingdom.com/luz-you-are-and-will-be -persecuted-severely/.

436 See her messages of May 3, 2023, and August 25, 2006, https://www .countdowntothekingdom.com/novena-to-the-queen-and-mother-of-the -end-times/.

437 https://www.countdowntothekingdom.com/luz-going-from-aberration-to -aberration/.

438 See "Luz—An Event Will Occur. . . ," https://www.countdowntotheking dom.com/luz-an-event-will-occur/, retrieved October 3, 2023.

439 The left-wing secular British newspaper *The Guardian*, which has published skeptical news articles on Gisella Cardia, reports that her real name is Maria Giuseppe Scarpulla, originally from Sicily, and that "Gisella Cardia" is an alias used by her "followers." The word "cardia" is Italian for "heart." It is very difficult to find reliable basic biographical information on Cardia printed in English, even her birth date.

440 In an extraordinary personal coincidence (perhaps providential), during my family's first visit to Italy in June 2014, we stayed at a villa in Trevignano Romano. This seems an especially remarkable coincidence because the village is not on the radar as an immediate choice for a family looking for a house to rent when visiting Italy. My wife, however, came upon the house and village through a popular online site for home rentals abroad. For whatever reason, we ended up in Trevignano Romano, which struck us as a nice, quiet, historic village within an easy drive of Rome and not far from towns like Assisi and others of interest. Cardia's mystical experiences began happening well after we visited the village. Unfortunately, our timing was such that I could not be there to investigate any of the claims of apparitions by Cardia and those who began following her. I have not returned to the village. I certainly have never met Cardia.

441 The best online archive for Gisella in English is the posting at Countdown to the Kingdom. See https://www.countdowntothekingdom.com/why-gisella-cardia/#messages.

442 See "Esudazione olio stimmate Gisella Cardia con testimonianza Dr Chifari /Gisella Cardia stigmata oil," https://www.youtube.com/watch?v=gMZ5_WMZroQ. The video is also posted and kept at https://www.countdowntothekingdom.com/why-gisella-cardia/#messages.

443 See "Gisella Cardia stigmata March 24, 2023 - Dr Rosanna Chifari/Peter Bannister," https://www.youtube.com/watch?v=5Iam0Eq_RT4. The video is also posted and kept at https://www.countdowntothekingdom.com/why-gisella-cardia/#messages.

444 See "The Gisella Cardia Conflict Relating to Discernment - Episode 5," posted at https://www.youtube.com/watch?v=ATTbZroY5ko.

445 Angela Giufridda, "'The Saint' leaves Italian town after case opened into statue's 'tears of blood,'" *The Guardian*, April 11, 2013.

446 The official statement from the diocese is posted at https://www.countdowntothekingdom.com/on-gisella-diocesan-statement/.

447 https://www.countdowntothekingdom.com/gisella-cardia-a-revolution-is-ready/.

448 https://www.countdowntothekingdom.com/gisella-cardia-they-want-to-separate-you/.

449 https://www.countdowntothekingdom.com/gisella-cardia-do-not-be-far-from-god/.

450 https://www.countdowntothekingdom.com/gisella-cardia-the-warning-will-soon-arrive/.

451 https://www.countdowntothekingdom.com/gisella-cardia-everything-will-fall/.

452 https://www.countdowntothekingdom.com/gisella-a-special-easter/.

453 https://www.countdowntothekingdom.com/gisella-ecclesial-freemasonry-wants-a-single-church/.

454 https://www.countdowntothekingdom.com/gisella-be-strong-cling-to-jesus/.

455 Countdown to the Kingdom notes this prediction (without quoting, dating, or linking to it) at its seer page on Gisella Cardia. For the CNS piece reposted by *Crux*, see Robert Duncan, "Mary foretold COVID-19 pandemic, alleged visionary claims," Catholic News Service, August 8, 2020, https://cruxnow.com/church-in-europe/2020/08/mary-foretold-covid-19-pandemic-alleged-visionary-claims.

456 As noted earlier, most of those dead under communist governments perished in that period when Stalin ran the Soviet Union and Mao spearheaded China.

457 Pastoral Letter of Bishop John Shojiro Ito, April 22, 1984, posted by the Marian Library/International Marian Research Institute, at the University of Dayton, at https://udayton.edu/imri/mary/a/apparitions-approved.php and

also at https://web.archive.org/web/20110813223303/http:/campus.udayton
.edu/mary/resources/akita_apparition.html.

458 Wikipedia entry on "Our Lady of Akita," https://en.wikipedia.org/wiki/Our
_Lady_of_Akita#cite_ref-:0_4-2, retrieved August 26, 2023.

459 See John Ata, "A Message from Our Lady–Akita, Japan," EWTN.com,
https://www.ewtn.com/catholicism/library/message-from-our-lady--akita-
japan-5167.

460 Pastoral Letter of Bishop John Shojiro Ito, April 22, 1984.

461 Ata, "A Message from Our Lady – Akita, Japan."

462 Caution must be exercised to distinguish between reliable videos and those
that are not. With careful, cautious searches, one can find online video footage
of Japanese documentaries that include interviews with Sr. Agnes and also with
Bishop Ito. Perhaps the best such effort was a 1992 documentary, *Marian Apparitions of the 20th Century*, narrated by respected actor Ricardo Montalban.
See the IMDb post at https://www.imdb.com/title/tt23552608/. The video
can be viewed online at https://www.youtube.com/watch?v=IafhGTVOhvI,
among other links. An excerpted video pulled from the documentary is posted online as "Our Lady of Akita (1973)," https://youtu.be/CAOFe1p26xk,
which also includes a few minutes of a Japanese-language interview with Sr.
Agnes as an add-on.

463 See Pastoral Letter of Bishop John Shojiro Ito, April 22, 1984. Iro was bishop
from 1962 to 1985. He died in March 1993. See post at Diocese of Niigata:
https://www.cbcj.catholic.jp/english/japan/diocese/niigata/.

464 See, among others, Graham, *Compendium of the Miraculous*, 102, 440.

465 See Joseph Pronechen, "Our Lady of Akita, Japan, and Today's Crisis," *National Catholic Register*, September 13, 2018.

466 The text of this message and the two from the subsequent apparitions are tak-
en from the official April 22, 1984, Pastoral Letter of Bishop John Shojiro Ito.

467 This is the message shared verbatim from the official April 22, 1984, Pastoral
Letter of Bishop John Shojiro Ito.

468 Pastoral Letter of Bishop John Shojiro Ito, April 22, 1984.

469 See Pronechen, "Our Lady of Akita, Japan, and Today's Crisis."

470 Pope Paul VI said this in a June 29, 1972, homily. For an analysis, see Jimmy
Akin, "The Smoke of Satin Homily," November 13, 2006, posted at his website, www.jimmyaking.org.

471 See Bishop Ito's April 22, 1984, Pastoral Letter.

472 See Graham, *Compendium of the Miraculous*, 440.

473 See Bishop Ito's April 22, 1984, Pastoral Letter.

474 *Diary of Saint Maria Faustina Kowalska*, 83

475 Quotation is found in Rt. Rev Msgr. William C. McGrath, "America! . . .
Sodom or Nineveh?" *Divine Love*, July–September 1957, vol. 1, nos. 1, 5.

476 This statement by Sr. Elena Aiello was also later reported by Fr. Albert J. Hebert, SM, in his book *The Three Days' Darkness*. Hebert quoted her this way

(the slight difference from the *Divine Love* version is surely due to a differing translation from the original Italian): "Clouds with lightning rays of fire and a tempest of fire will pass over the whole world and the punishment will be the most terrible ever known in the history of mankind. It will last 70 hours. The wicked will be crushed and eliminated. Many will be lost because they have stubbornly remained in their sins. Then they will feel the force of light over darkness." Fr. Hebert's book includes an official Church *nihil obstat* and *imprimatur*, as well as an introduction by Archbishop George Pearce. Unfortunately, Hebert does not provide a citation for this quotation from Sr. Elena, though in his bibliography he lists among his book's sources the biography of Sr. Elena by Fr. Spadafora and the *Divine Love* newspaper as his two sources on the Calabrian nun. As this chapter shows, the quote can be found in the *Divine Love* newspaper of July–September 1957 (page 5). See Fr. Albert J. Hebert, SM, *The Three Days' Darkness: Prophecies of Saints and Seers* (Dublin, Ireland: Fatima/ Rosary Promotions, 1986), 26. This book can be viewed online at https:// archive.org/details/TheThreeDaysOfDarknessByAlbertJ.Hebert/img089.jpg, retrieved July 27, 2023.

477 Among such alleged seers today, see the statements by Pedro Regis (who is not a stigmatist) posted at the website of Countdown to the Kingdom. Regis conveyed this in a March 20, 2021, alleged message from the Blessed Mother: "You are living in a worse time than the time of the Flood." See that and Regis's other dire March 2021 messages posted at https:// www.countdowntothekingdom.com/pedro-you-are-important-to-the-tr iumph/. In a December 18, 2021, message, also allegedly from the Blessed Mother, Regis again stated, "You are living in a time worse than the time of the Flood." See message posted at https://www.countdowntothekingdom.com /pedro-there-is-no-peace-without-jesus/. Regis has shared this message often. The most recent as of the time of the writing of this book was August 19, 2023: https://www.countdowntothekingdom.com/pedro-men-and-women-of-faith -will-lose-their-freedom/. Once again, I certainly cannot confirm nor endorse these. I am merely reporting what is being said.

478 See Graham, *Compendium of the Miraculous*, 353–55.

479 See https://www.mysticsofthechurch.com/2009/12/blessed-anna-maria-ta igi-wife-mother.html; https://en.wikipedia.org/wiki/Anna_Maria_Taigi; https://www.newadvent.org/cathen/14430b.htm; https://catholicexchange .com/blessed-anna-maria-taigi-housewife-mother-saint/; https://www.ewtn .com/catholicism/library/blessed-anne-marie-taigi-5888, all retrieved July 25, 2023; Cruz, *The Incorruptibles*, 246–49; and Bob and Penny Lord, *Visionaries, Mystics, and Stigmatists*, 286–318.

480 Fr. Albert Bessières, SJ, *Wife, Mother & Mystic: Blessed Anna-Maria Taigi* (Charlotte, NC: TAN Books, 2012). The book was translated by the Rev. Stephen Rigby and edited by Douglas Newton. The book received the *nihil obstat*

and *imprimatur* in 1952. It was originally published by Sands & Co. (Publishers), Ltd., 3 Trebeck St., London, W1, England, in 1952. It was reprinted by TAN Books, an imprint of Saint Benedict Press, LLC, in 1970, 1978, 1982, and then again in 2012.

[481] Bessières, *Wife, Mother & Mystic*, 126.

[482] Bessières, 154.

[483] See https://en.wikipedia.org/wiki/Three_Days_of_Darkness#cite_note-Taigi 1863-1, retrieved July 25, 2023.

[484] See, for instance, Edward Healy Thomson, ed., *The Life of Venerable Anna Maria Taigi, the Roman Matron* (New York: Fr. Pustet, 52 Barclay Street, 1873), 397. The Wikipedia citation references "Anna Maria Taigi, *Private Prophecies* (Rome, 1863)."

[485] Mark Mallett, founder of the website Countdown to the Kingdom, uses an almost verbatim quote (though he does not cite a source): "There shall come over the whole earth an intense darkness lasting three days and three nights. Nothing can be seen, and the air will be laden with pestilence which will claim mainly, but not only, the enemies of religion. It will be impossible to use any man-made lighting during this darkness, except blessed candles." He further quotes Taigi: "All the enemies of the Church, whether known or unknown, will perish over the whole earth during that universal darkness, with the exception of a few whom God will soon convert." See Mark Mallett, "Three Days of Darkness," Countdown to the Kingdom, August 17, 2007, https://www.markmallett.com/blog/three-days-of-darkness/, retrieved July 27, 2023.

[486] Bessières, *Wife, Mother & Mystic*, 143–44.

[487] Bessières, 144.

[488] Bessières, 156.

[489] Sr. Lucia later described the hell that the Fatima children saw as a "sea of fire," filled with "demons and souls in human form, like transparent embers, all blackened or burnished bronze, floating about in the conflagration, now raised into the air by the flames that issued from within themselves together with great clouds of smoke. . . amid shrieks and groans of pain and despair, which horrified us." They were also told by the Blessed Mother that "many souls go to hell." See, among others, Paul Thigpen, *Saints Who Saw Hell*, 59–62; and Fr. Andrew Apostoli, *Fatima for Today* (San Francisco: Ignatius Press, 2010), 106–07. Bessières, *Wife, Mother & Mystic*, 158n.

[490] Bessières, *Wife, Mother & Mystic*, 158n.

[491] Bessières, 158–59n.

[492] Regrettably, too, little is known in English about Marquis de La Franquerie. There is a French Wikipedia page on him, quite brief, that trashes him with all sorts of aspersions, calling him "far right" and other things.

[493] The book can be accessed online at https://ia800307.us.archive.org/14/items /PropheciesOfMarieJulieJahenny/marie-julie-jahenny-prophecy3.pdf. Unfor-

tunately, what is posted from this edition includes no title and copyright pages. In 2015, an updated Kindle edition of the book was published by KIC and is available on Amazon.

494 See, for instance, Hebert, *The Three Days' Darkness*, 36; and the entry on Jahenny at the Mystics of the Church website: https://www.mystics ofthechurch.com/2015/07/marie-julie-jahenny-breton-stigmatist.html, retrieved July 28, 2023.

495 See E. A. Bucchianeri, *We Are Warned: The Prophecies of Marie-Julie Jahenny*, published as a free e-book (December 2011) by Scribd, www.scribd .com, and posted at https://archive.org/details/WeAreWarnedMarieJulie Jahenny/page/n9/mode/2up, retrieved July 28, 2023.

496 Marquis de La Franquerie, *Marie-Julie Jahenny: The Breton Stigmatist*, 44.

497 Marquis de La Franquerie, *Marie-Julie Jahenny*, 44–45.

498 Marquis de La Franquerie, 45.

499 Excerpt taken from Bucchianeri, *We Are Warned: The Prophecies of Marie-Julie Jahenny*, and posted at the Mystics of the Church website, retrieved July 28, 2023.

500 Jimmy Akin, who I respect and trust, wrote a piece for *Catholic Answers Magazine* relating his unsureness about the three days of darkness claims. It is a good piece, though it does not have as much research as is presented here in this book. Still, I appreciate his healthy skepticism. Too many people are not careful. I hope that this book has exercised proper caution. See Jimmy Akin, "Will There Be Three Days of Darkness?" Catholic Answers, May 31, 2023, posted at https://www.catholic.com/magazine/online-edition/will-there-be-three-days-of-darkness.

501 A mere Google search will show this clearly. I could list numerous examples in this endnote. Those who do the search will come upon letters attributed to Padre Pio, but those alleged statements should not be reflexively assumed to be accurate. I could not confirm them. Interestingly, in my most recent search I had difficulty finding the purported letter from Pio's Capuchin Order. Previously, articles featuring that letter popped up easily. That letter aside, it must also be noted that I found nothing on Pio and the days of darkness in the major biographies of him published by reputable sources.

502 Martin interviewed by Freze. See Freze, *They Bore the Wounds of Christ*, 295.

503 The book of Revelation is an obvious example. See also 2 Peter 3:7, which states, "But by the same word the heavens and earth that now exist have been stored up for fire, being kept until the day of judgment and destruction of ungodly men."

INDEX

276